LEONIDAS B. LELLOS

GREECE

HISTORY · MUSEUMS · MONUMENTS

ATHENS 1973

GENERAL BIBLIOGRAPHY

1. Reports on excavations and finds exhibited in Museums, published in Archaiologike Ephemeris, Archaiologikon Deltion, and Athens Annals of Archaeology.
2. Guide de Grèce, of the series Guides Bleus.
3. Kirsten-Kraiker, Griechenlandkunde, 5th edition.
4. Guides of Museums and Sites, published by Sp. Meletzis - H. Papadakis.
5. Apollo Guides, published by E. Tzaferis.
6. Archaeological Guides of Museums, published by the General Direction of Antiquities and Restoration (T.A.P. Service).
7. Brief Guides (leaflets) published by the National Tourist Organization (E.O.T.).
8. Guide of Museums and Collections of Greece, published by the National Bank of Greece. Athens, 1970.

This book has been approved by the

GENERAL DIRECTION OF ANTIQUITIES AND RESTORATION
OF THE MINISTRY OF CULTURE AND SCIENCES.
(Doc. No. 30801/26.10.72).

Translated by Helen Zigada and Brian de Jongh

A BRIEF HISTORY OF GREECE

PREHISTORIC TIMES

Geography and climate

Greece is a land of unique natural beauty. An attractive scenery of endless variety and a transparent atmosphere of dazzling clarity make a real pleasure the visiting of this country from one end to the other. The landscape encountered everywhere is cheerful and serene.

The mild climate of Greece is the most ideal in Europe. Skies are blue and days sunny for the greatest part of the year. Because of its small area and meager soil, life has not been easy for the people who have inhabited this land for thousands of years, and conditions forced them to a constant search for means and ways to secure their survival.

There are few high mountains on the mainland — Mt. Olympos, the highest (2918 m.), Mt. Taygetos (2407 m.), etc. Mountain ranges, however, have harmonious contours and their appearance is not oppressive like that of massifs encountered in other countries. Approximately 80 % of the land is mountainous, but there are passes which make possible communication from place to place.

The landscape presents an astonishing variety : one suddenly comes across picturesque valleys separated by soft hills from plains of a normally small extent. Few of the rivers traversing them have abundant water all year round. On the other hand, there are many torrents or rivulets, and springs, when present, are a real blessing. Rains are not frequent. Although vegetation is not luxuriant, it shows great variety because of successive changes in altitude. Thus, the general picture of the landscape is dominated by a wide range not only of colours but also of delicate shades ceaselessly changing with the hour of day. In spring and autumn thousands of wild flowers grow everywhere.

Greece has neither towering mountains nor deeply shaded forests. Everything is of modest proportions and to human scale, so that nothing inspires fear or oppression. Nature is ever welcoming man. As the area of the country is small, even the highest mountainous district does not lie farther than 70 kms. from the sea. Thus, the horizon is always free.

Almost the entire mainland, except for its north side, is washed by the sea. Gentle shores, golden beaches and the boundless beauty of sparkling blue waters are the delight of swimmers.

A whole chain of small and large islands, each with a character of its own, girdle the Greek mainland. Six of the Ionian islands, the one more beautiful than the other, lie parallel to the west coast of the mainland. On the south, Crete, the largest island, with mainland features and a noble background, creates an unforgettable impression on the visitor. On the east, clusters of small islands (the Cyclades, the Sporades, etc.) offer with their diverse scenery a surprise and a pleasant interval during cruises.

The peculiar geography of the Greek territory played a role of paramount importance in its historical destiny. The situation of the country at the southeast end of Europe afforded since very early times easy access to the other two continents, Asia and Africa, where the two most important of the oldest civilizations had grown.

PALAEOLITHIC PERIOD

The Palaeolithic age lasted several thousands of years and during its middle period (100000 - 50000 B.C.) man made his appearance for the first time in Europe. Traces of Palaeolithic man have come to light in Greece (a skull was found within a cave near Petralona in Chalcidice). As shown by the few investigations carried out so far, men lived (between 40000 and 10000 B.C.) in caves and used tools made of flint or bone. Signs of life from that vast chronological phase have been found in Epirus (in the caves of Asprochaliko, Kastritsa, Kokkinopilos), in Macedonia, in Thessaly (on the banks of the river Peneios), in Kopais (in the cave of Seidi), in Megaris, Argolis, Elis, etc.

MESOLITHIC PERIOD

Palaeolithic man lived on game, fruit and plants. In the next brief chronological phase which is called Mesolithic (10000 - 7000 B.C.), the climate changed and a very primitive form of agriculture was introduced, while hunting continued to supplement man's diet. The artefacts employed during this period were of small size (microlithic). Traces of this phase have been attested in Thessaly, Kopais and the Ionian islands.

NEOLITHIC PERIOD

The Neolithic period (7000 - 2600 B.C.) was marked in Greece by an astonishing for those times degree of progress. Systematic cultivation of the soil began and men became tied to the piece of land they cultivated. They acquired a permanent dwelling and domesticated several animals (sheep, goats, oxen, pigs), which made them independent of the uncertain results of their hunting expeditions. Stability of life had important consequences. Small settlements were founded near rivers or springs which ensured supply of water (at Nea Nikomedeia near Veroia, in various locations of Thessaly, particularly near the present village of Sesklo, where the earliest fortified acropolis of Europe was uncovered, and in other parts of the Greek territory), while dwelling in caves was continued in some places (on Crete, at Diros in Mani, etc.).

The civilization which grew during that age was very significant. In addition to stone artefacts, clay vases were soon manufactured. These were later decorated with red and black paint or incised ornaments. They were made and shaped into attractive forms by hand and then exposed in the sun or on the open fire of the hearth. Finds dating to that age include stone weapons, and a great many clay and stone statuettes (idols) representing a female figure with very pronounced features of fertility (breasts, belly, buttocks); usually the entire lower part of the body is oversized. Male idols are rare. One of the female figures is seated carrying a baby in her arms ('kourotrophos'). These were cult idols. Since cultivation of land was the main source of livelihood for man in those times, fertility of nature and, hence, of animals and men was worshipped. The steatopygous idols represent the goddess of fertility whose worship is encountered in all primitive agricultural societies.

Initially men dwelt in square or round huts made of reeds, which were gradually replaced by small houses with stone foundations and brick walls, consisting of one or two rooms. Some of these houses show probable traces of a second storey.

Since life at that age was not evenly organized everywhere in Greece, the menace of hungry hordes was quite frequent. Dwellers of settlements, therefore, felt the need to erect fortifications and make themselves safe against sudden invasions. So they built walls around their acropoleis, where, in case of emergency, they sought refuge near the local ruler. These enclosures often consisted of double or even multiple walls.

Many cultural elements of that period present great similarities with the corresponding features revealed in the Neolithic settlements of Asia Minor and the Balkan peninsula. The type of the average quadrilateral house ('megaron'), with a principal room and open front porch formed by projection of the side walls, had perhaps originated in the Near East. With constant effort and ceaseless toil, Neolithic man laid the foundations of civilized life in the world through the radical changes effected on the economy and mode of living by the growth of agriculture.

BRONZE AGE

Early Helladic period

The knowledge and wide use of metal caused a great change in the way of life. Copper was discovered in the Near East, from where it spread to the Greek territory.

Originally, copper was used in the pure state. Very soon, however, man thought of adding tin to copper, thereby obtaining a harder metal — bronze.

The use of metal had very significant consequences. Tools and weapons were more durable and far more easily manufactured. The first rudimentary industries were then established and trade contacts with other peoples grew. Merchants travelled to the metal-producing places to purchase the material required, and communication between countries of the then known world increased. Settlements became better organized and acquired an urban character. Some villages of that age began to look almost like little towns with a rudimentary town-plan, and architecture was developed.

Mainland Greece, the Aegean islands and Crete attained great progress. Settlements had the general features of that age, though characteristic differences appeared from place to place. Again, some of the settlements were fortified (Lerna in Argolis, Asketario in Attica).

Although the Greeks had not yet descended on the peninsula —they reached the north of the Greek territory in about 2000 B.C. — one may well say that the Early Bronze Age marks the beginning of the miracle accomplished later by Greece.

Cycladic civilization

During the earliest phase of the Bronze Age, a civilization of exceptional interest and singular substance and form was developed on the Cyclades — the Cycladic civilization. The fact that gold, silver (Siphnos) and, most of all, marble (Paros, Naxos) were available on these islands, probably played an important role. Melos was a source of the precious obsidian, a hard volcanic stone which was easily shaped into tools, weapons and even vases. Owing to the geographic position of the islands between Greece and the East, the islanders became the first famous mariners of the world. They were the first to fit their small ships with keels, which enabled them to sail safely on the open seas. Their main occupation was seafaring and trade. Excavations revealed that they had founded small settlements in various sites along the coast of mainland Greece. Their settlements were built by the sea. Houses were constructed of stone and had a rectangular or apsidal shape, with two or three rooms. Their citadels were surrounded by double fortification walls (Chalandriani on Syros). They manufactured vases of dark clay and decorated them with incised patterns. Their most typical ware were the so-called 'frying-pans' bearing on the outer surface incised representations of ships. But the most representative products of Cycladic art are the marble statuettes. These are indeed remarkable, even by present-day standards, for their type as well as the means of expression and the solutions adopted by those early artists in representing the human figure (some fine examples are exhibited in the rooms of the Cycladic Collection at the National Museum, Athens). Their height varies. Some are very small, while a few are over one metre in size. They have neither plastic depth, nor pronounced fertility traits like the Neolithic figurines. On the contrary, they are characterized by marked abstraction and schematization. Some represent the human figure clearly, while others show a remote resemblance to it, which is rather reminiscent of a violoncello ('violin-shaped'). In addition to the works of larger size, the finest specimens include two statuettes, the one representing a standing flute-player and the other a seated harp-player (both have come from Keros). Attractive (white) marble vessels in open shapes were also manufactured on the Cycladic islands. Other products included bronze and silver jewellery, bronze weapons and tools, and some articles of beautification.

Middle Helladic period

The first Hellenic races, the Achaians, Aiolians and Ionians, descended from the north in about 2000 B.C. The use of horses was most important for successive movements in those times. Some of these races reached by stages as far as the southernmost end of the peninsula. They settled permanently on the Greek territory and prevailed almost everywhere, having imposed themselves on the older inhabitants who are given today the general name of Pre-Hellenes. They did not, however, cross over to Crete immediately. Archaeological investigation has proved that the transition from the Early Helladic to the Middle Helladic period was a peaceful process in some settlements, while in others the change was abrupt which denotes prevalence of the newcomers after struggle. The civilization of Greece during that period was again of an agricultural type. Except for a few instances, the settlements had no fortification walls, which indicates that the new settlers felt safe from external menaces. Houses were simpler than those of the previous period, but equipped with a circular hearth in the middle of the room or by one of the side walls.

Life then was marked by neither a higher standard nor material prosperity. Nevertheless, the principal characteristics of the Greek race begin to be distinguishable in that age : the organized productive activity, the pure and steady line (clearly seen in the shape of vases which acquired a solid base). The search for precision and stability dominated every aspect of daily life or art. The use of the ceramic wheel and kiln spread during that period. This was a very important step in the sphere of production and progress in general, for it facilitated greatly, both as regards speed and solidity, the manufacture of pottery which was an essential commodity of everyday life.

Minoan civilization

While the standard of living on mainland Greece showed no particular progress, an astounding flowering appeared on Crete, which was not yet inhabited by the Greeks. This was undoubtedly the most important and splendid civilization of Prehistoric times, not only in Greece but the whole of Europe. Assimilating influences from other earlier or even contemporary civilizations of the East, the brilliant people who created this culture gave it unique features of incredible fineness. Remarkable remains have been discovered since the beginning of our century in Central and Eastern Crete. Very recent discoveries in Western Crete do not stand comparison with the contemporary products of outstanding beauty and importance found in Central and Eastern Crete.

Crete was favoured by her proximity to the countries where great civilizations had flourished since early times (Egypt, Syria, Asia Minor). The active inhabitants of the island soon became excellent seafarers and gained supremacy over the Aegean and the Eastern Mediterranean. They exported the natural and industrial products of their island and imported gold, bronze, textiles and precious stones from West Asia, the Near East and Egypt. During their voyages they saw and learned a lot. Being themselves intelligent and productive people, they assimilated outside influences and with the passing of time created an outstanding civilization of their own, which has been named 'Minoan' by its discoverer, Sir Arthur Evans.

The main centres of the period between 2600 and 2000 B.C., lay in the fertile plain of Messara and in Eastern Crete. A remarkable creative activity prevailed in that age. Although showing apparent influences from Egypt, Asia Minor, the Cyclades and other places with which the Cretans maintained contacts, all Cretan works of art have a distinct character of their own.

Houses had two or three rooms and were rectangular in shape. Their walls were decorated with painted plaster. There was a great variety of styles in pottery, and polychrome decoration appeared by the end of the 3rd millennium B.C. Some of the vessels were given human or animal form. Elegant stone vases were also produced and given superb intricate shapes. The fine artists who made them knew how to put into advantage the natural veins of the stone adapting them to the shape of the vase. Goldwork was admirably developed and a great number of jewels made of fine gold, rock-crystal, or precious and semi-precious stones have come to light. Exquisite small seals were made of ivory or steatite. These were worn round the neck or the handwrist and used for sealing boxes, pyxides etc., serving both as a sort of amulet and personal seal of the owner. The surface used for sealing bore abstract motifs or representations of animal and human figures.

Marble statuettes were imported from the Cycladic islands and copied in the local workshops. The Cretans apparently lived in great comfort thanks to the growth of trade and navigation. They became distinguished as the best navigators of Prehistoric times and made contacts and transactions with the entire then known world.

In about 2000 B.C., the first palaces were built on the island. The emergence of a central authority made necessary the existence of administrative buildings that would also serve as residence for the ruler. Moreover, these palaces housed the most famous artistic workshops. The development of administration made possible a swift pace of progress, and trade and seafaring reached an unprecedented expansion. The first palaces were destroyed in about 1700 B.C., probably from earthquakes, but were immediately replaced by larger and more magnificent buildings.

Minoan architecture is one of the most màrvellous accomplishments of the Cretans. Large complexes with majestic propylaia, grand staircases, colonnades, light-wells, many corridors and courts, long rows of store-rooms, several storeys and a great number of amenities, afforded a most comfortable and pleasant life. Palaces were vast and several of their rooms were decorated with exquisite frescoes. Art flourished under every form and reached its zenith.

Separate villas built in the vicinity of palaces served as residence for the nobility. Around these villas were built the dwellings of the common people. Knossos, Phaistos, Mallia and Zakro were the most important urban and artistic centres.

Architectural remains, movable finds and wall-paintings dating to this period, which lasted until approximately 1500 B.C., literally amaze people of our times with their elegance, rich colour and beauty. The Cretans who were masters of the seas, apparently never experienced the fear of invasion. Their cities had no fortification walls. They must have spent their lives amidst intense commercial and artistic activity, in peace, tranquillity and joy. Being a sensitive people, they sought to attain comfort and be surrounded by beautiful objects. They were particularly fond of nature and represented its floral, faunal and marine world in superb fashion. They knew how to enjoy a life, in which men and women participated equally. They were a peaceful people and war scenes are totally absent from their works of art.

The Cretans were devoutly religious, but their religion did not exert pressure on man. They worshipped a great goddess (Nature), who was associated with a variety of symbols and depicted under various forms. She was honoured with many festivities and joyous celebrations, which are represented in the exquisite frescoes of the palaces.

There exists no corresponding civilization of such high standard and such freedom and joy in every manifestation. It has not yet been possible to decipher their script, the Minoan Linear A.

All this wonderful world was destroyed in about 1450 B.C. As proved by Professor Sp. Marinatos, the formidable eruption of the volcano of Thera which devastated the splendid local civilization — currently unearthed by his excavations — caused tidal waves which literally swept the northern coasts of Crete. Simultaneously, large quantities of volcanic matter (pumice) and sulphur were ejected at a distance of many miles. These terrible catastrophes were followed by earthquakes and fires. Thus, the most magnificent palaces of Crete were destroyed and the splendour of the Minoan civilization was extinguished.

In about 1400 B.C., the Achaians began to cross over to Crete in successive waves. They became masters of Knossos and provisionally repaired parts of its old palaces without building new ones. Cretan maritime supremacy came to an end and commerce passed into other hands.

In approximately 1300 B.C., large buildings resembling the Mycenaean houses of mainland Greece were erected at Hagia Triada, Palaikastro, Gournia, Tylissos, etc. Decline continued throughout the 12th century B.C., and when in 1100 B.C. the first waves of Dorians landed on the island, they prevailed without encountering resistance. Those of the old inhabitants who refused to submit to the conquerors, sought refuge on the mountainous districts.

Mycenaean civilization

The civilization of mainland Greece during the Late Helladic period, as well as this entire age, have been named 'Mycenaean', for this outstanding civilization of Greek origin was first uncovered at Mycenae —the most splendid and mighty center of the times— through the excavations carried out by Heinrich Schliemann. Until then (1876), no scholar believed in the existence of this civilization which was regarded merely as a product of Homer's poetic imagination. To this greatest of Greek poets, we owe a comprehensive picture of life in the Mycenaean age. In his two epic poems (the *Iliad* and the *Odyssey*), composed four centuries after the fall of the Mycenaean world, Homer does not record purely historical information but the reminiscences of later Greeks from that glorious era. Nevertheless, the veracity of his writings has been attested by the excavations carried out in the various Mycenaean centers.

Large palaces were built on fortified acropoleis protected by very strong walls at 'rich-in-gold' Mycenae, Tiryns, Pylos, Thebes, Arne (Gla), Iolkos in Thessaly, etc. Palaces were no longer many-storied buildings, as in Crete. Specialists presume that they had only two storeys; but they had a great many rooms and corridors, the typical 'megaron' with a hearth in the centre and a front porch with two columns overlooking an open court, flanked by other compartments. Walls were decorated in the interior with polychrome frescoes.

The king, who was the supreme authority, lived in the palace on the acropolis, and his kinsmen and high officials dwelt in separate villas nearby. The high and strong walls surrounding the acropoleis were constructed of huge blocks and were hence named 'Cyclopean' by the ancient Greeks, who believed that only superhuman beings, such as the Cyclops, would have been able to move and handle this heavy material. The inhabitants of every city dwelt in houses built around the acropoleis.

Despite common points between the Mycenaean and the Minoan civilizations, the former is of an entirely different character from the latter. The Mycenaean civilization is a Greek product marked by vigour and reason, created by a race who descended on the Greek territory with superior weaponry, imposed themselves on the older inhabitants as a military nobility, and founded several small states. The Achaeans who created this civilization were a people fond of hunting and war, which accounts for the representation of relevant scenes in their works of art. The naturalistic tendencies of Minoan art gave way to organized and disciplined motifs befitting the virile world which created them. The various rich finds of this period show remarkable accomplishments in all fields of art : metalwork, jewellery, seal-engraving, painting, sculpture, the working of precious stones, gold, ivory, etc. The products of Mycenaean art include the well-known bronze daggers bearing on their blades inlaid representations executed in other precious metals attached on the bronze surface (fine examples are displayed in the Mycenaean Collection at the National Museum, Athens).

Whereas the inhabitants of Crete never experienced the fear of enemies, the dwellers of cities in the Late Helladic period were constantly aware of outside menace. This is clearly denoted by their fortified acropoleis. People therefore must have lived in constant vigil, daily military training and strenuous effort in order to maintain the fruits of their labour. They were not, however, lacking in imagination or creative disposition.

With the passing of time, the Mycenaeans reached a remarkable degree of progress and their centres enjoyed an exceptional material prosperity and artistic flourishing. It is believed that in about 1400 B.C., following the destruction of the Minoan centres, the Mycenaeans found an opportunity to occupy and settle in Knossos.

The huge Mycenaean citadels were erected after 1400 B.C., when the so-called 'Mycenaean empire' became established and the Mycenaeans founded colonies or trade-posts on the Cyclades, Cyprus, Rhodes, and in Syria, Palestine, South Italy, Sicily, etc. Their works of art reached as far as Spain and the Balearic islands. This phase of the Mycenaean civilization was marked by an astonishing commercial expansion and material prosperity.

HISTORIC TIMES

In about 1200 B.C., perhaps, the famous Trojan War broke out. Many Greek cities participated in this campaign against Troy in Asia Minor. Immediately afterwards, and without our having any knowledge as to what exactly happened and which was the course of events — for the written monuments of that age, the Linear B tablets, are only lists of objects offering no historical data — disasters and a certain decline occurred in some Mycenaean centers, probably as a result of internal disorder or raids of the so-called 'peoples of the sea'. Following that, the gradual descent of various groups of Dorians, who were strongly armed with iron weapons, probably led to the final destruction of the Mycenaean civilization by the late 12th century B.C.

GEOMETRIC AGE

The final predominance of the Dorians in several regions of the Greek territory marked the beginning of a new era noted for some important changes in social structure, religion and other realms of life.

1) Writing was forgotten. The difficult Linear B script, known only to a few scribes, disappeared completely after the destruction of the Mycenaean civilization. Another form of writing, no longer syllabic as the Linear B, but phonetic, was introduced in the late 9th and early 8th centuries B.C. The Greeks learned it from the Phoenicians and altered a few symbols of the Phoenician alphabet to render certain vowels of the Hellenic language. This early use of the alphabet is known from inscriptions incised on pottery of that age. The absence of writing is, of course, a serious drawback for our knowledge of this period, during which many upheavals and changes took place, which gave rise to entirely new conditions. Historic times begin after the invasion of the Dorians in Greece; their beginning is roughly dated to approximately 1000 B.C.

2) All Hellas was 'iron-clad', to quote Thucydides.

3) In some districts of Greece the old rural settlements ('komai') were abandoned and the largest part of the population moved to cities. This movement probably began in the 10th century B.C. or even earlier —no historic evidence exists as to the date.

4) In most Greek cities kingship was abolished during that period, and authority was taken over by the aristocrats (the 'aristoi').

5) An important change occurred in religion, too. The Pre-Hellenic goddess of fertility was no longer the dominant deity. The twelve Olympian gods prevailed, and chief among them, a male divinity, Zeus, the 'father of men and gods', as Homer

calls him. Separate temples were founded next to or near the old Mycenaean palaces. Some of the twelve Olympian gods appeared in Mycenaean times.

6) Cremation of the dead became a general practice.

The first Greek colonization

Many of the earlier inhabitants were subjugated by the Dorians who finally stopped, having conquered the largest part of the Peloponnese. They did not settle in Attica, a fact stressed by the ancient Athenians in every period of their long history. The Doric settlement in Laconia was of a harsh and singular type.

Meanwhile, those of the old Hellenes who did not wish to live under Dorian rule, left Greece in successive waves in search of a land suitable for permanent settlement. Thus, the most lively and valiant element of the old Hellenic population began moving eastwards and settling by stages on the Cycladic islands and the coasts of Asia Minor. This migration is known in history as the First Greek Colonization. With the passing of time a number of Dorians, too, left mainland Greece and passed onto Thera, Melos, Crete, Kos and Rhodes. Some remained on these islands, while others crossed over to the southernmost part of the coast of Asia Minor. Export trade, which had given life and prosperity to the country, almost ceased in the first centuries after the so-called descent of the Dorians, and the inhabitants of Greece were restricted to agriculture and animal husbandry. Life became very difficult. Each house had to provide for itself the essentials of life.

Geometric art

The art of this period was based on a different spirit and assumed an absolutely disciplined and dynamic form. The entire civilization of those times was named after the decorative motives of pottery which were pure geometric patterns : circles, lozenges, triangles, squares, etc., initially executed with the help of rulers and compasses. The most typical motif is the meander, which appears in endless variations. After the two earliest centuries of that period, pottery was profusely decorated and the so-called dread of emptiness became the dominant trend (i.e. they avoided leaving undecorated space on the surface of the vase).

Geometric art is a purely Greek art, the product of the people who sprang from the fusion of the Achaeans and the Dorians. The vases of that age were well - shaped, with harmonious and solid contours, and their decoration aimed exclusively at enhancing their shape. Ornamental patterns were executed in black paint on the surface of natural clay. From the 9th century B.C., figures of birds and animals were included in the decoration. Human figures were added only in the 8th century B.C., but these, too, were completely ruled by the geometric spirit and characterized by marked abstraction.

The statues that have survived from that period are of small size. Representations of figures show sturdiness but lack plasticity. Proportions of the various parts of the body are not correct. Statues were made of clay, bronze, lead or ivory. The most noteworthy example is a small statuette of ivory representing a woman wearing on her head a 'polos' (adorned with meander). Manufacture included fine weapons, large and small bronze vessels, jewellery, mostly pins, fibulae etc. (The presence of gold is scant. Fine gold plates decorated with various motives were sometimes deposited in the graves of the rich as funerary offerings).

The buildings preserved reveal the simple architecture of the Geometric times. They were lightly constructed with stones and consisted of two or three quadrilateral rooms with a courtyard (Andros, Kastro at Siphnos). Temples similarly display a very simple form. The temple of Artemis Orthia at Sparta is dated to the Geometric period.

The second Greek colonization

The second colonization, undertaken chiefly during the 8th and 7th centuries B.C., was the most significant event in the history of Greek antiquity. It gave tremendous impetus to the evolution of civilization and resulted in a completely unexpected prosperity and expansion of the Greeks over the whole then known world. This was indeed one of the most magnificent accomplishments of Hellenism, although it had resulted from the restless situation prevailing within certain city-states.

From the small city-states that had been formed on Greek territory, active and determined men were sent out to found colonies in all sites important for trade along the coasts of the Black Sea, the Aegean and the Mediterranean. Large Greek cities grew in the new settlements. These cities attained great prosperity, which was due to the wealth of resources in the new colonies as well as the activity of the Greek colonists. With remarkable insight and knowledge of the situation, the new cities were built on locations selected not only for their significance in the trade with the East or Africa, but also for their access to areas abounding in raw materials, or wheat and other goods. A glance at the map of that period shows that the Greeks succeeded in planting strong new cities from the Black Sea to the coasts of North Africa and from Asia Minor to Gibraltar.

The outcome of this movement was of immense importance to Hellenism. As recorded by the ancient historian Herodotos, the Greeks did not undertake voyages, as the Phoenicians did, only for trading purposes; their purpose was both commercial growth and acquaintance with the world around them. And as contact of the colonists with the metropolis (the mother-city who sent them out) never ceased, ties remained strong and relations close between the Greeks of the mainland and those of the colonies.

Thus, Hellenism benefited in more than one ways. Not only abundant raw materials and goods were acquired for the development of commerce and craftsmanship, but through close observation a profound knowledge was gained of the new cultures that emerged on the lands where the great Eastern civilizations had grown. Many of these cultural elements were adopted by the Greeks, who outgrew rapidly the stage of imitation of foreign types and forms and reached the phase of creative assimilation leading to a remarkable evolution and flowering in every domain of life and particularly art.

ARCHAIC CIVILIZATION

Thus emerged a new cultural phase, the Archaic (700 - 480 B.C.), preparing the way for the development of the Classical civilization as fashioned in the 5th century B.C., which raised Greece to the highest spiritual sphere of antiquity.

The Archaic age is a revolutionary period in every respect. The evolution of architecture produced great temples and two dominant styles : the Doric and the Ionic. Great technical works were carried out (aqueducts, such as the one built by Polykrates on Samos, the Diolkos in Corinth, etc.). Art reached an exceptional flowering in all its branches. Large-sized and lively statues were for the first time produced by anonymous sculptors who competed with each other for the presentation not so much of novel forms as of perfect figures. In a short while, statues of smiling nude young men (kouroi) and elaborately dressed maidens (korai) filled the Greek sanctuaries and the cemeteries of cities. The discovery of the method of melting bronze and casting it in moulds, led to a great development of bronzework. Coins — which were also notable works of art — were minted in the powerful Greek cities. Ivory, metals, various precious and semi-precious materials, filled the Greek workshops to be fashioned by artists into fine weapons, elegant vessels, attractive statuettes and countless other works of art. Superb woven textiles and fine tissues were produced in Corinth and sold on the Greek and foreign markets. The development of pottery was no less impressive. Inspired by age-old Greek myths, the vase-painters represented various mythical scenes on the elegant vases produced in their workshops. The entire Greek world was literally vibrating with artistic creation.

It was then that for the first time the Greek mind began to wonder about the meaning of life, and philosophical thought emerged in Ionia (Asia Minor). In the early Archaic period (8th - 7th century B.C.), Homer, the greatest of Greek poets, composed his two magnificent epic poems, the *Iliad* and the *Odyssey.* These were truly national sagas, projecting Hellenism and its message in every form and describing the adventures of the Greek race in search of a land for settlement. The type of Odysseus, representative of the keen and determined Greeks, became familiar and liked all over the Greek world. These two great epic poems were the Bible of the Greeks during antiquity, taught to children at school and giving them the first incentive to thinking.

History writing was then developed and so were didactic poetry (Hesiod), as well as lyric poetry, which was developed under various forms in Greece.

The absence of dogma — an unprecedented instance for a civilized people — allowed the free evolution of religion. As the standard of civilization became higher, deities emerged with finer features and more profound significance. Zeus, Apollo, Athena, Hera and Demeter were the first gods and goddesses to whom a fully divine nature was attributed, as it appears in the beautiful *Homeric Hymns,* which were mostly poetical works of that period.

Intense activity and the evolution of all social classes in cities, contributed to the development of man as an individual. Once again, it was here that for the first time in the world the individual acquired consciousness of his own value and demanded the rights to which he felt entitled.

Forms of government were developed in rapid succession and legislations written by worthy men, most of whom were among the famous Seven Wise Men of Greece. There exists in the modern world no form of government which cannot be traced to ancient Greece; for, the Greeks had lived through every stage of political evolution : monarchy, oligarchy, tyranny, aristocracy, democracy.

As was natural, commercial activity led to remarkable maritime growth. The types of ships were perfected. Nevertheless, conditions in the city-states of ancient Greece became at times difficult. For, as life progressed, enmities and rivalries arose between them, eventually leading to wars. In order to meet the necessities of war, strong military bodies were organized : the phalanx of hoplites, who when properly trained proved of surprising strength with their infrangible formations.

In spite of internal conflicts the cities prospered, each creating a distinct type and organizing a complete world of her own. Among the Greek cities (Argos, Corinth, Sikyon, Chalkis, Eretria, Aigina, etc.), two were distinguished as the leading powers of Hellenism : Sparta and Athens. During the Archaic period these two cities developed along different lines their ideals and cultures with their unique essence and message, which have remained to our days as examples to the Western World.

The remarkable achievements of this era were nearly irretrievably lost in 490 B.C. The great expansion of Hellenism and its wide-spread activities disturbed the mighty Eastern empire of the Persians. Following their policy of expansionism with determination, impetuousness and stubborness, the Persian monarchs, wishing to enlarge the boundaries of their vast empire into European territory, decided to invade Greece, whose small and restless city-states were an obstacle to their plans of world domination.

The Persian Wars (490 - 479 B.C.)

The danger of race extinction was great. All the more so, since Greece had never known until that age the fruits of unity, but was harassed by endless fratricidal wars. There existed, therefore, a probability — on which the Persians' initiative must also have been based — of the dissolution of Hellenism and whatever it had so far achieved, and the conversion of Greece into a small Persian province following its eventual conquest by the barbarians. Fortunately, however, Greece was saved thanks to the cultivation of the ideal of liberty and the full awareness of the fact that in spite of mutual differences all Greeks belonged to the same race, sharing in common the same language, religion and ideals. Patriotism was fully awakened, so that all Greeks joined in a common struggle 'for all', determined to preserve their world or perish.

10.000 Athenian hoplites led by great men — Miltiades with Aristeides and Themistokles — and joined by 1.000 Plataians faced the Persian armies and quite unexpectedly won a brilliant victory in the battle of Marathon (490 B.C.). In 480 B.C., the united Greeks (they had founded in 481 B.C. the Panhellenic Alliance under the leadership of Sparta) achieved outstanding victories, both moral and military, demonstrating to the barbarians the unconquerable spirit of Hellenism and its determination never to surrender. The king of Sparta, Leonidas, with 300 Spartans fell in the battle of Thermopylai (480 B.C.) leaving for posterity an immortal example of supreme heroism.

Again, in 480 B.C., the navies of all the Greek states under the leadership of both Sparta and Athens (Eurybiades and Themistokles) won at Salamis the greatest victory of the Persian Wars. In the next year, 479 B.C., once more united and led by the Spartan general and regent Pausanias, the Greeks triumphed at Plataiai. Following their defeat, the Persians decided to leave Greece and never again try an invasion of the Greek territory.

Victory was final. The great national struggle 'for all' had been won. The Greeks, a people of very limited resources as compared to their mighty and rich opponents, had succeeded with their valour, high moral and superhuman heroism to repel the menace of the barbarians who had imperilled the very existence of the whole Hellenic world. Greece, and with her the whole of Europe, had been saved. If the Greeks had been vanquished, the cource of history would have been entirely different and consequences would have been dramatic for the present Western civilization.

THE CLASSICAL ERA

The consequences of victory were inestimable. The great surge of pride and optimism that filled the victorious Greeks had miraculous effects in every manifestation of life over the whole Hellenic world and, particularly, Athens. The Greeks became aware of the value of national unity, for they had clearly perceived during the Persian Wars that when a handful of united men are determined to fight for their national liberty, they may well succeed to repel an opponent superior in number and power. The unique flowering of all the Greek cities, and, above all, Athens, was the immediate outcome of the confidence and elation that prevailed in the Hellenic world following the defeat of the Persians.

To protect themselves against the perils of another attack which the Persians might eventually undertake against Greece, the Athenians organized the First Athenian Alliance, which was gradually joined by most of the cities of Asia Minor, the Aegean islands, the Hellespont, etc. During its peak years the Alliance numbered approximately 170 member cities. This enterprise was the most important confederation ever formed in ancient Greece until the age of Alexander the Great. Leadership was assumed by Athens, the undisputably greatest naval power of the Greek world. Later, in addition to other obligations imposed on the allies, the use of Athenian coins, weights and measures was adopted by all, a fact which facilitated to a great extent commercial transactions between them.

The outcome of the tremendous power and prosperity gained by the Athenians through the Alliance, was the unique cultural accomplishment of the 5th century B.C. in the city of Athens, which became the greatest artistic and intellectual centre, enjoying Panhellenic prestige. These achievements were realized thanks to the excellent statesmanship of Perikles, who retained the leadership of the democratic party of Athens from 462 B.C. until the year of his death in 429 B.C., being annually elected as general from 443 B.C. onwards. His wise administration established the Athenian democracy and made it an unparallelled example of this form of government till present times. The deme of Athens, the deme with the highest cultural standard ever attained, voted at the Assembly with absolute sense of responsibility, deciding which of the propositions advanced by the politicians would serve the state best.

Art and letters in the Classical period

The fact that the age of Perikles immortalized the name of Greece for times to come was not merely due to the outstanding political and economic development of Athens, but principally to the splendid cultural flowering that the city experienced under his leadership.

From all the Greek city-states gathered in Athens the most distinguished men of that age : Philosophers like Anaxagoras, named 'the Mind', and Gorgias; the historian Herodotos, 'the father of History'; Hippodamos of Miletos, the first town-planner in the world, etc. All these celebrated figures joined the intellectual and artistic circles of Athens which included already outstanding men of letters and artists, and they each left as an invaluable legacy to mankind the fruits of their creative ability. Thus, the 5th century B.C., the most important of Greek antiquity in all fields of accomplishment, was justly named 'Golden Age' and associated with the name of the great Athenian politician and general, Perikles.

Some decades had already passed after the Persian Wars, and the cherished goddess and great patroness of Athens to whom the city owed her prosperity, as the ancients believed, still lacked a temple befitting her majesty on the Acropolis. The earlier temple of the goddess destroyed by the Persians had not been replaced. Perikles decided to reconstruct the shrines of the city, including, of course, the temples of the Acropolis, where he appointed the greatest sculptor of the century, Pheidias of Athens, as overseer of the works. The majestic marble Propylaia, the monumental entrance to the sanctuaries of the Acropolis, were erected on plans designed by the architect Mnesikles, while Iktinos and Kallikrates were the architects of the Parthenon, the supreme masterpiece of Classical architecture. The sculptured decoration of the temple, designed by Pheidias, was executed by himself and a group of talented artists working under his direction. Shortly afterwards was built the Erechtheion, the most extraordinary temple of Greek antiquity, which housed the cult of Athena Polias together with the old cults of Athens. At the south-west corner of the Sacred Rock was erected the elegant Ionic temple of Athena Nike. Countless bronze and marble votive offerings of superb artistic quality (among which the statues of Athena Promachos, Athena Lemnia — both works of Pheidias — Athena Hygieia, and many more) were set up in the area of the Acropolis, where the sanctuary of Artemis Brauronia, the Chalkotheke and some lesser shrines were also founded.

In addition, magnificent temples were built in the centre of Athens and the large demes of Attica : the temple of Hephaistos at Kolonos Agoraios, the temple of Nemesis at Rhamnous, the temple of Ares in the deme of Acharnai, the temple of Poseidon at Sounion, the Telesterion in the sanctuary of Demeter at Eleusis. The Odeion of Perikles was constructed on the south-east slope of the Acropolis.

The 'asty' of Pallas Athena became the most beautiful city of Greece; not only the sanctuaries but also the city itself was embellished with superb monuments. All branches of art reached their zenith (sculpture, painting, bronzework, minor arts, pottery etc.). The works of the great tragic poets Aischylos, Sophokles and Euripides, were among the most outstanding intellectual products of those times. Citizens attended gratis (the polis offered them this opportunity for educational purposes) the theatrical performances included in the celebrations of festivals in honour of Dionysos. It was during this century that Herodotos wrote the history of the Persian Wars — the most glorious war adventure of the ancient Greeks — and Thucydides, the greatest historian of antiquity, the history of the Peloponnesian War.

Athens became the 'school' of the Hellenic world, but art and letters reached a high level in other cities too, both on mainland Greece and the islands as well as in Magna Graecia.

THE PELOPONNESIAN WAR AND THE 4TH CENTURY B.C.

This astonishing pace of progress was checked by the Peloponnesian War (431 - 403 B.C.), in which the greatest Greek cities participated, siding either with Athens or with her rival, Sparta. This war and other hostilities during the 4th century B.C., caused such extensive disasters all over Greece that by 350 B.C., most of the Greek cities were more or less exhausted. It became obvious then, that local rivalries had been severely detrimental to Greece and that Greeks should unite into a single Hellenic power setting aside their mutual differences.

The kingdom of Macedon, which had remained neutral during the conflicts of the other city-states of Greece, aspired to realize this significant objective. In spite of their political genius, however, neither king Philip II, at first, nor, after his death, his son and successor Alexander, succeeded in uniting the Greek cities into one great power. Philip's vision was to unite the city-states of the Greek mainland under the leadership of Macedon and subsequently launch an expedition in

Asia against the Persian empire. His premature death put an end to his ambition, which was however realized, even more gloriously, by his son Alexander named 'the Great' for his astounding triumphs.

ALEXANDER THE GREAT

Alexander's objective was to liberate the Greek cities which were under Persian yoke and avenge the Greeks for the many calamities they had endured because of the Persians.

In 334 B.C., when Alexander's army set off from Macedon, Darius III Codomanus was king of Persia. With an infantry of 30,000 soldiers and a cavalry of 5,000 horsemen, Alexander crossed to Asia Minor. His army was outnumbered by the Persians, but he proceeded boldly according to the ingenious plan he had conceived. Victory was on his side from the start.

Following a series of brilliant victories —first on the river Granikos (334 B. C.), then at Issos (333 B.C.), where in addition to rich spoils he captured the family of Darius— he conquered Asia Minor. He did not stop there, however. He advanced, always victoriously, against Syria and Palestine. The cities of Phoenicia surrendered to the Macedonian army, and so did the cities of Palestine — only Gaza fell after a siege of two months.

The Persian king took fright. He could not understand what Alexander's aim was. He proposed peace, ceding all territory west of the Euphrates and offering his daughter as wife to the Greek king.

Nevertheless, wishing to free Egypt from the Persian rule, Alexander proceeded, victorious as ever, to the realization of this objective, too. He then founded Alexandria at an important site of the Nile Delta on plans of the engineer Deinokrates.

After his triumph in Egypt, Alexander set out for the conquest of Persia. The Greek army clashed at Gaugamela with the far more numerous Persian troops who were, moreover, equipped with elephants and 200 scythed chariots. With his heroic spirit and infallible military genius, fighting with his phalanx in oblique arrangement, Alexander annihilated his enemies. The heart of Persia lay open before him, while the frightened Persian monarch was retreating inland of his vast dominion. One after the other, the three Persian capitals fell to Alexander. Every conquered city added new treasures into the hands of the Greeks. With the quantities of gold found in the royal treasury of Persia, Alexander minted and put into circulation gold coins. Meanwhile, in the upheaval precipitated by the successive victories of the Greeks, the Persian king was assassinated. Alexander ordered that the king be buried with great honours and proclaimed himself successor of the Achaimenids, i.e. the Persian dynasty.

The measures taken by the young Greek conqueror for the administration of the vast Persian empire are indeed worth of admiration. He respected the local customs and religion and treated the vanquished Persians in the best of ways, so as to discourage any ideas of uprising against him.

Between 329 and 328 B.C., Alexander conquered Sogdiana and Bactria in Upper Persia. In 327 B.C., he marched against India, attracted by the mystery of this country. He advanced unrestrainable towards the valley of the Ganges and prepared to reach the Hyphasis. There, he stopped at last, for his army was exhausted from the long march. The return was full of adventures and terrible hardships. But Alexander faced them bravely, always at the side of his soldiers, deprived even of water, as they were.

In 323 B.C., delegations from all nations came to visit Alexander to congratulate him, crown him and express their admiration for his achievement. He had indeed become a legendary figure. Scythians, Aithiopians, Gaules, Spaniards, Carthagenians, etc., gathered before him, astounded by his youth and indomitable valour. In spite of his youth, however, Alexander's life was nearing its end. Shortly afterwards he fell ill with a fever and died a few days later.

The magnificent undertaking of Alexander the Great stands as a unique phenomenon in history for its success and extent. A great leader and a brilliant general, he won with his noble character and keen intelligence the confidence of those around him. His aim was a synthesis of the Greek and Persian civilizations. He founded a great many new cities in the most important sites of Persia and the other conquered countries, where the Greeks settled forming nuclei of the Greek civilization.

He was tolerant and respected the way of life in the lands he occupied. He was also endowed with remarkable administrative abilities. He knew how to win the love of people. He expanded most widely the frontiers of Hellenism and brought the Macedonian coinage to the confines of the world. For a short while trade reached an unprecedented peak.

The most outstanding of all his accomplishments, was perhaps the civilizing influence he exerted. The Greek language was spoken by multitudes and penetrated deep into Asia and Egypt. It became the instrument of both written and oral expression, and had already taken roots when it was employed for the spreading of Christianity, thus contributing immensely to the propagation of the new religion.

Alexander was interested in every aspect of life. He was accompanied by a group of educated men, whom he instructed to study the soil, subsoil, fauna and flora of the countries he occupied. The relevant sciences were thus greatly developed. He became interested in the irrigation system of Mesopotamia with a view to make possible the cultivation of arid lands, and send out exploratory missions from Babylon to find a sea-route to Egypt.

Dying at the age of 33, he left a new world, a world filled with the message of the Greek spirit. He was, indeed, justly named Alexander the Great.

THE HELLENISTIC PERIOD

Following the death of Alexander the Great, his chief generals and assistants took over the administration of the vast empire he had created by his glorious campaigns in the East. Each of them became ruler of a large section, and soon afterwards proclaimed himself king. Thus the regions under their command became independent kingdoms; these included the kingdom of Egypt, Syria, Thrace, Pergamon and Macedon. This partition of the empire was a necessary step for its survival in those difficult times. The ambitious, former generals sought to develop their states in the best possible way. Fairly soon, however, they waged wars against each other, while the various city-states of mainland Greece, reminiscent of their irretrievably lost old glory, tried to rid themselves of the Macedonian mastery. Sparta was becoming less and less important. A brief revival in the 3rd century B.C. under the kings Agis and Kleomenes was only temporary. Thus, whilst the ambitious Macedonian rulers of the Greek overseas kingdoms were entangled in endless wars that weakened their states, mainland Greece followed strenuously her historic course amidst economic adversities.

Two noteworthy confederacies formed in those times — the Achaian and the Aitolian Leagues — appeared for a short while as capable of saving Greece. Unfortunately, however, they lost sight of their main objective and spent their energy in wars against each other.

The worst peril for Greece emerged in the 2nd century B.C. The Roman state which had attained great prosperity and developed unrestrainable tendencies of expansion, became interested in the Hellenic territory. Taking advantage of the constant rivalries between the Greek cities, the Romans succeeded in gaining supremacy first over Macedonia, and, in 146 B.C., over the whole of Greece.

After the Greek mainland, the Greek kingdoms of the East from Pergamon to Egypt fell in turn under Roman sway. The misleading evidence of events showed that Hellenism was forever extinguished.

HELLENISTIC CIVILIZATION

Yet, the Greek race was not destined to perish. The campaigns of Alexander the Great had opened the boundaries of the then known world to Hellenism. Science, art, literature, all important intellectual activities, as well as trade, had advanced to a remarkable extent. Thus, with their superior civilization the vanquished Greeks 'subdued their harsh conquerors', to quote the Roman poet Horace. Greece became a small province of the vast Roman empire. Nevertheless, the young Romans of noble descent were sent to the Greek cities to acquire education and culture. The philosophical schools of Athens, Rhodes, Alexandria, etc., had many Roman students. Roman families employed Greek tutors for the education of their children. Moreover, the works of Greek art were plundered or copied and transported to Italy to adorn the villas of eminent Romans. By reason of its high standard Greek civilization prevailed, and the Greeks did not disappear from the face of the earth. The restoration of Hellenism was merely a matter of time, as it soon became apparent. The Greek language which had spread to the remotest places of the then known world, served for the preaching of Christianity. Even though no longer appearing on the map of the world as a free state, Greece continued to offer her spiritual gifts. The Early Christian times were hard and dramatic for Greece, whose geographic position exposed her to every invasion from the East. When the great barbarian invasion started in Europe in the 3rd century A.D., Greece went through a most trying period. Disasters, massacres, plunders were the results of every enemy raid against Greece, who had already been suffering this fate from the 2nd century B.C. But the Greek nation survived again, following the division of the Roman empire into East and West, necessitated by the prevailing difficulties. Once more, thanks to the splendid civilization of the past, and without war struggle, Greece emerged as Byzantium, not only free but also a great power in the world.

THE BYZANTINE EMPIRE

Its name, beginning and character

Byzantine history is essentially the history of Mediaeval Hellenism. It not only constitutes one of the most interesting phenomena in world history, but also illustrates the vigour and inner force of Hellenism. The Byzantine empire was in fact the East Roman state, officially christianized (from the Edict of Milan to the formal establishment of Christianity by Theodosios the Great) and fundamentally hellenized to such a degree that in spite of its over-millennial duration, vast extent, unstable frontiers and population composed of various nationalities, the Greek language and character together with the Christian Orthodox faith formed the cohesive force which gave the empire its ultimate features. By its nature, Byzantine history has no definite beginning, since it evolved from a process of gradual conversion of the Roman to a Greek Christian state. The foundation of Constantinople (A.D. 324 - 330) was certainly a landmark designating the transference of the centre of the empire from Latin to Greek territory. The selection of the site of Byzantium — after which the whole empire was named by modern historians — was indeed most fortunate, for New Rome (Constantinople) was founded on the crossroads of both land and sea routes connecting Europe with the East. Another date that may be regarded as the beginning of Byzantine history is the year A.D. 395, when the Roman empire was divided into East and West.

THE MEDIAEVAL HISTORY TILL THE AGE OF JUSTINIAN (A.D. 395 - 527)

The earlier period of Byzantine history was marked by struggles against the barbarians : the Huns, Ostrogoths, Vandals and Persians. By repelling them, Byzantium succeeded to preserve the tradition of Western civilization. At the same time, with the Oecumenical Councils (the first in A.D. 325 at Nikaia, the second in A.D. 384 at Constantinople, the third in A.D. 431 at Ephesos, the fourth in A.D. 451 at Chalcedon) the Orthodox creed was more clearly defined and safeguarded from various heresies.

During that period was produced the Codex Theodosianus (438), which became the basis for legislation in the states of the West. An event of great importance for the development of the letters was the foundation of the University of Constantinople, the 'Pandidakterion', where the Greek and Latin languages were chiefly taught.

Art followed in the steps of ancient tradition. Churches of the basilica type (an oblong building divided by rows of columns into an odd number of naves and terminating on the east side into a semicircular apse) prevailed and marked the triumphal advance of Christianity. Fine examples of this magnificent style — undoubtedly of Roman origin — have survived in Thessaloniki (St. Demetrios, Acheiropoietos), while remains have been brought to light by archaeological excavations at other sites (Philippi, Anchialos, Nikopolis, etc.). Splendid mosaics, strongly reminiscent of Hellenistic art, adorned the floors and walls of basilicas and other religious and secular buildings (the Rotunda, St. Demetrios, Hosios David at Thessaloniki, the floors of the Palace of Constantinople, the floors of basilicas at Nikopolis, etc.).

THE OECUMENICAL STATE OF JUSTINIAN

Some of the most glorious chapters of Byzantine history embracing all manifestations of culture were written during the reign of Justinian (A.D. 527 - 565). This great emperor, assisted by worthy collaborators, and particularly his wife, the Augusta Theodora, aspired and — during his lifetime, at least — succeeded in giving Byzantium an oecumenical character. Following the victories of his generals Belisarius and Narses over the Persians, Vandals and Ostrogoths, the empire expanded from Spain and the coasts of Africa deep into Asia. After the famous riots of Nikas (532), peace and order were restored in the internal political life. Circumstances, then, permitted the emperor to devote time to his great legislative and constructive work, and take measures for the protection of the Orthodox creed by summoning the fifth Oecumenical Council (at St. Sophia, in A.D. 553) and striking the last blows on the remnants of paganism. His legislative work (Corpus Juris Civilis — the Institutes, Digest, Codex Justinianus and Novellae), which provided the basis for the codification of the Roman law and the organization of justice of the whole European world to our days, has been characterized by a foreign historian as the most important book, after the Bible, for the evolution of humanity.

The church of St. Sophia in Constantinople, where the problem of crowning a square building with a circular dome was given an ingenious solution, reflects the stability of the imperial authority and constitutes the most perfect architectural expression of the Orthodox faith : the huge dome depicts the universe, which is the throne of God, and at the same time represents the incarnation of the Word of God, i.e. the coming of Christ into the world. A number of buildings with fine mosaics were erected throughout the empire — from the biblical Mt. Sinai, where the Monastery of St. Catherine was adorned with the apse mosaics, to Ravenna in Italy, where St. Vitale's was decorated with gold-trimmed mosaics representing the majestic processions of Justinian and Theodora, and the island of Paros in the Aegean, where the imposing church of Katapoliani was built. On the other hand, castles, large aqueducts, reservoirs, etc., were constructed during that age. A parallel flourishing was noted in all branches of art (decorative and plastic art, illuminated manuscripts, portable icons — in the encaustic technique applied in Mt. Sinai — and metalwork).

HERACLIUS AND HIS STRUGGLES AGAINST THE PERSIANS AND THE ARABS

Heraclius, the emperor-soldier (A.D. 610 - 642), carried on the age-long tradition of fighting against the Persians, which now took the form of a crusade and ended in 'everlasting' peace (629) and the recovering of the True Cross (630). In 626, when the emperor was fighting against the Persians far from his capital, Constantinople went through very trying times, besieged as it was by the Arabs and Slavs. The defence of the Vasilevousa was conducted by the Patriarch Sergius and the patrician Bonus, who saved the city with the help of the 'Hypermachos Strategos', the Virgin. It was then that the people of Constantinople sang the 'Akathistos' hymn of thanksgiving to the Theotokos, one of the most exultant and beautiful works of ecclesiastical poetry. Though the Persians ceased to be a problem for the Byzantine empire, another people, the Arabs, emerged at this age and became a source of menace for the Orthodox emperors in the following centuries.

The year of the Hegira (622) marks the beginning of the history of the Arabs. Their expansion was rapid and deprived the Byzantine empire of vitally important territories, such as Egypt, Palestine and Syria; Alexandria, one of the most prominent centres of Hellenism, fell into foreign hands — an event of grave consequence in the course of Hellenic history. This age also witnessed the appearance of other races (Slavs, Bulgars), whose invasions harassed the empire for centuries.

THE ISAURIANS AND THE ICONOCLASTIC MOVEMENT

The dynasty of the Isaurians, founded by Leo III Isaurus (717 - 741), ruled during the 8th century. Being himself a tough soldier, this emperor faced bravely the Arabs and saved Europe from the peril of an Islamic domination with his victorious battles on land and sea (battle of Constantinople).

A most peculiar event disturbed the Byzantine empire at this age and lasted till the first half of the 9th century : the Iconoclastic movement, i.e. the dispute over the role and significance of icons in the life of the church. Iconoclasm had several phases. In brief, the course of events was as follows : In 726, the emperor forbade the worship of icons. This interdict provoked revolts and some of the rebels proclaimed themselves emperors, but failed to impose themselves. In 754, the Council of Hiereia pronounced the dogmatic establishment of Iconoclasm. However, the seventh and last Oecumenical Council at Nikaia in 787, condemned the Council of Hiereia and pronounced the iconoclasts as heretics. Again, in 815, another council revived Iconoclasm, until icon-worship was finally restored in 843.

Historians give many and varied interpretations to the iconoclastic movement. Some regard the movement as an attempt of the Isaurians at social reform; others as an instrument for restricting the influence of the clergy and particularly the monks. It seems, however, that the root of the problem was of a purely religious and spiritual context. Under cover of the dispute over the icons, lurked the dissensions over the nature and person of Christ. Moreover, the Oriental Isaurians could not grasp easily the concept of the icon. Had their ideas prevailed, the exquisite art of wall-paintings, mosaics, movable icons and illuminated manuscripts would have never existed. The few monuments that have survived from this tumultuous period in remote regions, such as the Mani, the island of Naxos, etc., demonstrate the kind of art which the iconoclasts wanted to create. Finally, however, as an eminent Greek historian remarks, «the failure of Iconoclasm secured the future of the distinct Byzantine civilization as related to the civilizations of antiquity, within the community of Christian Europe» (D. Zakythinos).

THE MACEDONIAN REVIVAL

After the Isaurians and the triumph of Orthodoxy, the Macedonian dynasty ascended the throne of Constantinople. This dynasty led Byzantium to one of the highest pinnacles of its glorious history, so that most historians would later speak of a Renaissance, which had already been announced from the reign of the last emperor of the Amorian dynasty, Michael III (842 - 867). This was the age of the great scholars Theodore Studites and the Patriarch Nikephoros, and of the first eminent scientists, like Leo the Mathematician, who became the soul of the Pandidakterion of the Magnaura, one of the earliest universities.

The conversion of the Slavs to Christianity during this period (862) was a most important event, in which the enlightened brothers, Constantine - Cyrillus and Methodius of Thessaloniki played a leading role. In addition to Orthodoxy, they presented the Slavs with an alphabet. The Gospels, liturgical books, and the Digest of Laws prepared during the reign of the Isaurians were translated into the Slavonic language. A few years later (864), the Bulgars, too, were converted to Christianity and their sovereign Boris was christened and given the name of Michael.

During the reign of the Macedonian dynasty, inaugurated by Basil I the Macedonian (867 - 886), Byzantium reached its highest peak. Brave and wise emperors, valiant warriors or prominent scholars, such as Leo VI the Wise, Constantine Porphyrogenetos, Nikephoros Phokas, John Tsimiskes, Basil Bulgaroktonos, etc., wrote the 'Byzantine saga' with their campaigns against the Arabs, the Bulgars and other enemies of the empire, and restored the frontiers of the realm in East and West. Thus, with the reconquest of Italy, Byzantium became once again a notable power and an important factor on the European political scene. At the same time, the fine arts attained their most remarkable expression and most beautiful form, while the letters reached a singular flowering.

Military magnates and emperors, such as John Kourkouas, Nikephoros Phokas, John Tsimiskes and George Maniakes, regained Greek territories from the Arabs (Crete in 961, Cyprus in 965) and restored the Byzantine empire to its former eastern frontiers, with a parallel expansion of its boundaries as far as Armenia. Another focal point in the heroic campaigns of the Macedonian emperors was their struggle against the Bulgars. The final victory of the emperor Basil Bulgaroktonos (976 - 1025) at Kleidi (in 1014), dissolved the Bulgar state, dispelled Samuel's ambitious views and put an end to his cruelty with a chastisement which by today's standards appears particularly harsh. However, the Christian World was shaken by two events during that epoch : the two Schisms of the Church. The first (in 867), the so-called Photian after the name of the protagonist, Photius the Great, Patriarch of Constantinople, did not last long (it ended in 880), but the second, in 1054, ended in a final rupture between the Church of Constantinople and the Church of Rome with sad consequences lasting to present days. This date marks the official recognition of the latent dogmatic, liturgical and other differences between the Greek Orthodox Church and the Roman Catholic Church. The Schism occurred in the reign of Constantine IX Monomachos (1042 - 1055), while the powerful and haughty Michael Cerularius was Patriarch and Leo IX Pope, though the latter died shortly before the anathema.

The letters and arts were greatly developed during that age. Authors and scholars, like Michael Psellos, John Mauropous, Arethas of Kaisaria, restored the study of ancient Greek Classics and established modern Humanism, while the sciences were similarly promoted (Mathematics, Astronomy, Physics). Constantine Monomachos founded the 'School of Law', where eminent professors, such as John Xiphilinos, lectured. It should be noted at this point that the Macedonians produced an important legislative work (Procheiros Nomos, Epanagoge, Basilika, Eparchikon Biblion, and several other handbooks of law). In ecclesiastical literature emerged outstanding figures, among whom Symeon the New Theologian, the most celebrated mystic poet of the East. The conversion of the Russians to Christianity was one of the achievements of the Church, and stands as an event of singular importance, for it brought so vast a nation into Orthodoxy and under the influence of the Byzantine state.

Monuments of art attest to the prosperity and glory of the Macedonian dynasty. The architectural type of the cruciform domed church, also known as Byzantine, evolved during that period. This type combines the cross of Christ, since the arrangement of roofs is in the shape of a cross, and the boundlessness of the universe, as symbolized by the semicircular dome. A variant is the octagonal type of church, where the dome is enlarged and the interior better unified. Fine examples of this type have been preserved in Greece : Hosios Lukas, Nea Moni of Chios; Kapnikarea, Sts. Theodoroi, the Gorgoepekoos in Athens, and many other churches in Mani, Argolis, Naxos, etc. Mosaic decoration reached its zenith (Hosios Lukas, Nea Moni of Chios, Daphni). Theological maturity and dogmatic purity found their most remarkable expression through art. The illumination of manuscripts developed into an exquisite art, which impresses the modern viewer for the artists' skill in miniature work and aesthetic perfection. In addition, marvellous small sculptures in ivory depicting religious subjects, as well as secular themes or motifs inspired from ancient art, are now displayed in various museums along with fine specimens of goldwork, silverwork, etc.

THE COMNENES AND THE CRUSADES

Signs of decline appeared during the last years of the Macedonian dynasty, until a new vigorous dynasty of soldier-emperors ascended the throne and led the empire to one of the last phases of acme. The Comnene Dynasty gave emperors like Alexios I (1081 - 1118), John II (1118 - 1143), Manuel I (1143 - 1180), etc. Although these wise emperors succeeded in opposing the many enemies of the empire, new peoples entered the stage of History, and demanded a role during this period. The Normans, Turks, and, above all, the Crusades became the major and most difficult problems of the reign of the Comnenes. Byzantium was already being pressed on all sides and losing territory, when the Crusaders of the Fourth Crusade took advantage of certain dynastic rivalries among the Byzantines and altered their initial intention and objectives. They destroyed the Byzantine empire, conquered Constantinople and founded several small Frankish states throughout the realm.

The letters and arts continued to be of a high standard. Eustathios of Thessaloniki proved a great philologue and profound commentator of Homer. Anna, daughter of Alexios Comnenos, was a historian of value. Other historians (such as Anna's husband Nikephoros Bryennios, John Kinnamos, Niketas Choniates), philologues (such as Choniates' brother Michael, Archbishop of Athens), poets (like Theodore Prodromos, known as Ptochoprodromos) and a constellation of other scholars and scientists, lent brilliance to the 12th century and made it «the era of the first Greek Renaissance», as stated by a foreign historian.

THE FRANKISH OCCUPATION

After the fall of the Vasilevousa (Constantinople), the emperor transferred his seat to Nikaia, whilst the empire was partitioned into several small Frankish and Greek states : the Latin empire of Constantinople, the Latin kingdom of Thessaloniki, the hegemony of Achaia, etc. On the Greek side, in addition to the empire of Nikaia which was, in a manner of speaking, the continuation of the Byzantine empire, were founded the empire of Trebizond, the despotat of Epiros, etc. In 1261, the emperor of Nikaia, Michael VIII Palaeologos (1258 - 1282) reconquered Constantinople and founded the dynasty of the Palaeologues, who were destined to be the last emperors of the thousand year old empire.

THE PALAEOLOGUES

During the two centuries of the reign of the Palaeologues, Byzantium, surrounded as it was by menacing enemies, followed a difficult and often dramatic course. The last of the most Serene emperors, Andronikos II (1282 - 1328) and Andronikos III (1328 - 1341), John V (1341 - 1391), Manuel II (1391 - 1425), John VIII (1425 - 1448) and the heroic Constantine XI (1449 - 1453) tried desperately, both on battlefields and through diplomacy, to save the empire. The Union of the two Churches, formally achieved by the Council of Florence - Ferrara (1439) proved of no avail, since it was actually accepted by no one in the empire. Thus, the young state of Ottoman Turks encircled more and more tightly Constantinople and the region to which the once vast empire of the Romans had shrunk, as well as that part of the Greek territory where the despotat of Mistra was flourishing. On Tuesday, the 29th May 1453, Mohammed the Conqueror put an end to the Byzantine empire, while its last tragic emperor perished honourably fighting on the ramparts. It should be noted, however, that in the last centuries of its existence, in spite of continuous loss of territory and diminution of the political and strategic importance of its role in European history, Byzantium presented an admirable development in the letters and arts. Great ecclesiastical authors, such as Gregory Palamas and Nicholas Kabasilas, expounded the Orthodox mysticism known as the Hesychast movement. Historians, like Phrantzes, Dukas, Kritobulos, Chalkokondylis, the emperor John Cantacuzenus, Pachymeres and Nikephoros Gregoras recorded valuable information on that age, while the first four authors described the unhappy event of the fall of Constantinople. Also notable among other writers was Demetrius Kydones. The legendary philosopher of Mistra, George Gemistos Plethon, was held by his contemporaries as the wiser scholar after Plato. Plethon acquainted the West with Plato and in this way contributed greatly to the Renaissance.

True masterpieces were produced in art, such as the mosaics of the Monastery of Chora (Kariye Djami) in Constantinople (executed under the patronage of the very learned humanist Georgios Metochites), the wall-paintings of the churches of Mistra (the Metropolis, Peribleptos, Aphentiko, Pantanassa), the paintings of the so-called Macedonian school in the monasteries of Mt. Athos, where the outstanding painter of this school, Manuel Panselinos, embellished with his works the church of the Protaton. Other painters of the same school (Kallerges, Eutychios and Michael Astrapas) made fine wall-paintings in the churches of Macedonia and Serbia (Veroia, Achris, etc.), starting from Thessaloniki (St. Euthemios, St. Nikolaos Orphanos, mosaics of the Holy Apostles). The painting of portable icons gained particular significance. Some of them (the Crucifixion, the Archangel, the Virgin, now in the Byzantine Museum) clearly illustrate the aesthetic trends of the Palaeologan period, which combined the Orthodox spirituality with Greek elements of beauty. In architecture, elegant and attractive churches, such as the Holy Apostles' and St. Catherine's in Thessaloniki, and the churches of Mistra and Constantinople, provided the last fine examples of age-long types.

THE IMPORTANCE OF BYZANTINE HISTORY

In the course of its millennial history, Byzantium gave humanity the purest expression of Orthodox Christianity. It preserved and transmitted the ancient Classical culture. It converted to Christianity and set the bases for the civilization of the Russians, Serbs, Bulgars, Hungarians, Rumanians, etc. It created the most important art in Mediaeval painting and (partly) architecture. And when it finally fell under the Turkish rule, with the help of the church and tradition in general, it armed the Greek nation —and the other Balkan nations— in a way which permitted Greece to survive 400 years of slavery and rise again with the great War of Independence in 1821.

MODERN GREECE

Any other nation with such a long history and after such devastating blows would have perished; but not Greece — a nation destined to guard for many centuries the frontiers of Western civilization, to fight against the barbarians of the East, to be wounded and suffer every calamity, and then, like the mythical bird, the phoenix, to be reborn out of its own ashes.

The first decades after the Turkish occupation had been a most trying period for Hellenism. The Turks did not dominate over the whole Greek territory simultaneously, for the Cyclades, the Dodecanese, Crete and Cyprus were under other foreign rulers. In spite of the privileges accorded to the subjugated people, the Turkish yoke was almost unbearable and often exterminatory. Thousands of Greek children were taken by force from their families and trained to serve in the formidable legions of the Janissaries, in order to fight later even against their own parents, having lost from an early age every contact with their home, language and national tradition. The 'paidomazoma' (abduction of children), as this cruel action of the Sultan has been named, was a sort of horrible blood levy imposed on the conquered Greek people.

The historic course of the nation during that period was twofold. The regions occupied by the Turks declined economically (the Turks had taken the most fertile lands and driven away the Greeks to the mountainous and arid districts). Commerce was restricted. The letters declined, too, for shortly before or after the Turkish domination all the educated Greeks had left for Italy, where they played an important role in the Italian Renaissance —particularly in Florence— by teaching Greek literature and especially the philosophy of ancient Greece.

Similarly, art dwindled gradually, for conditions did not permit the production of great works that would create new types. The Turkish conquerors forbade the building of churches. The subjugated Greeks could not be taught freely even their own language. It was only in secrecy that children were instructed on some basic knowledge of their language and history by simple priests who acted also as teachers. Hence, mainland Greece fell into a sad state of illiteracy, while the splendid monuments of the past were turning to ruins through lack of preservation. Production in the major arts stopped, but instead a moving fact was noted : popular artists and craftsmen, —painters, masons, carpenters, etc.— preserved and developed the popular tradition in art. In spite of prohibitions, a little church was often built within a few nights (usually outside the cities or in villages where the control of the occupants was not so tyrannical) and its interior adorned with wall-paintings. Ancient sculptures were often built into the walls of churches — inscriptions, funerary stelai, architectural members and other marble fragments— connecting in this peculiar way the glorious days of the past with the then dramatic situation of the nation.

While life dragged amidst hardships and pains on mainland Greece, conditions on the Cyclades, the Dodecanese, Crete, Cyprus and the Ionian islands were quite different. Life there continued briskly, for the European rulers had not been harsh like the Sultans. The 16th century was an era of great flowering of religious art, both architecture and painting, as well as any other branch of art that served ecclesiastical purposes. At the same time, the growth of trade, which brought much wealth and became a source of prosperity, made possible the construction of fine mansions and other buildings. So, these islands enjoyed an active life until the time when they passed into the hands of the Turks — with the exception of the Ionian islands which were never submitted to the Turkish rule.

After the occupation of Crete by the Turks in the 17th century, Cretan artists and scholars migrated to the Ionian islands, where a remarkable artistic growth was noted within the framework of Greek tradition, while new types and styles were introduced from nearby Italy as a result of trade contacts.

In the second half of the 18th century the situation changed in Greece. The serious disorganization in the administration of the Ottoman empire gave educated Greeks the opportunity to occupy important positions in the Turkish adminis-tration, while many other Greeks developed most active commercial transactions with Europe. Thus, in the dark years of slavery, while local uprisings and attempts at liberating the nation were made on repeated occasions, a surprising commer-cial activity was carried out. Guilds of merchants and craftsmen were established —at Ambelakia in Thessaly, etc.— and the rich merchants became owners of fine many-storied lordly houses decorated in the interior with beautiful wall-paintings. This activity was particularly pronounced in the hegemonies by the river Danube (in the area of Eastern Rumelia, i.e. the present Rumania, Bulgaria and Eastern Thrace), in Macedonia and in Thessaly.

The Orthodox clergy, who had not only preserved the moral of the nation, but also taught letters to the Greek youths for centuries, included in the second half of the 18th century very learned members, who imparted their knowledge to laymen. Thus, the modern Greek Renaissance began in the second period of the Turkish domination. As was to be expected, attempts to liberate the nation from the Turkish yoke became subsequently more intensive, and the unsuccessful upris-ings of the subjugated Greeks were both frequent and costly in bloodshed. Those of the Greeks who could no longer endure the yoke took to the mountains, where they were free to practice with arms. They became known as 'klephtes' and, when-ever their enslaved brothers suffered from a particularly harsh measure of the Turks, they launched punitive raids.

The European travellers who visited Greece quite often in the late 18th and 19th centuries, offered a great service to the Greek nation : by writing on their re-turn their travellers' memoirs and describing the great monuments of the past, they projected the Greek cause and made it one of the most interesting pursuits of the intellectual circles of Europe.

The War of Independence started in 1821 without support from abroad and without supplies. It was inspired by an ardent wish for liberty, and developed into a miraculous achievement which forced the Holy Alliance (of the powerful states of Europe, who had been opposed to every national movement for liberation in those times) to consider the Greek cause and accede to the demand of all the Greeks for 'sweet freedom', to use the expression of the national poet, D. Solomos. Blood, sacrifice and superhuman struggles secured the survival of Greece and enabled her to continue her life as a free nation among the other free nations of Europe.

PLATES

1. Acropolis Museum, Athens.
   Relief of the «Mourning Athena».

2. National Archaeological Museum, Athens.
Bronze statue of Poseidon from Artemision.

3. National Archaeological Museum, Athens.
   The Ephebos of Antikythera.

4a. National Archaeological Museum, Athens.
    Gold cups found at Peristeria Kyparisias.

4b. National Archaeological Museum, Athens.
    Gold masks from the royal graves of Mycenae.

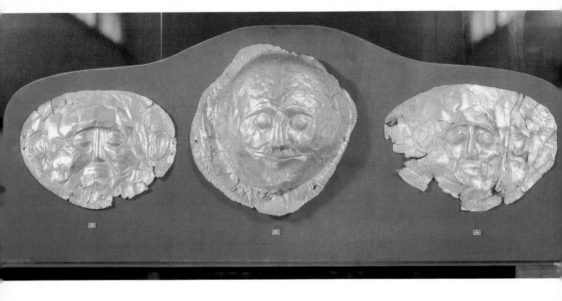

5. National
Archaeological
Museum,
Athens.
Bronze
statuette
from
Dodona.

6. Byzantine Museum, Athens.
The Virgin and Child.

7. Attica, Monastery of Daphni.
   Mosaic with representation of an angel and Hierarchs.

8. Ancient Corinth.
   The Archaic temple of Apollo.
   Acrocorinth is visible in the background

10. Mycenae.
Lion Gate.

11. Mycenae.
The «Treasury of Atreus».

12. Epidauros.
Statue
of the god
Asklepios.

13a. Epidauros.
    The sanctuary of Asklepios (restored).

13b. Epidauros.
    The ancient theatre.

14. Mistra.
Church of the Pantanassa.

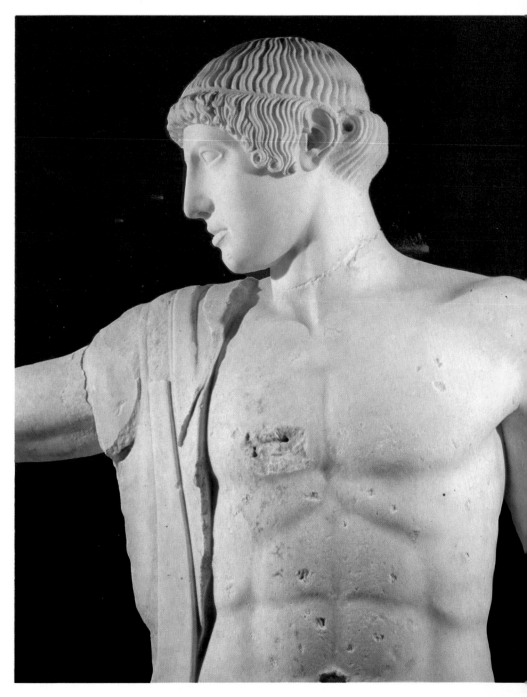

15. Olympia.
Statue of Apollo from the west pediment
of the temple of Zeus.

16. Olympia.
The Hermes
of Praxiteles.

17. Museum of Delphi.
    The Charioteer (detail).

18. Delphi.
   General view of the archaeological site.

22. Meteora.

21. Thessaloniki, Archaeological Museum.
Bronze crater from Derveni.

20. Hosios Lukas, Phokis.
   Representation of Christ.

19. Dodona.
The ancient theatre.

23. Pella.
Mosaic floors of a house
with restored columns.

24. Delos.
   Mosaic with representation of a panther.

25. Delos.
   Archaic lion.

26. Samothrace.
   The «Sanctuary».

28. Thera.
    Fresco
    of the
    Boxing
    Children.

29. Thera.
Fresco of the Spring.

30. Crete, Knossos.
    Fresco of the Gift-bearers.

31. Crete,
   Archaeological Museum of Herakleion.
   Sarcophagus from Hagia Trias.

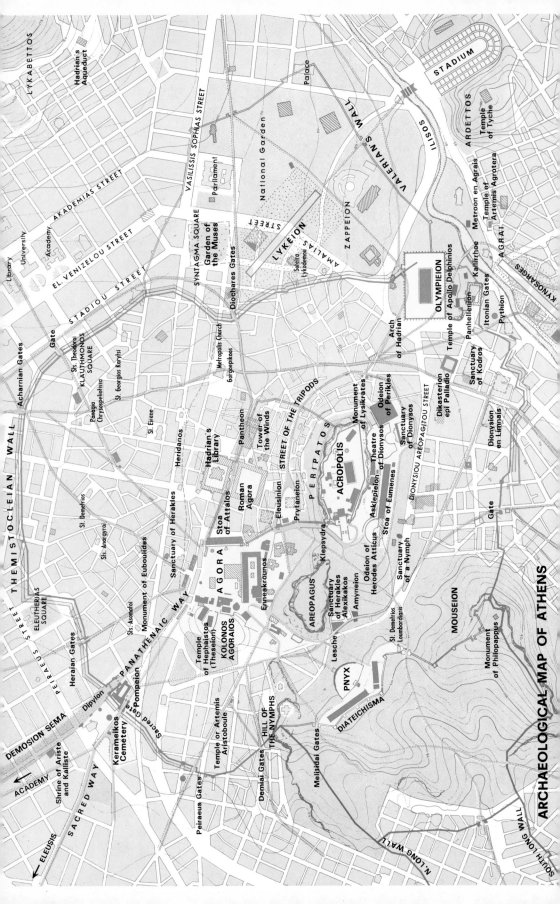

ARCHAEOLOGICAL MAP OF ATHENS

ATTICA

ATHENS

Athens is a city of unique character. Her remarkable beauty is linked with reminiscences of a very old past, covering not just one but many periods across the centuries. Her outstanding feature is the age-long nucleus of the city, the *Acropolis,* crowned with the precious and venerable remains of the most important stage in the history of antiquity.

The history of Athens is closely associated with the history of her Sacred Rock. As revealed by archaeological investigations, the caves on the northern slope of the hill had been occupied in the Stone Age by the earliest inhabitants to whom tradition ascribes the name of Pelasgoi. When faced with danger, the settlers sought refuge in the fortified top of the hill. (Small settlements must have existed in other locations as well, as denoted by the Pre-Hellenic name of the site : *Athenai).*

In the Mycenaean Age the Acropolis became the seat of a small strong state. The rock remained the centre of the settlement and was later fortified with a strong wall. The palace of the sovereign was on the Acropolis. Traces of Mycenaean houses and graves have been uncovered below and around the Sacred Rock (in the area of the ancient Agora, the Pnyx, and as far as the Kerameikos). The city extended in the Mycenaean period southwards and northwards of the Acropolis. At the foot of the hill, three springs secured water supply to the inhabitants.

In about the 12th century B.C., the Acropolis ceased to be the king's stronghold. With the passing of time, the most important and sacred buildings of the city were founded on the rock, which no longer served as dwelling-place of the supreme archon. The Acropolis became once again the political center of Athens for a brief interval in the 6th century B.C., during the tyranny of Peisistratos, who had his residence there. At that age (6th century B.C.), were erected the first fortification wall around the whole city, and the first Propylaia on the south slope of the Acropolis, the only side from which the Sacred Rock is accessible. The sanctuaries and rich votive offerings, which were an eloquent sign of the profound piety of the ancient Athenians towards the patroness goddess of their city, were destroyed in 480 B.C., during the barbaric invasion of the Persians. When the Persians were driven away, the pious Athenians dug pits at the top of the Acropolis and buried the mutilated statues and other offerings. Later, in 448 B.C., in the age of Perikles, the restitution of the sanctuaries began under the supervision of Pheidias, the greatest sculptor of all times, and the Acropolis acquired the most magnificent buildings of Greek antiquity : the *Parthenon,* the masterpiece of Classical architecture —in the Doric order— decorated with exquisite sculptures designed and executed by Pheidias and his disciples. The *Propylaia,* the monumental marble entrance to the sacred precinct of the Acropolis, were also erected at that time, in more majestic fashion, on plans of the architect Mnesikles. By the end of the 5th century B.C., another two architectural masterpieces with superb sculptured decoration were completed : the *Erechtheion,* the temple which housed the oldest cults of the Athenians, and the *temple of Athena Nike* both splendid examples of the Ionic order. All these buildings adorned the Sacred Rock with their magnificent appearance and elegant form. West of the Parthenon were founded the *Chalkotheke* and the *sanctuary of Artemis Brauronia.*

Countless votive offerings filled once more the entire space of the sacred precinct. Inside the Parthenon was set up the chryselephantine statue of the goddess

Athena, the masterpiece of Pheidias' magic art and the pride of the city. The *Odeion of Perikles* was built on the south-east slope of the Acropolis and the *theatre of Dionysos* on the NE slope, next to the *temple* of the god. Further to the west was founded the sacred precinct of the healing god *Asklepios,* a *sanctuary* of world-wide renown whose cult survived as late as the 5th century A.D. In brief, Athens reached during that age the highest peak in every field : artistic, intellectual and political. On the south slope of the Acropolis a great stoa was erected later, by *Eumenes* II, the art-loving king of Pergamon; to the west of it, was built in the 2nd century A.D. the *Odeion of Herodes Atticus,* where very interesting concerts and performances of ancient drama are now organized every summer by the National Tourist Organization (EOT) in the framework of the annual Festival of Athens.

The unsurpassed civilization that had grown in ancient Athens contributed to the preservation of her radiance in later times, when the city of Pallas Athena declined economically and her citizens lived on memories of the glorious past. From 38 B.C. to the 6th century A.D., when by decree of the Byzantine emperor Justinian her philosophical schools were closed, Athens remained a brilliant educational centre attracting young people from remote places of the West and the East.

Athens survived through the Roman and Mediaeval age, but only the various monuments still standing on the Acropolis and the city bore witness to the splendour of the old days. During the Frankish occupation, the foreign rulers resided on the Acropolis, and so did later, during the Turkish domination, the Turkish governor as well as several Turkish families. The Athenians never forgot —not even in the trying period of the Turkish rule— the outstanding importance their city had in the past, and kept alive in their souls the hope of her revival. Following the great War of Independence in 1821, when Greece was partly liberated after centuries of bondage, the soul of the freed nation made Athens the capital of the free sate (in 1834).

Athens is in our days a singular and fascinating city for tourists. In her center and over her entire area, visitors encounter remarkable monuments of every period of her age-long history.

At the beginning of Syngrou Avenue, the 'Columns' stand as a landmark of the entrance to the centre of the city. These towering columns belong to the gigantic *temple of Olympian Zeus,* whose construction, begun in the 6th century B.C., was completed in the 2nd century A.D., at the expence of the philhellene Roman emperor Hadrian. When finished, the temple looked like a forest of columns (104 in number), within which stood the large chryselephantine statue of Zeus, a copy of the god's statue at Olympia. Another characteristic monument nearby, is the *Arch of Hadrian*, which separated the ancient city from its extension of the Roman period. This gate was also built at the expense of the emperor Hadrian.

The circular *monument of Lysikrates*, at the end of the present homonymous street, is an example of the splendid monuments erected in antiquity by the 'choregoi' (wealthy Athenian citizens who defrayed the cost of preparation of a tragedy performance), if the play they had financed had been awarded a prize.

Beyond the south-west end of the Acropolis rises the *hill of Philopappus*, crowned by the remains of a monument erected by the Syrian prince who was made Athenian citizen and Roman consul. The view from the summit of the hill is panoramic, embracing Mt. Hymettos, the sea, the hill of the Pnyx and the Acropolis.

Right opposite the west side of the Acropolis stands the low *hill of the Pnyx*, which served for a long period as gathering-place during the political meetings of the ancient Athenians. Between the Pnyx and the Acropolis, lies the even lower *rock of the Areopagus*, the seat of the council of nobles initially, and the supreme judicial court later. It was from this site that the whole of humanity was taught the philanthropic principle that «equality of votes is in favour of the accused».

At the end of Aiolou Street stands one of the best preserved monuments of antiquity : the *Tower of the Winds*, the hydraulic clock of Andronikos of Kyrrhestos, built in the 1st century B.C. The tower was surmounted by a weather-vane and included a sundial and a water-clock. An interesting frieze with reliefs representing the winds extends along each side of the building, hence called at present 'the Winds' (Aerides).

Some fine monuments of the Mediaeval age have also been preserved in Athens, most important among them a number of churches of the 11th century A.D.: the *Sotera Lykodemou* (known as the Russian church) on Philhellenon Street, the *Kapnikarea* on Ermou Street, the *church of Hagioi Theodoroi* on the homonymous square at the beginning of Euripidou Street, the *church of the Holy Apostles* on the site of the Agora of the Classical period. In the outskirts of Athens, the *Monastery of Kaisariani, Omorfocclesia, Moni Asteriou and Ayios Joannes Kynegos,* are worth a visit.

In the 19th century, during the Romantic movement, a great love and admiration for the Classical monuments of Greek antiquity prevailed in Central Europe, and a strong tendency was noted to imitate their style in modern public buildings. Foreign architects visited Greece with that purpose in mind, studied the ancient monuments and inspired from them produced in Europe —in Vienna and Munich— the so-called 'Neoclassical style'. This style was adopted by Greek and foreign architects alike and Neoclassical buildings were also erected in Athens. Examples of these are : the church of St. Paul (Anglican church) on Philhellenon Street, the Zappeion, part of the Grande Bretagne Hotel, the Old Palace (Parliament), the Iliou Melathron (where the Areopagus is housed at present), the church of St. Dionysios (Catholic church), the Ophthalmiatreion, the University, the Academy, the Library, and the buildings of the Polytechneion and the Museum on Patision Street.

Athens is a beautiful city, clean and tidy. Walking in the narrow streets of the Plaka and the Aerides —where the ancient city was situated— one may see a capital, part of a column or an architectural marble fragment built into the walls of the houses or standing in the typical old courtyards. In the heart of modern Athens are the two most important archaeological sites after the Acropolis : the *Kerameikos,* the official cemetery of ancient Athens, and the *ancient Agora* (to the east of which are the imposing ruins of *Hadrian's Library* and the *Roman Agora)*.

The ancient Agora

The Agora (which had originally occupied the area between the Areopagus and the Propylaia) was the religious and political centre of the ancient city. The site of the Agora is bounded on the west by the great *Temple of Hephaistos* (known as the Theseion), built in the 5th century B.C. on the summit of the hill of Kolonos Agoraios, and on the east by the *Stoa of Attalos*, a vast two-storied building, erected at the expense of the philhellene king of Pergamon Attalos II (159 - 138 B.C.) and his wife Apollonis, as recorded on the dedicatory inscription. This monument has been restored (inaugurated in 1957) and serves as local Museum for the finds that have come to light during the extensive excavations on the site, and offices of archaeological services (Greek and American). In antiquity the Stoa had 21 shops opening on a double colonnade in each storey.

Excavations of the Agora were begun by the Greek Archaeological Service in about the middle of the 19th century, continued for a short time by the German Archaeological Institute, and conducted, from 1931 onwards, by the American School of Classical Studies.

The west side of the Agora is occupied by the ruins of the most important administrative, judicial and religious buildings of the site, just below the hill where stands the temple of Hephaistos. The latter was dedicated to the worship of Hephaistos and Athena, the patron deities of the arts. The sculptured decoration of this temple, which has been preserved in excellent condition, represents the Athenian hero Theseus, founder of the Athenian state —he was the originator of the synoecism. The other buildings appear in the following sequence from south to north : the *Tholos*— a circular building which served as the Prytaneion, and for the performance of political and religious ceremonies. The Council (Boule), an executive body numbering 500 members, held sessions in the *Bouleuterion* (its entrance is on the north of the Tholos). In front of the Bouleuterion is the *Metroon*, the temple dedicated to the mother of the gods, also used as repository of the state archives. Opposite the façade of the Metroon was a fence enclosing a high base surmounted by the bronze statues of the Eponymous Heroes (after whom the Athenian tribes had been named). Official state announcements were posted on that base. Northwards of the Metroon stood the *temple of Apollo Patroos*, the father of Ion — who gave his name to the great Hellenic race of the Ionians, from whom the Athenians derived their descent.

Farther to the North was the *Stoa of Zeus*, and next to the railway the *Stoa Basileios*, seat of the archon basileus.

The several stoas surrounding the site of the Agora were most useful to Athenian citizens, offering shelter from sun, rain or wind in all seasons of the year. They apparently served no particular purpose, though at times groups of judges etc., held sessions in their space. It was there that youths gathered to be instructed on the theories of philosophers. Sokrates is known to have frequented the Stoa of Zeus. On the north side of the Agora were the *Stoa of the Herms* and the *Stoa Poikile*, a building decorated in antiquity with superb frescoes (it has not been uncovered yet). The stoa is known to have given its name to the philosophical school (Stoic) founded in Athens in about 300 B.C. by the philosopher Zeno.

From the south-east to the south-west end of the Agora stood monumental fountains and in the central part of it was erected the *Odeum of Agrippa*.

On the north side of the Agora two large *stoas*, the *Middle* and the *South*, served as law-courts. Near the south-west fountain was the law-court of *Heliaia*. In later times, the *Library of Pantainos* was built to the south of the Stoa of Attalos. Opposite the Stoa of Zeus (to the east) stood the *altar of the twelve gods*, a most sacred part of the Agora, marking the starting point of road distances measured by the Athenians in antiquity.

In the Imperial age, two temples were removed by the Athenians to the site of the Agora and reconstructed there for purposes of preservation : the *temple of Ares* (from Acharnai, today's Menidi), and another temple on the south-east end of the Agora, by the east end of the Byzantine church of the Holy Apostles, which was erected on the site of an ancient *Nymphaion*. On the south side of the church of the Holy Apostles was the *Mint* of Athens.

The site of the Agora was diagonally traversed by the *Panathenaic Way*, i.e.

the official way used in antiquity for the procession of the Panathenaic festival, the most important feast celebrated in Athens. This way started from the Dipylon and passing through the Agora terminated on the south-west end of the Acropolis. The ship carrying as sail the *peplos* of the goddess stopped at this point, the priests lowered the peplos, folded it and carried it ceremoniously on the Acropolis, to dress with it the wooden statue of Athena, the patroness goddess of the city.

Agora Museum

The exhibits of this representative Museum show in a most lively fashion the daily life, art and cults of Athenians over the various periods of the city's history from 4000 B.C. down to the 19th century A.D. In the colonnade of the ground-floor are exhibited statues, architectural members and inscriptions found in the course of excavations on the site. The Museum includes characteristic collections of pottery, bronzes, ivories and other works of the minor arts; a large number of objects, as well as drawings and maps, illustrate the private and public life of the ancient Athenians.

From the upper gallery of the Stoa, the visitor has a general view of the site and the excavated area, and gains a clear idea with the assistance of detailed drawings and plaster models : one of these represents the site of the Agora, another depicts the Stoa of Attalos, still another large-sized plaster model shows the Acropolis and its sanctuaries in every detail. Busts, remarkable inscriptions on marble and other sculptures complete the collection of exhibits.

Kerameikos

The Kerameikos is one of the most important archaeological sites of Athens. It was situated at the point of convergence of the three main roads leading to the ancient city of Athens. The *Academy road* terminated at the *Dipylon*, the double gateway, which was the main gate of the city. (The Dipylon is flanked by remains of the city walls dating from various periods : the wall of Themistokles, of Konon, of the Macedonian era). The *Sacred Way* connected Eleusis with Athens and terminated in the Sacred Gates. Between the latter and the Dipylon lie the ruins of a large building, the *Pompeion*, used for storing the sacred objects needed in processions during the city's festivals.

At the beginning of the Academy Road is part of the *Demosion Sema*, where the Athenians buried in common graves the dead that had fallen in battle and the eminent citizens benefactors of the city in various ways. The ancients founded their cemeteries outside the city walls, along the edge of large roads. Excavations on the site, carried out by the German Archaeological Institute, have brought to light remarkable graves with fine stelai, huge marble or clay vases serving as 'semata', and countless funerary offerings included in the graves. Most of the finds, and the best, have been transferred to the National Archaeological Museum (they were found in graves uncovered in the Sacred Way, the Academy Road, and the so-called *Street of the Tombs*).

Kerameikos Museum

This is a small but representative Museum, containing funerary monuments (stelai) dated from the early Archaic period to the late 4th century B.C. Among them is exhibited the superb inscribed stele of Dexileos, a young Athenian nobleman, who fell in the Corinthian War (394 B.C.) with four other Athenian horsemen.

Of the remaining rooms of the Museum, those open to the public contain an interesting collection of funerary offerings found in the graves of the Kerameikos cemetery, dating from the early Geometric times down to the Roman age. The main exhibits are : clay vases with decoration characteristic of every period, bronze weapons and ornaments, gold and silver bands, clay statuettes and small objects made of glass.

OTHER MAJOR MUSEUMS OF ATHENS

There are about 40 public and private Museums and Collections in Athens, which include works of Ancient, Byzantine and modern Greek art. The most important state Museums are the following :

Acropolis Museum

The Museum is situated on the Sacred Rock; it has been purposely built low so as to be invisible from below the hill and not interfere with the sight of the splendid monuments of the Acropolis. It is a local Museum containing finds from excavations carried out (by Greek archaeologists) on the Sacred Rock and the slopes of the hill. In its nine rooms are exhibited mostly stone and marble sculptures, while bronzes, clay vases and many inscriptions have been transferred to the National Archaeological Museum. Vases and other clay objects found in excavations south of the Acropolis (1955 - 1961) are also displayed in separate cases.

The Acropolis Museum includes unique masterpieces of ancient Greek art and gives the visitor the opportunity to follow step by step the evolution of Attic art from the early 6th to the late 5th century B.C. Some later works are shown in the ninth room.

Exhibits are arranged in chronological order. The first five rooms contain various works of the 6th century B.C.: limestone and stone pediments of buildings unknown to us, architectural sculptures, votive inscriptions. Outstanding among them are the pediment portraying Herakles slaying the Lernaian Hydra (No. 1) the Trisomatos Daimon (Three headed Monster) (No. 35), the Moschophoros (Calf - bearer) (No. 624), the pediment showing lions attacking a bull, the Rampin Horseman, a hunting-dog depicted with great artistic skill, and the exquisite and major series of Archaic Korai —statues representing dressed maidens with traces of rich colouring— offered by the Athenians as dedications to their beloved patroness goddess.

The fifth room is dominated by the large marble pediment representing the Gigantomachy; the centre of the representation was occupied by the figures of Athena and Zeus, each of whom was fighting against a Giant. The pediment belonged to an earlier temple of Athena, dating to the age of the Peisistratids.

In the sixth room are displayed works of art dating from 490 B.C. to approximately 450 B.C., which include some masterpieces: the Boy by Kritios (No. 698), the head of the Blond Ephebos (No. 689), the Kore of Euthydikos (No. 609).

The seventh and eighth rooms contain works of the highest artistic peak of Athens, that have come from the Parthenon, the Erechtheion and the Temple of Athena Nike. In the seventh room visitors may see in plaster models a reconstruction of the two pediments of the Parthenon. The eighth room includes the splendid

Acropolis Museum, Athens.
Archaic Kore.

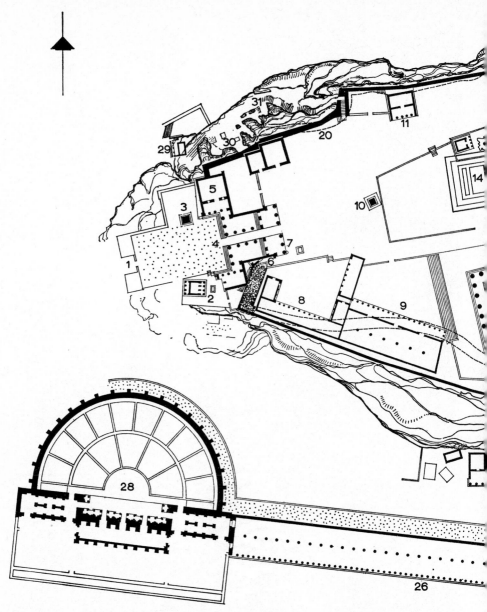

1 Beulé Gate 2 Temple of Athena Nike 3 Foundations of the Agrippa Monument 4 Propylaea 5 Pinacotheca 6 Remains of the Pisistratid Propylaeum and of the Pelasgian Wall 7 Sanctuary of Athena Hygeia (Health) 8 Temenos of Artemis Brauronia 9 Chalcotheke and Temenos of Athena Ergane 10 Athena Promachus 11 House of the Arrephoroi 12 Pandroseum 13 Erechtheum 14 Ancient Temple of Athena Polias 15 Altar of Athene 16 Parthenon 17 Temple of Rome and Augustus 18 Shrine of Zeus Polieus 19 Temple of the Hero Pandion 20 Pelasgian Wall 21 Odeum of Pericles 22 Old and New Temple of Dionysus Eleutherium 23 Theatre of Dionysus 24 Monument of Thrasyllus 25 Monument of Nicias 26 Stoa of Eumenes 27 Sanctuary of Asclepius 28 Odeum of Herodes Atticus 29 Clepsydra Spring 30 Cave of Pan 31 Ancient Stairway 32 Shrine of Eros and of Aphrodite "in the Gardens"

For this plan of the Acropolis we are indebted to the architect and archaeologist, John Travlos, Athens.

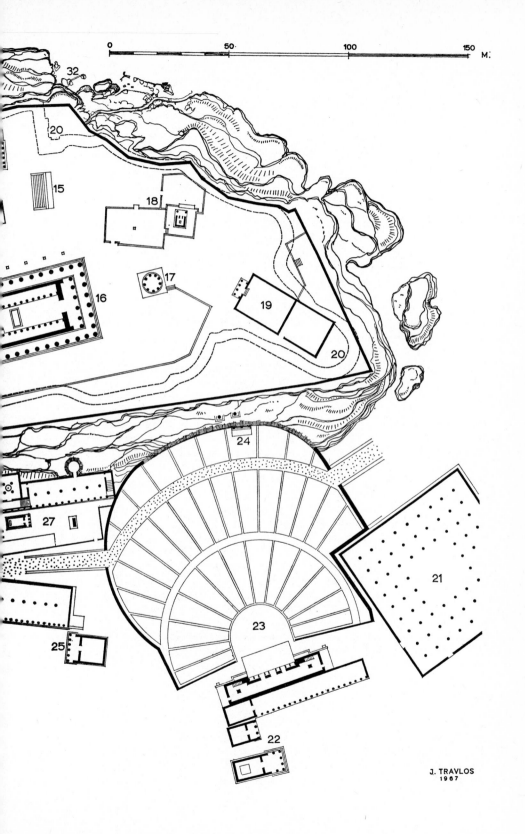

J. TRAVLOS
1967

sculptures of the Parthenon frieze, and sculptures from the parapet of the temple of Athena Nike.

The ninth room comprises remarkable exhibits, among which the head of Alexander the Great, possibly a work of the sculptor Leochares (4th century B.C.); the statue of Prokne (No. 1358), a work of Alkamenes, Pheidias' outstanding disciple; and the head of an old philosopher (No. 131), a fine work of late antiquity (circa A.D. 400).

National Archaeological Museum

For the acquaintance of the ancient Greek art, this is the most important and rich Museum in the world. It is housed in a typical Neoclassical building, one of the few preserved today in Athens, built (1866 - 1889) on plans of the architects Lange and Ziller (the latter was responsible for some modifications to the original plan). The east and south sections are later additions.

According to the foundation statute, the National Archaeological Museum gives a comprehensive picture of ancient art as developed not only in Attica but in the whole of Greece. It is a known fact that in antiquity each city-state, particularly the great ones, gave its proper character to art; hence, exhibits from various regions present a great variety.

The Museum includes collections of Prehistoric art and works dating to every period of antiquity until the Byzantine age. There are stone and marble works, clay vases and statuettes, bronze statues and countless objects of the minor arts made of various materials.

Prehistoric Greece is represented by the exhibits in the three rooms of the ground floor: these date to the Neolithic times and the two earliest periods of the Bronze Age (left). The central room offers a rare and most impressive picture of Mycenaean art and civilization. The room on the right (south) comprises characteristic finds of the singular art of the Cycladic islands in Prehistoric times, particularly the early Bronze Age (Early Cycladic art).

The splendid exhibits of the Mycenaean room fascinate the visitor : finds from the royal graves of Mycenae (bronze weapons with inlaid decoration, exquisite metal and clay vases, gold masks, various metal objects, and a vast number of jewels made of precious and semi-precious materials —gold rings with superb decoration, beads of gold or other precious matter from necklaces, seals and a multitude of other ornaments). Following the order of exhibits in the several cases, the visitor may appreciate the artistic production of the various centers where Mycenaean art had flourished. Particularly impressive examples are the finds from the Mycenaean graves of Mycenae, Messenia and many other sites. The clay tablets of Linear B script, found in the palace of Nestor at Englianos in Messenia (Pylos), are of exceptional interest. This room also includes the remarkable frescoes (fragments) from the palace of Tiryns, and other typical works from all over Mycenaean Greece.

The small north room left of the Mycenaean hall contains interesting examples of Neolithic objects. Noteworthy is a clay statuette by the west wall. Thessaly is represented with characteristic finds (clay vessels, tools, and stone or clay figurines), and so are the regions of Central Greece. The careful viewer may observe in the exhibits of this room, the efforts of early men in the remote Neolithic times or the early phases of the Bronze Age to give their vessels a beautiful appearance and elegant shape, to render in plastic fashion the female goddess they worshipped, to make ornaments and jewels from various materials. The gold ornaments

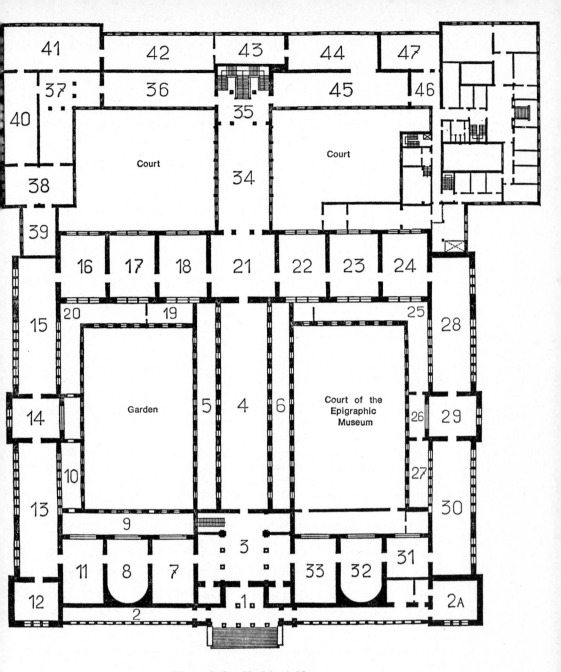

Plan of the National Museum

1 Entrance   2A Exhibition of mouldings   3 Entrance-hall   4 Mycenaean hall   5 Neolithic finds   6 Cycladic finds   7-13 Archaic Art   14 Early 5th century   15 Early 5th
century, Poseidon's hall   16-20 Classical Art, 5th century. Gravestone stelae and votive
reliefs   21 Diadumenos' hall   22 Sculptures from the sanctuary of Asclepios at Epidauros   23-24 Gravestone stelae, 4th century   25-27 Votive reliefs, 4th century   28
Youth of Anticythera's hall   29 Themis' room, 3d century   30 Hellenistic Art   32 Stathatos Collection   34 Votive sculptures, Hall leading to the new building of the museum
35 Stairs to the upper floor. Ceramic collection   36 Carapanos Collection, Dodona   37
Bronze Collection   45 Bronze Sculptures   38-44, 46, 47 Rooms closed for rearrangement

from Lemnos, shown in a separate case, are quite impressive and constitute unmistakable evidence of an exceptionally high artistic standard. After the loss of the 'Treasure of Priam', a collection of finds ascribed to the same date from Schliemann's excavations at Troy, these jewels are the only source of knowledge for the art of that age, for they are closely related to the Trojan jewellery.

Marble, the typical raw material of the Cycladic islands, prevails in the Cycladic room. The large marble statue by the west wall is a work of astonishing vigour, depicting with marked abstraction a nude female figure. Two small statues, the one representing a standing flute-player and the other a seated harp-player, denote the islanders' love of music. Clay and stone implements, jewellery, fine vases with characteristic shape and decoration, and frescoes of outstanding naturalism from Phylakopi, Melos, complete the picture of the Cycladic art and civilization.

The first eight rooms of the left wing of the Museum show the development of plastic art from the 7th century B.C. to 450 B.C. Fine statues of Kouroi (nude young men) of life-size or larger than life-size, illustrate the successful attempt of artists at a plastic rendering of the nude male body. Archaic art in various regions of Greece is represented here : the Kouros of Sounion, the Dipylon Head, the Kouros of Valomandra, Kroisos and Aristodikos, are examples of the talented skill of Attic sculptors in the Archaic age. The Kouroi of Melos, Kea, Megara, and Boiotia are parallels from other sites.

Exhibits include statues of seated female figures and a series of fine relief grave stelai. Worthy of attention in the first Archaic room is the statue of a standing woman, found on Delos, a votive offering of Nikandre of Naxos, as recorded on the inscription on the side of the statue.

In the corner room (N.W.) are displayed the remains of sculptures from the east pediment of the temple of Aphaia on Aigina. In the next large room, behind the Kouros Kroisos, a fine relief base of a statue shows characteristic athletic scenes.

The Late Archaic room contains representative sculptures from various places which illustrate the artistic visions of the times.

The superb bronze statue of Poseidon, found in the sea off Cape Artemision, dominates the room of the 'Severe Style'. This is indeed a masterpiece of Greek bronzework. Noteworthy in the same room is the large relief from Eleusis representing the goddess Demeter, the Kore Persephone and the young hero Triptolemos.

Three rooms with sculptures come next. The first and the third show the development of Attic funerary stelai in the 5th century B.C. A fine example is the stele of Hegeso, in the second room of Classical funerary monuments. In the intermediary room are displayed the remarkable architectural sculptures from the Argive Heraion, the head of Hera and, opposite, the sculptured decoration of the base of the statue of Nemesis at Rhamnous. Three small rooms west of the above, contain excellent copies, which give the visitor an idea of the lost great works of the Classical age.

In the garden of the Museum are exhibited several relief grave stelai —many of them dedicated to children— a remarkable funerary monument representing a lion, and statues from the shipwreck of Antikythera. The centre of the garden is occupied by the fine mosaic head of Medusa, found in Piraeus.

On the central axis of the Museum, a large room has been arranged to reproduce an ancient open-air sanctuary, with an altar in the middle and various votive offerings around. In the preceding room one may see the statue of Hermes of

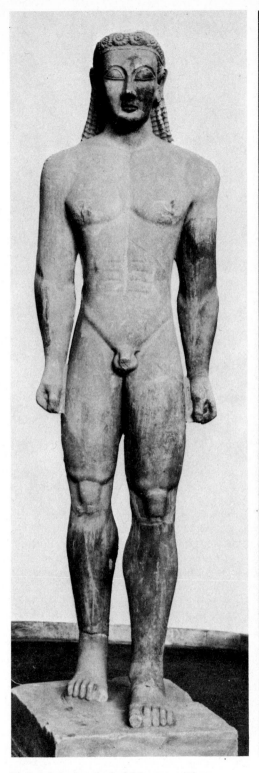
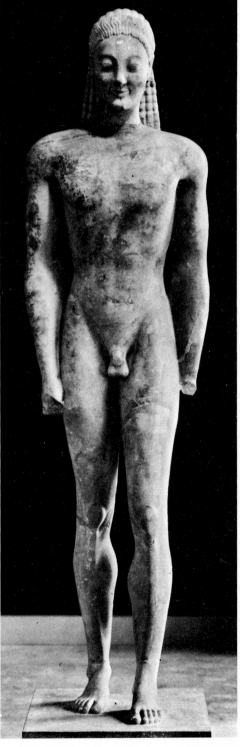

National Archaeological Museum, Athens.
a) Larger than lifesize statue of the Kouros from Sounion.
b) The Kouros from Valomandra.

Andros, a copy of the Diadoumenos imitating the original by the sculptor Poly-kleitos, and statues of two women of Herculanum.

Further south there is a whole room with the fine pedimental sculptures from the temple of Asklepios at Epidauros. Three small rooms contain very interesting decrees and dedicatory reliefs, and two large rooms show the development of Attic funerary stelai in the 4th century B.C.

In the next room are exhibited the large funerary relief of Aristonautes, and another unusual funerary relief with the representation of a horse and a little negro, bearing abundant traces of colouring. To the west stands the principal exhibit of this room, the exquisite bronze statue of the Ephebos of Antikythera (said to be the Paris of Euphranor). Finally, the visitor may see in the same room fine sculptures by Skopas from the temple of Athena Alea at Tegea, and the well-known head of Hygieia.

The next small room contains the statue of Themis from Rhamnous, the relief bases of Mantineia, and the very remarkable sculptures from Lykosoura.

The last room of the south side has in the centre the marble statue of Posei-don from Melos, three fine bronze heads —of a boxer, a philosopher and a third one from Delos— of astonishing liveliness. It also contains the statue of the priest-ess Chairestrate from Rhamnous, an interesting and fine work of the 3rd century B.C., and the statue of Aphrodite with Pan and Eros among other masterpieces dating to the latest centuries of antiquity.

In a room of the west wing is displayed the Hélène Stathatos Collection, which includes precious jewellery from various parts of Greece.

The east wing of the Museum is occupied by the Karapanos Collection —with remarkable finds from the sanctuary of Dodona— and the Museum collection of Archaic bronzes from various regions of Greece. Three rooms contain sculptures of the Roman age and another room, right of the staircase, includes the bronzes found near the Panathenaic stadium, as well as the bronze statue of Apollo and the statues of Athena and Artemis, which are the three most characteristic finds from Piraeus.

This wing will also house the Egyptian collection of the Museum.

In two rooms of the upper floor are exhibited the splendid finds from the ex-cavations of Professor Marinatos at Akrotiri on the island of Thera. Frescoes of unparallelled beauty (Fresco of the Spring, Fresco of the Boxing Children, etc.), pottery with fine painted decoration and a great number of other objects denote the great importance of art in Prehistoric Thera.

The remaining of the upper floor contains in chronological order the rich Museum collection of pottery dating from the Protogeometric and Archaic times to the end of the 4th century B.C. The collection of ivory plaques from the sanc-tuary of Artemis Orthia at Sparta, and the fine collection of Attic white-ground lekythoi are of great interest. Several painted metopes from Kalydon and Thermos give an idea of Greek painting in the Archaic age.

The National Archaeological Museum also houses two independent and most important collections : the Epigraphical and the Numismatic.

Epigraphical Collection

Entrance is from Tositsa Street. The collection consists of about 14,000 inscrip-tions dating from the 6th century B.C. to the 3rd century A.D., very finely pre-sented. In the two front rooms open to visitors (admittance in the remaining rooms is restricted to specialists only), are exhibited inscriptions of particular significance either for their content or their form, as well as inscribed bases of statues that have been lost, bearing the signatures of great sculptors of various periods of antiquity.

A room to the west includes the huge and impressive tax lists, where the Athenians recorded, from 454 B.C., their income from taxes paid by each city member of the First Athenian Alliance.

Numismatic Collection

This excellently presented Collection is in the upper floor of the National Archaeological Museum (entered through the Museum Offices from Tositsa Street) and includes all kinds of coins that had been in use in Hellenic cities from the 7th century B.C. to the latest times of antiquity.

The Collection also comprises Roman, Byzantine and modern Greek coins (down to those currently used in our days), as well as coins of other European states displayed in a special case. There is also a characteristic series of lead seals, ancient bronze and lead symbols and gems.

Byzantine Museum

The Byzantine Museum, the only of its kind in the world, is in the centre of Athens (22, Vasilissis Sophias Avenue). It is housed in the villa built in 1848, in the style of a small Florentine palace, by the well-known architect Kleanthes for the eccentric French Duchesse de Plaisance, who lived in the years of king Otto's reign.

In the Museum are displayed works of Christian art, covering all periods and every branch (architecture, sculpture, painting, and the minor arts). In the ground-floor of the central building, three rooms have been arranged to reproduce the main types of church corresponding to the three phases of religious architecture (Early Christian, Byzantine and Post-Byzantine), decorated with sculptures from various monuments belonging to these periods. Thus, the visitor is offered a clear picture of the evolution of Christian architecture and sculpture. In the first room of the upper floor are exhibited the most important icons of the Museum collection (12th - 16th century), and illuminated manuscripts; in the second room, wall-paintings and bronze objects, mostly liturgical vessels; in the third room, works of the minor arts; in the fourth room, textiles, mostly vestments, etc. The left wing of the Museum includes three rooms with icons. In the first room the icons have been displayed according to iconographical type, so that visitors may see the same theme executed in several styles and study the similarities and differences between them. The second room contains for the most part icons of the 16th century, and the third room a collection of icons by Greek popular painters and Russian artists.

In the court of the Museum are exhibited Early Christian and Byzantine sculptures.

Benaki Museum

This Museum (1, Koumbari Street, opposite the Royal Garden) is a donation of the national benefactor Anthony Benaki, housed in the Emmanuel Benaki residence, which is an interesting Neoclassical building with later additions on the north wing to house new acquisitons.

The Benaki Museum includes several collections. The collection of Greek art dates from Prehistoric times to present days (painted vases, bronzes, a great number of jewels).

The collection of Greek popular art is of special interest (local costumes of various Greek regions, wood and bronze utensils, jewels, embroideries, all displayed in the Museum basement). There is an important collection of Byzantine and Post-Byzantine icons, as well as manuscripts, ecclesiastical embroideries and religious relics that had belonged to the Greek populations of Asia Minor, Pontos and Eastern Thrace; a characteristic collection of weapons, and historical relics and mementos from the War of Independence of 1821; an interesting collection of 18th century paintings and engravings with Greek subjects. Other collections are the Coptic, Moslem and Turkish (comprising textiles, embroideries, carpets, weapons, jewellery, metalwork, pottery, etc.). There is also a remarkable collection of Chinese art with works from the Neolithic period to the 19th century. Finally, one room contains personal objects, manuscripts, photographs and other souvenirs of Eleutherios Venizelos.

Museum of Greek Popular Art

The Museum is situated at Monasteraki Square and housed in an 18th century mosque. The visitor wishing to have a comprehensive picture of Greek popular art is advised to visit this Museum, which completes, in a way, the collection (in the basement) of the Benaki Museum. Here are displayed attractive and rich collections of textiles, embroideries, laces and beautiful local costumes from various Hellenic regions, all very finely presented. The visitor has the opportunity to see also a large collection of jewellery in precious and semi-precious materials, made by popular goldsmiths, a great many metal objects, fine wood-carvings and products of popular pottery as developed in various parts of Greece. (Those interested in popular musical instruments, may visit the private collection of Ph. Anogeianakis, which includes some 300 popular musical instruments of the last three centuries).

National Museum of History

The Museum is housed in the impressive building of the Old Parliament, on Stadiou Street, built in 1858 on plans of the architect Boulanger. It comprises a large collection of every kind of relics associated with the nation's history in modern times. After the Benaki Museum collection of war mementos of 1821, a visit to this Museum completes the range of historical activities in Greece.

Relics and mementos of the national strifes are exhibited here, with explanatory labels : documents and personal objects of people who played a role in the preparation of the War of Independence and other historical personalities until the First World War. There are also some sculptures and engravings.

This is the third Museum, besides the Benaki Museum and the Museum of Greek Popular Art, which has a collection of local Greek costumes. Also displayed are a series of seals of eminent persons associated with the history of the nation, as well as war mementos from the Byzantine era to the period of the Turkish rule. (A complete picture of the hard struggles for the nation's freedom, will be given by the War Museum; this Museum is presently under construction at the junction of Vasilissis Sophias avenue and Rizari Street).

The National Museum of History also possesses collections of various Greek handicrafts.

National Gallery and A. Soutzos Museum

Situated at the beginning of Vasileos Constantinou Avenue, opposite the Hilton Hotel, the National Gallery and A. Soutzos Museum comprise a remarkable collection of sculptures, paintings and engravings by Greek artists of the 18th, 19th and 20th centuries. The Gallery includes four paintings by Domenikos Theotokopoulos (El Greco), and works of the European schools of painting of the last four centuries (Dutch, Italian and Flemish schools). There is also a noteworthy collection of studies and engravings by foreign artists (Dürer, Rembrandt, Watteau, Van Dyck, Braque, Picasso, etc.).

Exhibitions are quite often organized in the National Gallery.

PIRAEUS

The ancient harbour of Athens is today a big city, full of life. Built on the site of the ancient town, the modern city does not permit the uncovery of antiquities. The two smaller harbours in the area of Piraeus, *Zea* and *Munichia*, are very picturesque and delight visitors. No trace has been preserved from the Long Walls which ensured communication between Athens and her harbour in antiquity. On the other hand, there exist entire stretches of the wall along certain parts of the coast, built in the age of Konon (4th century B.C.) upon the fortifications erected according to plans of Themistokles. The *sanctuary of Artemis Munichia* occupied in antiquity the site where the Royal Yacht Club is at present.

The Hellenistic theatre of the city, where performances are given in our days, and, of course, the Museum are of special interest.

Piraeus Museum

The Museum is housed in a newly constructed building on Philhellenon Street, and contains a notable collection of sculptures of the Classical, Hellenistic and Roman periods. On the upper floor is exhibited an important series of Classical funerary reliefs. Also included are vases of the Classical age, clay and bronze figurines, coins and several works of the minor arts. The bronze statue of Apollo, the statues of Athena and Artemis, a large bronze votive shield and the finds which have come to light during the 1959 excavations will be exhibited in this Museum.

Naval Museum of Piraeus

The Museum is situated on the bay of Phreattys. Exhibits are carefully arranged so as to give a characteristic picture of the nation's naval history from antiquity to present times.

In groups of historical unity are displayed ship models, relics of naval battles, paintings with naval subjects, historical documents, prints, maps, drawings, and a number of commemorative objects of important personalities of modern Greek history, along with a great many photographs.

Archaeological Museum of Piraeus.
Classical grave stele of Chairedemos and Lykeas.

SOUNION

In antiquity, Cape Sounion was a remote part of the city-state of Athens; today, it is one of the most attractive archaeological sites. As attested by finds from excavations, the site —one of the most beautiful in ancient Attica— was a cult center since the 3rd millennium B.C. It was natural for the god of the sea to be worshipped on this 'divine promontory', as characterized by J. Moreas. The power and prosperity of ancient Athens were based on her navy, and Cape Sounion was a most appropriate site for the foundation of a sanctuary dedicated to the god whose favour would ensure protection of the city's mercantile marine and war fleet.

Owing to its commanding position, Cape Sounion offered the possibility of surveying the movement of ships entering the Saronic Gulf, of controlling the south of Attica and guarding the precious silver mines of Laurion; it even afforded easy control over the sea routes towards Euboia and the Cycladic islands.

The south and east coasts of the promontory are inaccessible, but fortification was necessary on the other two sides, where a strong polygonal wall was erected in antiquity. Thus, Sounion became a major strong fortress in Attica, manned by a selected garrison under the command of the local general-governor.

The Athenians also fortified the small harbour on the west. A square temenos with a temple of Poseidon was founded in the Archaic age on the headland formed at the highest point of the rocky promontory. The temenos was separated from the remaining area of the fortress by an individual wall built along the north and west side of the square precinct. The site was approached by a road leading from the harbour to the Propylaia. Along the road were several buildings, which probably served as living quarters for the garrison of the fort.

The *temenos of Poseidon* is entered from the N.E. end. The *Propylaia* had three entrances. To the right of the Propylaia is a small construction believed to have been the guardhouse. Further to the right, a *stoa* extends along the north side of the square precinct, with nine Doric marble columns on the facade and six limestone columns in the interior. The stoa was enlarged in later times to include part of the west side of the temenos.

The first *temple of Poseidon* was founded in 488 B.C., but its construction remained incomplete. The building was destroyed during the Persian invasion of Attica in 480 B.C. The temple now seen by the visitor was founded in the mid-4th century B.C. (in 444 or 440 B.C.). It is a Doric peripteros. Restoration has included as many columns as possible. Lord Byron's name can be seen carved on one of the columns standing on the facade. The metopes of the temple had no relief decoration, but were, perhaps, painted. Very few fragments have survived from the pedimental sculptures, which are now exhibited in the National Archaeological Museum in Athens. The frieze lining all four sides of the pronaos was probably decorated with representations of the Centauromachy and the Gigantomachy, as it appears from a few slabs preserved in very poor condition — they are in the shed in front of the Propylaia.

On the lower level, approximately 400 m. from the temple of Poseidon, is the *temenos of Athena Sounias,* which is earlier in date than that of Poseidon. A wall of limestone blocks surrounds the temenos. Apparently the site was a sacred precinct from the Early Helladic period. On the north slope of the low hill there exists a circular peribolos, which is thought to have been a very old open-air shrine of an olive-tree standing at the centre of the precinct (tree-worship). In any event, the goddess Athena was worshipped in the temenos from the 6th century B.C. Like that of

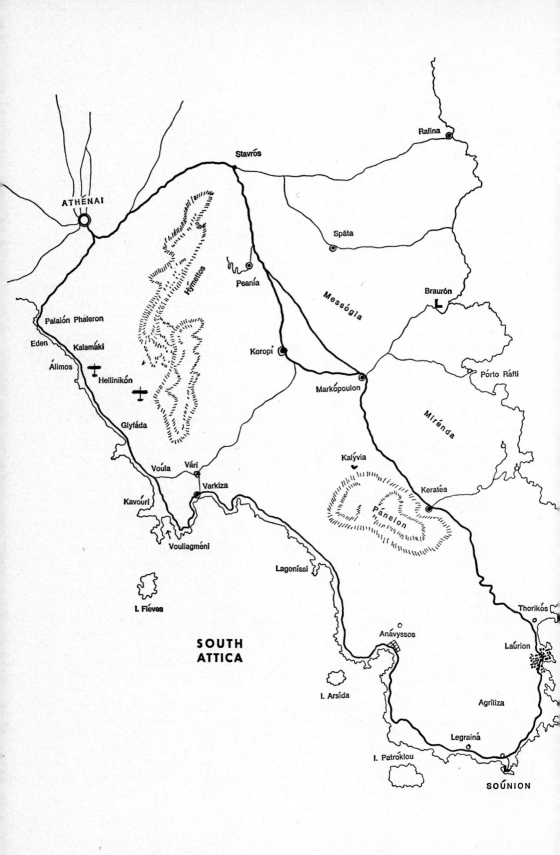

ATHÉNAI

Stavrós

Rafina

Spáta

Peanía

Hymettos

Messógia

Braurón

Palaión Pháleron

Eden

Kalamáki

Koropí

Pórto Ráfti

Álimos

Hellinikón

Markópoulon

Mirénda

Glyfáda

Kalývia

Voúla   Vári

Keratéa

Kavoúri

Varkíza

Pánelon

Vouliagméni

Lagoníssi

I. Fléves

Thorikós

Anávyssos

**SOUTH
ATTICA**

Laúrion

I. Arsída

Agríliza

Legrainá

I. Patróklou

SOÚNION

Attica. Sounion.
The temple of Poseidon.

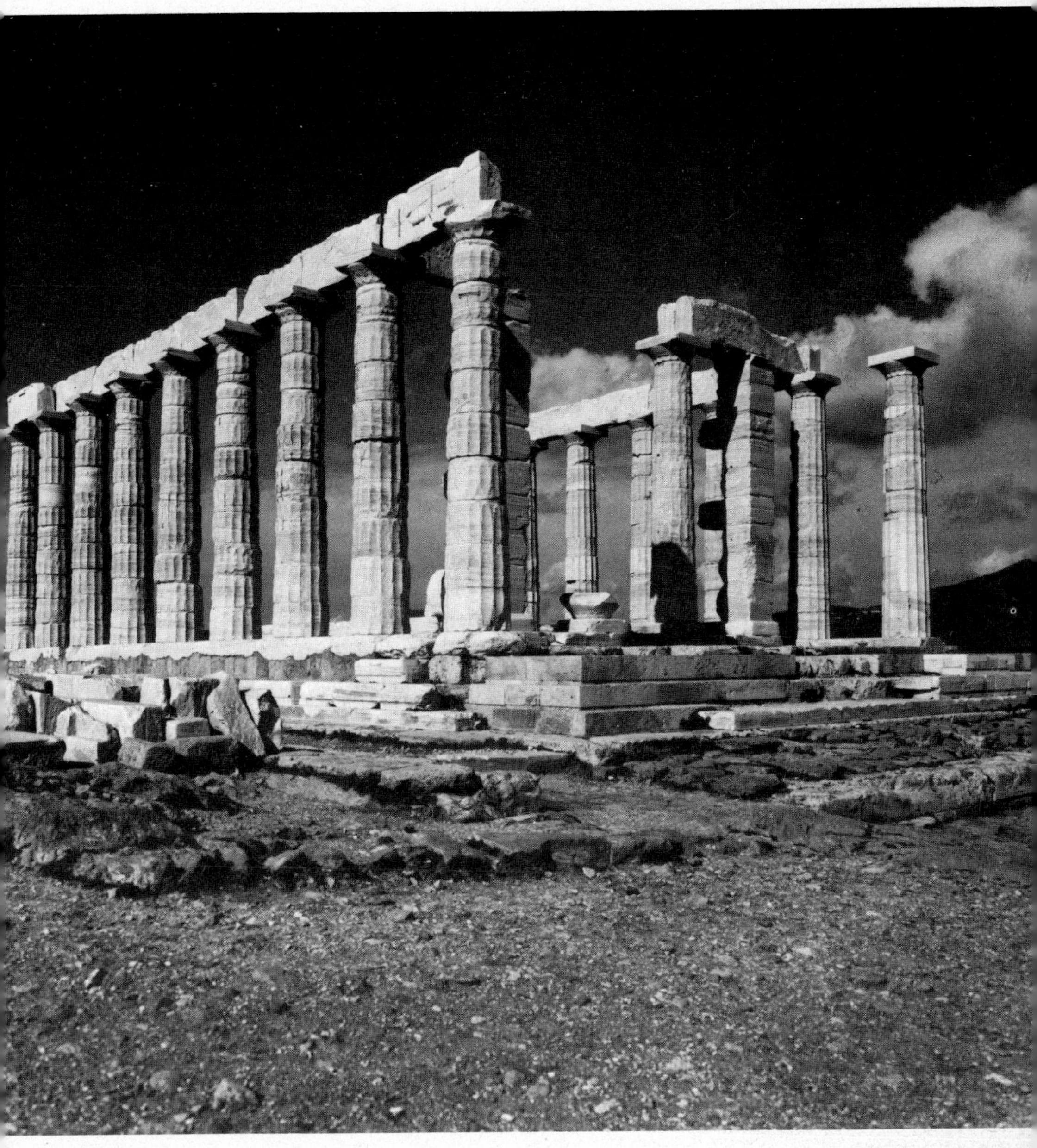

Poseidon, her earliest *temple,* the Archaic, was destroyed by the enemy in the Persian Wars, and was later replaced by a larger Ionic temple dedicated to the goddess.

Naval contests were performed at Sounion every quinquennium. In addition to Poseidon and Athena, *Hermes* and *Zeus Sounieus* were worshipped there. There was also a grove dedicated to *Asklepios* and a small *Herakleion* on the site of the little bay of Zeza.

Two of the most remarkable Archaic statues found so far, have come from the temenos of Poseidon (the two large Kouroi of Sounion, exhibited in the National Archaeological Museum).

THORIKOS

Antiquities of the deme of *Thorikos,* one of the earliest demes of Attica, are located at a distance of 4 kms. from *Laurion.* The site was first occupied shortly after 2000 B.C. The ancient city was built on a hill and protected by a fortification *wall* 2 kms. long — part of the wall with a square tower has survived. The visitor may see the fairly well-preserved ancient *theatre* of Thorikos (of the 4th century B.C.), which could accommodate about 4,000 spectators. Near the theatre are the ruins of a small *temple of Dionysos.* South of the theatre are preserved some traces of the *temple of Demeter and Kore.* Two tholos tombs of the Mycenaean age have been found on the N.E. slope of the hill of Velatouri. Part of a Mycenaean wall and remains of Mycenaean houses have also been uncovered there.

In order to defend the Laurion mines, the Athenians erected in 412 B.C. a fortress with polygonal masonry (1 km. east of the theatre of Thorikos).

BRAURON

The *temenos of Artemis Brauronia* is located 38 kms. from Athens. Archaeological investigations have revealed that the site had been occupied since Prehistoric times. The sanctuary of Brauron is one of the most important in Greece, not only by reason of its major significance in antiquity, but also because of the fact that it has not been overlain by later buildings. Thus, when the excavations interrupted in 1963 will be completed, we shall have a unique example of an ancient sanctuary.

Artemis was worshipped there as a protectress of childbirth, and, hence, as patroness of the tribes of Attica. The temple of the goddess dates to the 5th century B.C., and is presently in a very ruinous state.

Nevertheless, a large (Π-shaped) *stoa* has survived admirably. Following its recent restoration, it has become the most impressive monument on the site. There were small couches in the rooms of the stoa, which is believed to have been the dwelling place for the young girls *(arktoi)* of the noble families of Attica, sent by their parents to attend the goddess for a while in the sanctuary. Behind the stoa of the arktoi are the ruins of another stoa that had been used for the display of the precious fabrics dedicated to the sanctuary by several pious Athenian ladies. The *heroon of Iphigeneia* lies to the east of the temple of Artemis and further beyond is the *oikos* of the priestesses.

Museum of Brauron

Excavations in the sanctuary have brought to light a great number of finds : statues, reliefs, clay figurines, sealstones, ceremonial vessels, bronze mirrors and in-

Attica. Museum of Brauron.
Statue of a young girl ('arktos').

scriptions. Finds from the district of Mesogeia (Anavyssos, Myrrhinous, Perati) are also included among the exhibits. A plaster model of the site can be seen in the anteroom. The first room to the left contains pottery found in the sanctuary, bronze mirrors and other products of the minor arts, displayed in chronological order. The second room (to the right of the visitor entering the Museum) houses the finest reliefs found in the sanctuary and other sites of Mesogeia. The majority are votive reliefs with inscriptions recording the name of the dedicant and stating that the relief is an offering to the goddess. In the third room are presented in atractive cases a great many terracotta figurines discovered during the excavations. (The remarkable Classical relief of the gods is also exhibited in this room). In the fourth room (left) are displayed the rich finds from the late Mycenaean graves at Perati. In the last room are shown some funerary stelai from Mesogeia and fine vases found in the course of various excavations, particularly in the large cemetery of Myrrhinous. Funerary monuments are displayed in the porch.

MARATHON

The site of Marathon is of great significance. To the right of the site, where the famous battle which saved Greece was fought in 490 B.C., stands the *Tumulus* (i.e. collective tomb) of the Marathon warriors. In the course of recent excavations conducted by Professor Sp. Marinatos, important Middle Helladic graves and the *Tumulus of the Plataians* who fell in the battle of Marathon were uncovered at *Vrana,* at a small distance left of the public road — these may be visited at present. Archaeological investigation carried out at times in the whole area has revealed finds dating to various periods, such as those from the *Cave of Pan,* situated on the slope of Mt. Pendeli overlooking the plain of Marathon.

Museum of Marathon

The Museum building, donated by Mr. Eugene Panagopoulos, consists of five rooms which contain finds from Marathon dating from Prehistoric times down to the Roman age and possibly the Byzantine period. Exhibits include finds from the Early Helladic necropolis at *Tsepi,* the Early and Middle Helladic necropolis at *Plasi,* and the Middle Helladic and Mycenaean 'royal' graves at *Vrana;* from the Cave of Pan (datable from the Neolithic to the Roman period); and from the Tumulus of the Plataians. There are also Geometric finds yielded by earlier excavations at the foot of Agrieliki. Among the Roman finds, the Egyptianizing statues are associated with Herodes Atticus, whose brithplace was Marathon.

The Museum includes plaster casts of other important works, such as the bronze statue known as the 'Boy from Marathon', now on display in the National Archaeological Museum, Athens.

RHAMNOUS

The *sanctuary of Nemesis* at Rhamnous is situated at a distance of 14 kms. from Marathon. The deme of *Rhamnous* was one of the remote coastal demes of Attica, opposite the island of Euboia. For the ancients, Nemesis was the goddess who chastised men who committed the sin of 'hybris' i.e. of excessive arrogance.

Two temples have been preserved on the site, an earlier one with fine wall-construction, and a later one which remained unfinished because of the Peloponnesian War. In the sanctuary, which is enclosed by a well-built peribolos, were found the statues of Themis and her priestess, as well as many inscriptions of great significance. But the most important finds were the fragments of the *cult statue of Ne-*

mesis, a work of Agorakritos, the outstanding disciple of Pheidias. The head of the statue is in the British Museum, and the sculptured decoration of the base in the National Archaeological Museum of Athens. Quite recently, a Greek Professor of Archaeology succeeded in restoring the statue of the goddess from the fragments preserved — an accomplishment of great importance, for this is the first cult statue of the Classical period of which we have knowledge through the original instead of later copies.

In the shelter at the back of the sanctuary are kept several small funerary inscribed stelai. From the sanctuary an ancient road led to the deme of Rhamnous. By the seaside stands a rocky hill (Ovriokastro), which was the *citadel of Rhamnous.* On the east slope and below the hill were the houses of the demots of Rhamnous. The acropolis was fortified with a wall, parts of which are still preserved to a height of 4 m.; for better protection, towers were added at intervals. The entrance, flanked

Attica. Marathon.
Prehistoric grave circles excavated by Professor Sp. Marinatos.

by two towers, is on the S.E. side. On the site of the ancient deme were uncovered a *theatre,* the *sanctuary of Dionysos,* a *gymnasion,* a small circular building and the *agora* of the demos.

The visit to the sanctuary of Rhamnous produces an unforgettable impression, because of the beauty of the landscape, which has not been spoiled by later building on the site.

AMPHIAREION

45 kms. from Athens, near the village of Kalamos, opposite the island of Euboia, the Amphiareion lies in a secluded pretty ravine, away from inhabited areas. The sanctuary belonged to *Oropos,* a coastal deme of Attica, and was dedicated to Amphiaraos, the healing hero particularly venerated and honoured by the ancients who believed that in his sanctuary they could be cured of any ailment, even psychic illness. Amphiaraos belonged to a generation of seers and, according to ancient mythology, he had participated in the war of the 'Seven against Thebes'. At the moment when he was in danger of being captured by his Theban opponent, he was saved by Zeus, who opened a chasm where the hero disappeared with his chariot.

The sanctuary gained renown in the 4th century B.C., when the Doric *temple* of the god was founded. The ruins now seen on the archaeological site are of this temple. A few metres beyond the east side of the temple, there is a long and narrow *altar,* where sacrifices were offered not only to Amphiaraos but to other gods as well (his 'symbomoi'). Beyond the altar there were three semicircular steps, where apparently the pilgrims sat and watched the performance of ceremonies. To the N.E. of the temple there was a *spring* into which coins were thrown by those visiting the temple to seek the god's healing power.

A great oblong *stoa* (the *Enkoimeterion*) was built at the S.E. end of the precinct. The patients slept there on the hide of the ram they had sacrificed to the god, who appeared in their sleep and indicated the way of their therapy.

Farther east of the Enkoimeterion, there was a *bath.* Behind the stoa, on an elevation of the ground, there is an excellently preserved small *theatre,* a true work of art, which could accommodate approximately 500 spectators. The proskenion of the theatre is very well preserved.

To the left of the visitor entering the sanctuary, stands a line of pedestals which were surmounted by statues in antiquity. Their inscriptions are very important.

In the small *Museum of Amphiareion* are kept a few sculpture fragments, some notorious inscriptions and architectural elements. The major finds have been transferred to the National Archaeological Museum of Athens.

SALAMIS

The island, popularly known as Koulouri, lies very close to Piraeus (1 nautical mile distance).The name of Salamis is associated with the famous naval battle won in 480 B.C., as a result of which the whole of Greece was saved from the Persian menace.

The island has a rich legendary background (tradition has it that Ajax departed from Salamis for the Trojan War). Popular architecture on the island has preserved a local character. On the west part of Salamis, the *Monastery of Phaneromeni* stands amidst a pine-clad area. The church of the monastery has a remarkable 17th century wall-painting representing the Day of Judgement.

Museum of Salamis

It is a small but very interesting Museum, containing a representative series of Classical funerary stelai, important inscriptions, and many vases and figurines of the Mycenaean period.

AIGINA

Lying at a short distance from Piraeus (1 hour and 10 minutes by steamer), Aigina is an island full of light, affording delightful impressions to the visitor. Excavation data have revealed that life began on the island in the 3rd millennium B.C.

According to a local legend, the island was named in very old time Oinone, and it was there that Zeus led the nymph *Aigina* whom he loved. The son born of their union, Aiakos, became king of the island which he named after his mother, and was regarded as the most righteous man of his age. When once Greece suffered from a rainless spell and the advice of the Oracle of Delphi was sought, the Pythia indicated Aiakos as saviour : if he were to ask his father Zeus to send rain, his request would be granted. So, Aiakos climbed on Mt. Oros and prayed to his father, the first of the gods, who at once sent the blessed rain to men. Subsequently, Aiakos founded an altar on the mountain and established the *cult of Zeus Hellanios.* Aiakos had two sons, Telamon and Peleus, who fathered two outstanding heroes of the Trojan War : Ajax and Achilles. On Mt. Hellanion, the highest on Aigina, there are traces of the ancient cult of Zeus.

The pursued nymph Aphaia also sought refuge on the island, and vanished with the help of the gods in a grove, where her sanctuary was founded. The site is 12 kms. distant from the town of Aigina and a visit to it is very pleasing. It is situated on a mound overlooking the pretty gulf of Hagia Marina.

The cult was initiated in the sanctuary in the end of the Mycenaean period. Having enjoyed the splendid scenery, the visitor may admire the ancient *temenos of Aphaia,* which is surrounded by a low peribolos. The site is entered from the *Propylaia,* to the right of which stood the dwellings of the priests. The *temple* of the goddess is of the Doric order and has been restored from whatever material has survived. There is a superimposed colonnade in the interior and an oblong *altar* in front. The temple was built in the late 6th century B.C. upon the remnants of two earlier temples. The pediments of the temple were decorated with fine sculptures, the figure of the goddess Athena dominating in the centre of the composition. Scenes were depicted from the Trojan War, where the two descendents of the royal house of Aigina, Achilles the son of Peleus and Ajax the son of Telamon, had become illustrious. By the end of the first decade of the 5th century B.C., the sculptured composition of the east pediment was destroyed, possibly struck by thunderbolt. It was then repeated in the style of that age, which accounts for the difference in artistic conception noted between the east and west pediments. Most of the sculptures preserved from both pediments are now exhibited in the Munich Glyptotek. The fragments exhibited in the National Archaeological Museum of Athens come from the earlier east pediment which had been destroyed.

On the north side of the modern harbour, which corresponds to the ancient commercial port, at the highest point of the promontory overlooking the bay of Karantina, where the ancient military harbour was *(Kryptos Limen),* a solitary Doric column marks the site of the *temple of Apollo.* This was founded on the ruins of a Prehistoric settlement which has been recently uncovered by the German

Aigina.
Temple of Aphaia.

Archaeological Institute. The site is now called *Kolona,* after the column preserved, and was in antiquity the center of the town which extended as far as the modern town and was surrounded by a fortification wall. Several monuments have come to light on the site : the *Attaleion,* the *monument of Phokos* (third son of Aiakos), the *theatre,* etc.

At a distance of 6 kms. from the modern town of Aigina, lies *Palaiochora* a ruined Mediaeval town built on a hill, where the Aiginitans sought refuge from the frequent raids of the pirates. In 1537, the town was sacked by Barbarossa, and its population massacred. It was rebuilt later, and again destroyed by the Venetians in 1654. Once more rebuilt, it remained as the capital of the island until 1826, when it was deserted by its population who moved and established themselves in the modern town of Aigina. Palaiochora has about 40 churches dating from Mediaeval times and the period of the Turkish rule. 16 of these churches are relatively well-preserved, some decorated with remarkable frescoes. Near Palaiochora is the Monastery of Hagios Nektarios. (He was born in Selymbria and became Metropolite of the Pentapolis of Egypt. He founded the Monastery of Hagia Trias and was buried there when he died in 1920 in Aigina. He was recently canonised by the Oecumenical Patriarchate).

It would be a mistake to leave Aigina without paying a visit to the *Omorphi Ecclesia,* a small basilica of the 13th century consecrated to the Sts. Theodoroi. Its interior is embellished with splendid wall-paintings.

In 1828, the Governor of liberated Greece, John Capodistria, made Aigina the seat of his Government for one year, before transferring it to Nauplion. It was then that some truly delightful mansions were built on the island.

Museum of Aigina

The Museum is in the town, near the Metropolis, and consists of two rooms and an anteroom. It was the first Museum of modern Greece, and has been housed since 1926 in this building which belonged to the compound of the Central School of the time of Capodistria.

The Museum contains sculptures, Prehistoric pottery and figurines, black- and red-figure vases, stone implements, metal objects, and some inscriptions of significance for the history of the island. In the first room (right) there are two important funerary stelai and a marble Sphinx, a masterpiece of great beauty, dated to about 460 B.C.

POROS

This island, with its conical hill covered with little white houses, presents a charming sight to visitors. This hill was probably the citadel of ancient *Kalauria.* A narrow strait separates the island from Galata, situated across on the coast of the Peloponnese, where a grove of lemon-trees adds in springtime an enchanting beauty to the resort.

The most notable site on Poros is the *sanctuary of Poseidon,* which was in antiquity the seat of an amphictyonic league including among its members Aigina, Hermione, Epidauros, Nauplia, etc. The site (named by the local population Palati) was excavated in 1894 by the Swedes. The sanctuary of Poseidon was a renowned place of shelter for political refugees, and it was there that the Athenian orator Demosthenes sought refuge when persecuted by the soldiers of Antipatros (322 B.C.).

The temple, built in the 6th century B.C., is not well-preserved, but the view from the precinct is indeed panoramic. A 40-minute walk to the *Monastery of Panaghia* rewards the visitor with another exquisite scenery. In the church of the monastery there is a 16th century gilt iconostasis, brought from Kaisaria of Asia Minor, and an icon of the Virgin painted by the Italian artist Seccoli.

The local *Museum of Poros,* a gift of the Al. Korizis family, has not been inaugurated yet.

HYDRA

Hydra is a bare island full of rocks, but it has an atmosphere of valour and virility. It has recently become the international summer resort of intellectuals and artists. Hydra has many well-preserved old mansions reminiscent of the times (18th - 19th cent.) when the island was rich and prosperous thanks to its large merchant navy, enjoying a form of independence even though it belonged to the Turks. The Hydriot captains were very active with the transportation of merchandise during the Napoleonic Wars, and they owned the fine mansions, which still embellish the island with their magnificent appearance. In the War of Independence the island of Hydra played a leading role, for it possessed weapons, a fleet and experienced sailors who proved capable of great deeds during clashes with the enemy. Eminent families, like the Kountouriotis, Tompazis, Tsamados, and particularly Miaoulis, were the terror of Turkish ships during the War of Independence. Later, with the evolution of steam navigation, the island declined.

By reason of the naval tradition of the island, an important Training School for officers of the mercantile marine has been founded in Hydra. The School is housed in the mansion of Tsamados, to the north of the harbour. On the opposite south side, is the mansion of Tompazis, now a hostel for artists of the School of Fine Arts. Along with the houses of Kountouriotis, Boudouris, etc., these provide fine examples of the Hydriot architecture.

The *Metropolis* of Hydra, on the central part of the port, was formerly (in the 17th century) the Katholikon of a Monastery. Its bell-tower is dated to 1808. The coronae of the church are adorned with the Bourbon fleurs de lis.

SPETSAI

Like Hydra, this island too, is impregnated with naval tradition. Its pine-clad hills and many other sites are suitable for pleasant walks. Recent archaeological investigations at Hagia Marina have revealed remains of Early and Late Helladic occupation.

Spetsai played an important role in the War of Independence of 1821, when the Spetsiot ship-owners offered their vessels for the liberation of the nation. The leading personalities of the island gathered at the fortified harbour of the Dapia. Further up stands the house of the local heroine Bouboulina.

Near the old harbour is the *Metropolis,* consecrated to St. Nicholas. The church belonged to a monastery and it is being said that Paul-Marie Bonaparte, the brother of Napoleon, was killed in one of the monastery cells. The church dates to the 17th century.

Museum of Spetsai

The Museum is housed in the mansion of Hadziyannis Mexis, and contains relics of the naval achievements of the Spetsiots: the flag of Independence, figures

Attica. Daphni.
Mosaic with representation of the Nativity.

decorating the prows of vessels, drawings and paintings of the Spetsiot ships, the bones of Bouboulina in a casket, weapons and other mementos of eminent families of the island.

The Museum also includes a small archaeological collection which comprises sculptures of the Roman and Early Christian age. Among the exhibits are some Post-Byzantine icons and an embroidered *epitaphios*. A small collection of popular art is also on display, consisting of a few local costumes, ceramics and other handicrafts.

DAPHNI

The Byzantine *monastery of Daphni,* dedicated to the Dormition of the Virgin, was founded on the site of the *sanctuary of Apollo Daphnephoros.* The scenery is very attractive, full of pine-trees and oleanders, and the site is associated with many traditions. The monastery, built in the 5th - 6th century A.D., was later deserted and renovated in the 11th century. The *church* we see at present was built at that time and has become famous for its mosaic decoration which is excellently preserved and shows the predominance of ecclesiastical tradition in Byzantine art. An imposing figure, the Pantokrator, looks down from the vault of the dome with his finger placed on the book of judgement. Stern figures of prophets, saints, and angels, and scenes from the life of Christ, are executed in vivid blue, pink and green colours producing an exquisite effect against the gold background of the mosaics.

A year after the conquest of Constantinople by the Franks, the monastery was occupied by the Cistercian monks, who were driven away by the Turks in the 15th century. In the 16th century, the monastery was returned to the Orthodox monks, who increased its land property. The Cistercians had already added the Gothic arches on the church facade, and the panels in the narthex, which was used as a library. On the north side of the narthex, there is a square tower with interior stairway.

The cloister with the monastic cells in the peribolos, the refectory, and a porch to the south of the church, added by the Cistercians, complete the compound of the monastery. In the courtyard there are two sarcophagi adorned with fleurs de lis, which contain the remains of two Frankish dukes: Othon de la Roche and Gautier de Brienne, who were buried at Daphni.

ELEUSIS

3500 years ago, the large plain of Eleusis was occupied by small settlements, each headed by its own ruler. The sovereign of Eleusis was generally recognized as the strongest and accepted as king among the others.

The location of Eleusis is indeed privileged, for it commands the road leading from Attica to Megara and the Peloponnese and has access to a protected bay offering shelter to ships. Rich corn crops from the land and abundant fish from the sea made the region self-sufficient. Thus, Eleusis remained independent over a long period and became the major rival of Megara and Athens.

Kings and high officials resided on the summit of the acropolis, which was surrounded by a fortification wall. The dwellings of the population occupied the south and east slopes. Water was always scarce in the city; hence, the only well at the foot of the acropolis was regarded as sacred and the maidens of Eleusis danced around it during ceremonies, which accounts for its name 'Kallichoron Frear' (Well of the Fair Dances).

The site of Eleusis had been closely associated with the cult of the goddess Demeter from the Mycenaean age. This factor determined the fate of the city, which became the centre of a mystery cult of outstanding importance in the religious life of the ancient Greeks until the age when Christianity prevailed.

The legend associated with the cult is very characteristic. Grieved by the loss of Persephone, who had been abducted by Plouto, the god of the Underworld, Demeter wandered from place to place in quest of her daughter. Tired and disguised as an old woman, the goddess came to Eleusis, where the king's daughters, who ignored her true identity, offered her hospitality in the palace. Metaneira, the consort of the king Keleos, entrusted her then with the care of her newborn son, the prince Damophon. In gratitude for this whole-hearted hospitality, the goddess decided to immortalize Damophon. The boy's mother, however, took such fright, when she suddenly witnessed the strange ceremony, that the goddess was forced to leave the palace, after revealing her divine identity to the Eleusinians and teaching them the mystery of agriculture. She also blessed them to be happy in both earthly and eternal life, on condition that they would keep her instructions and perform her cult according to all the rules. Demeter also commanded them to found a temple and an altar in her honour, which they did at once, and it was there that the Eleusinian Mysteries were performed as taught by the goddess herself.

The *Eleusinian Mysteries* were basically a religion, whose primordial element was the cult of the earth, which is, along with the sun, the source of life for men. It was believed that the goddess Demeter had revealed to men the secret of cultivating the soil, as well as the mystical process which would ensure not merely abundance of earthly products but also happiness in life after death.

The secret of the Eleusinian Mysteries has been kept so well, that we know nothing today of the mystical ceremonies performed in the Telesterion of Eleusis. The initiated were under strong vows, so that no one dared speak for fear of losing happiness in this life and the next. The Eleusinian Mysteries were instituted by Eumolpos and spread not only in Attica but over the whole of Greece. Eleusis has yielded finds dating to Prehistoric times, when there were small townships on the site with local rulers, chief among whom was the king of Eleusis. In remote times many wars were fought between the Eleusinians and the Athenians, who wished to include Eleusis in their state, particularly in the age of Theseus. It was only in 600 B.C., that the Athenians succeeded to conquer Eleusis and make it one of the great demes of Attica. During all subsequent periods and until the end of antiquity, the Athenian statesmen took special care of Eleusis and gave a singular splendour to the celebration of the Eleusinian Mysteries, which became the cult of the state of Athens.

Because of its important location next to enemy states, and particularly Megara, the Athenians erected a fortification wall to protect the city and secure her harbour. Thus Eleusis became a real stronghold.

Solon, Peisistratos, Kimon, Perikles and Lykourgos made their own contributions to the walling of the city and the buildings of the sanctuary. The shrine flourished until the 2nd century A.D., when it reached its greatest peak. It declined in the end of antiquity—it was sacked in A.D. 395 during the Gothic invasion of Alaric, and was given the final blow by the Byzantine emperor Theodosios I, who abolished the performance of the Mysteries.

In later times the Byzantine emperors showed interest in the fortification of the site, by reason of its key position. From the 14th - 15th century, however, tired of their constant struggles, the inhabitants began to abandon the town, which was gradually deserted and left an easy prey to the Turks. The site was raided in the 17th century by pirates. Thus, when in 1676 the French traveller Spon arrived there, he did not find a single house. From 1700 onwards Eleusis was inhabited again, and the small church of the Theotokos was founded on the site of the palace of the Prehistoric king. During the War of Independence the city took an active part and became the headquarters of G. Karaiskakis and other commanders.

Excavations on the site were begun by the British Society of the Dilettanti (1812) and continued later by the French archaeologist Lenormant (1860). From 1882 onwards the site has been systematically excavated by the Greek Archaeological Society, and investigations are still carried out.

Entering the paved great forecourt (at the terminal of the Sacred Way leading from Athens to Eleusis), the visitor sees on the right the *temple of Artemis Propylaia* and on the left the *Kallichoron Frear*. Nearby lie the ruins of the *Great Propylaia,* which were the main entrance to the sanctuary. Several walls belonging to subsidiary buildings of the sanctuary extend to the left. Passing through the *Lesser Propylaia,* the visitor has on the right the *Ploutoneion* (the cavern of Plouto, where the god of Hades was supposed to have abducted Persephone). Beyond the Lesser Propylaia is the sacred court (left), with a great quadrilateral building on the N.W. side, the *Telesterion,* where the ceremonies of the Mysteries were performed. Above the Telesterion rises the acropolis of Eleusis.

Museum of Eleusis

The Museum is located within the archaeological site. It is a local Museum which houses the movable finds of the excavations. A large Proto-Attic amphora with mythical representations is an impressive exhibit in the first room to the right. In this room and the anteroom there are various notable sculptures of the Archaic, Classical, Hellenistic and Roman periods. Also noteworthy are the Prehistoric finds from the large cemetery, uncovered near the football field of the town. They include pottery, gold and bronze jewellery and weapons. From the cemetery of the Classical period comes a bronze funerary urn which contained the bones of the dead wrapped in a cloth entirely preserved. Special cult vessels, the kernoi and kalathoi, are worth of attention, and so are various groups of funerary finds carefully collected and displayed in the last room on the left. There are also some remarkable Geometric vases (a small skyphos is decorated with the representation of a ship).

PERACHORA

11 kms. from Loutraki (a summer resort and spa) lies a most picturesque lagoon surrounded by pines, with the ruins of the *sanctuary of Hera* nearby. The excavations of the British School of Archaeology have brought to light important movable finds—votive offerings to *Hera Limnaia* and *Hera Akraia*. The sanctuary is situated on a rocky promontory overlooking two gulfs : the Corinthian and the Alkyonic. Although the superstructure of the temple of Hera has not survived, the ruins are quite impressive. Most remarkable, however, is the small but very elegant 'agora' of the precinct, as well as the small harbour *(Sacred Harbour)* which still serves its purpose in our days, offering shelter to fishermen's boats on the site were pilgrims anchored their ships in antiquity.

Museum of Perachora

This is mainly an archaeological collection which includes some movable finds from the site : bronzes and, mostly, Corinthian pottery that have come to light in the course of excavations at the Heraion. The other finds are exhibited in the National Archaeological Museum, Athens.

THE PELOPONNESE

CORINTH

Corinth was in antiquity the most extensive and prosperous city of mainland Greece. Homer names her ἀφνειός, i.e. rich, and she owed her riches to her privileged geographic position between two gulfs: the Saronic and the Corinthian. Corinth had two ports : *Lechaion* and *Kenchreai*. At the narrowest point of the strip of land separating the two seas, the Corinthians constructed an important work, the Diolkos, for the portage of both ships and cargoes from the one gulf to the other. The Corinthians charged a toll for this passage, which the ancient mariners preferred to the hazardous voyage round the Peloponnese, past the rough seas of Cape Maleas. Corinth also commanded the routes leading from the Peloponnese to Central Greece and vice versa.

Excavations have revealed that there existed settlements in Corinthia in Prehistoric times (Neolithic period), and that life continued uninterrupted down to historic times. Water was abundant on the site and the soil yielded rich crops—a factor which, in addition to her strategic position, contributed to the prosperity of Corinth. The Corinthians were the first to perfect the type of ship with 50 oars, which they employed for their voyages to East and West, where they obtained the raw material which the skilful Corinthian artists transformed into fine products of the minor arts : bronze weapons and pottery. The Corinthian vases which introduced the polychrome decoration were famous in the Archaic period.

Corinth attained great prosperity in the 6th century B.C., during the tyranny of Periander, who was one of the Seven Wise Men of antiquity. His age was marked by the construction of the *Diolkos* and the foundation of the *temple of Apollo,* which dominates the knoll rising above the ancient agora of the city. The Corinthians were illustrious for their clay sculpture and bronzework, and were the first to develop and advance the art of painting. The city became incredibly rich through commerce. On *Acrocorinth,* decicated to the cult of Helios, there was a *temple of the Armed Aphrodite.* Corinth began to decline in the 5th century B.C., when following the great flowering of Athens, the commerce of mainland Greece passed chiefly into the hands of the Athenians. This became the cause of enmity against the Athenians. Corinth prospered again at the time when Philip II was king of Macedonia. The huge *South Stoa* —an imposing two-storied edifice, the greatest of its kind on mainland Greece— was then built in the agora of the city. Philip, and later his successor Alexander, summoned at Corinth a Synedrion of the representatives of the Greek cities to ratify the leadership in the campaign against the Persians. The growth of Corinth in the Hellenistic age was remarkable. However, the prosperous city was suddenly extinguished, when in 146 B.C., after the last battle of the Greeks against the Romans (at Leukopetra), where the Hellenic forces were defeated, Corinth was mercilessly razed to the ground by the Roman general Mummius. On this occasion, the countless artistic treasures of the beautiful and rich city were savagely plundered.

In 44 B.C., the Roman general Julius Caesar built a new city on the ruins of the old one, which had been protected by a strong wall, and the city was colonised by manumitted Romans and Jews. Thanks to her important geographic position however, Corinth became soon the seat of the Roman pronconsul of Achaia. In A.D. 51 - 52, St. Paul, the Apostle of the Nations, arrived in Corinth to preach the Christian religion. In the Roman period the city was embellished with new edifices, the agora was adorned with fine buildings and it attained great prosperity anew. In A.D. 67, the Roman emperor Nero attempted the piercing of the Isthmus, but works were discontinued following his assassination. In the 2nd century A.D. the Roman emperor Hadrian supplied the city with fine buildings and an aqueduct for conveying water from Lake Stymphalia. Herodes Atticus was similarly a benefactor of the city. Thanks to the contributions of all these eminent men and the growth of commerce, Corinth experienced once again a great flourishing. It was at that period that the phrase 'A voyage to Corinth is not for everyone' became proverbial. A crowd of foreign travellers and merchants gathered in the city to spend a few pleasant days.

From the 3rd century A.D., Corinth played an important role in the expansion of Christianity — a fact attested by the large early Christian basilicas found on the site particularly the huge *basilica of Lechaion* (of the size of St. Peter's in Rome). The successive and devastating raids of the barbarians, the fire set by the Goth Alaric, and a number of earthquakes completed the destruction of the once splendid city. In the age of Justinian, the extensive Justinian Wall (the *Hexamilion*) was constructed along the length of the Isthmus, in order to prevent a descent of invaders on the Peloponnese. Architectural material for the construction of this wall was for the most part obtained from the great buildings of the sanctuary of Poseidon at Isthmia, and particularly the temple of the god.

In the Byzantine age, especially from the 9th to the 12th century, Corinth became again an important centre of craftsmanship and commerce, and the seat of the Byzantine general of the Peloponnese. In the mid-12th century the Norman invaders plundered the treasures of the city and occupied Acrocorinth. In 1208, the valiant local governor Leon Sgouros, having failed to prevent the conquest of the region by the Franks, jumped with his horse from the ramparts of Acrocorinth to avoid being taken alive. Until 1458, when Acrocorinth fell to the Turks, the place underwent successive occupations by the Franks, the Florentines, the Knights of St. John, etc. Between 1699 and 1715 the site was occupied by the Venetians and subsequently retaken by the Turks. Old Corinth then became a flourishing village which gradually developed into a city. Kiamel, the last Bey of Corinth, was very fond of the city and built a fine palace at the site known as 'The Baths of Aphrodite'. In 1822, following the defeat of Dramali at Dervenakia, the city was liberated from the Turks. For a brief period Corinth became the seat of the Greek Revolutionary Government. In 1858, the city was destroyed by a severe earthquake. It was thus slowly deserted by the inhabitants who moved to the coast, where New Corinth was founded. The disaster was repeated in 1928 and 1930. The village of Old Corinth still stands on the site of Ancient Corinth, next to the archaeological site.

From the ancient great city have survived the Doric *temple of the Pythian Apollo,* the *Fountain of Glauke,* the *Sacred Spring,* and the repeatedly remodelled *Fountain of Peirene.* These monuments together with the *Theatre* and the *Odeion* give a picture of the public center of the city and its shrines.

The aspect shown by the excavated site at present, is that of the period of the

Roman sway : the great Archaic temple to the north, and, below, the *agora* with the various public edifices, stoas, basilicas and small shrines. A moving sight is the *Bema,* where St. Paul the Apostle was taken to apologize before the Roman consul Gallio. The south side of the agora is dominated by the ruins of the Hellenistic *South Stoa,* while on the north side stand by the row of the *northwest shops,* the *Sacred Spring, the Captives' Façade* (a monumental entrance of a large two-storey building) and the *Great Propylon* giving access to the paved road of Lechaion. On the west side there are small shrines and the circular *monument of Babbius.* Further west is the *Fountain of Glauke.* As the visitor descends the road to Lechaion, he encounters (on the right) the *Fountain of Peirene* —which underwent nine modifications in antiquity— and the *peribolos of Apollo* — which contained the statue of the god and was painted on the south side with a representation of the 'Killing of the Suitors' as described by Homer in the Odyssey. The *theatre* was built in the 4th century B.C., but was later remodelled.

The *aphesis* of the Stadion has been identified at the east end of the area of the agora. Excavations on the site were begun in the 19th century and are still carried on by the American School of Classical Studies. What we see today is the aspect Corinth had in the 1st century A.D. Further north, by the road, lie the ruins of the *North Stoa* and the *Greek Bath.* Northwards of the archaeological site, near the wall, is the *Asklepieion* and next to it the *Fountain of Lerna.*

The ancient city extended on the foot of the north slope of Acrocorinth. The area it occupied varied in different periods. The perimeter of the wall measured 20 kms. and the population in peak periods numbered 20,000. Long walls connected Corinth with her two harbours.

ACROCORINTH

Acrocorinth is one of the finest citadels with imposing fortifications. Conquerors who occupied the site at times, restored or rebuilt walls above the ancient enceinte, parts of which are still visible. The main entrance is enclosed by a triple line of fortifications. In the interior, by the N.W. end of the wall, were uncovered traces of the small *temple of the Armed Aphrodite.* Walls belonging to buildings of various periods are encountered everywhere. An underground cistern at the south end of the site is thought to have been the *Upper Fountain of Peirene,* from which the ancients believed that water flowed to the *Lower Fountain of Peirene.* It is there that according to a local legend Bellerophon caught Pegasos, the winged horse.

Museum of Corinth

The elegant small building houses the finds brought to light during excavations at the Agora, the Asklepieion, and other sites of Corinthia. The first room to the left contains Prehistoric finds : vessels, figurines, implements and tools made of stone or clay. In the room to the right, the ceramic products of the unique and outstanding Corinthian workshops are displayed in chronological order, showing the development of Corinthian pottery. The finds have come from the Corinthian Kerameikos or from cemeteries. The room also includes a few characteristic works of large sculpture made of clay, marble objects (such as the fine head of a small kouros of the late Archaic times), small bronzes from the excavations at Isthmia, and a superb marble *perirrhanterium.*

A separate room contains finds from the Asklepieion of Lerna, which are indica-

Museum of Corinth.
Archaic vases.

tive of the medical knowledge of the ancients. In the Museum courtyard are exhibited inscriptions and metopes from the theatre.

The large room of the Roman period contains many statues, busts and other sculptures, as well as mosaics from Roman villas. There are also on display a collection of coins, Byzantine plates and vases, and an early Christian wall-painting.

ISTHMIA

Very little can be seen by the present-day visitor of the most important site of Isthmia, where the great Panhellenic Isthmian games were celebrated every quinquennium. Pindar, the incomparable poet of the 5th century B.C., composed odes for several victors of the competitions.

The archaeological site lies by the village Kera Vrysi, 5 kms. off the national road before reaching New Corinth. Excavations have been conducted by the American School of Classical Studies and have uncovered the foundations of the Archaic *temple* and *altar of Poseidon,* the *aphesis* (starting line) of the *Stadion* of the Classical period, and *stoas* enclosing the temenos. By the south side of the temple, there is another *temple* and *altar* dedicated to the hero *Palaimon;* the temple had an underground passage necessary for the celebration of cult. This popular hero was honoured with nocturnal ceremonies—excavations have brought to light hundreds of lamps. The major finds from the sanctuary of Isthmia are exhibited in the Museum at Old Corinth.

To the N.E. of the temenos there are rooms, hewn out of the soft rock, which served cult purposes, and the *theatre* of Isthmia.

NEMEA

31 kms. from Corinth, a crossroad leads to the village Heraklion, where, in antiquity, a *sanctuary* was dedicated to *Zeus Nemeos.* Great Panhellenic games were held there biennially. The best time to visit Nemea is at dusk, when the sun sets behind the mountains and the pretty valley appears in a rosy hue. Excavations have uncovered the *temple of Zeus* (dated to the 4th century B.C.) with its oblong *altar* to the east. The ruins of the *Palaistra* and the *Gymnasion* have also been identified.

Musical, dramatic, equestrian and gymnastic contests were performed during the Nemean festival in honour of the prince Opheltes, son of the king of Nemea Lykourgos. Remains of the ancient *theatre* and *stadion* are located on the slopes of Mt. Phoka. A cave at Korakovouni has been associated by local tradition with the lion slain by the hero Herakles.

MYCENAE

41 kms. from Corinth there is a crossroad where the route diverges towards Mycenae (at a distance of 4 kms.). The scenery with its grey steep rocks is peculiar. The legend that inspired the great Athenian dramatic poets of the 5th century B.C., haunts the site and reminds the visitor of the tragic fate of the house of Atreus— of Agamemnon, Aigisthos, Klytaimnestra, Orestes and Electra.

The excavation of Mycenae has been a sensational event. It was here that in the 19th century Schliemann, who strongly believed in Homer's tale of the 'rich-in-gold' Mycenae, searched and found five of the six royal graves. The discovery was of major importance and marked an epoch, for it revealed to science the hitherto unknown Mycenaean civilization. Excavations are still continued by the Greek Archaeological Society, under the direction of Professor G. Mylonas.

The Cyclopean walls surrounding the acropolis are very imposing, and the monumental entrance, the famous *Lion Gate,* surmounted by the lintel with the huge relief, can be seen from afar.

Immediately after entering the acropolis through the Lion Gate, the visitor sees on the right the ruins of granaries and houses, and farther on, the royal grave circle. A climb to the top of the hill leads to the royal palace. The frescoes and other objects of the palace and the rich finds of the royal graves are displayed in the Mycenaean room of the National Archaeological Museum of Athens. Within the walls were also uncovered the ruins of large houses, which had probably served as residence for the nobility. In fact, the acropolis was a palace-fort, complete with cisterns and large stores.

Another circle of shaft-graves, grave circle B, was discovered outside the acropolis and yielded rich finds, though not as sumptuous as those from the graves within the enceinte.

The huge tholos tombs —nine in all— are extremely impressive, the most remarkable one being the so-called *Treasury of Atreus* or Agamemnon. These tombs resemble enormous beehives. Large houses were also found outside the citadel; some of these yielded clay tablets with Linear B script.

ARGOS

Argos lies at a distance of 50 kms. from Corinth. The ancients believed that the city had been founded by Danaos, and it is certain that life existed there in Mycenaean times, particularly on the hill of Aspis. The city reached its greatest peak in the Geometric and, especially, the Archaic age, the most important period being the 7th century B.C., during the tyranny of Pheidon; he was the first to introduce coinage and institute games — the Heraia.

Hera was the patroness goddess of Argos and her sanctuary stood 7 kms. N.E. of the city. This major city of the Peloponnese is associated with many mythical traditions. Argos, Sparta and Thebes had been great centres before the growth of Corinth. After 494 B.C., when the Argives were defeated by the Spartan king Kleomenes, the city declined for some decades, but remained a famous center of sculpture and bronzework — the celebrated artist Polykleitos was an Argive.

A large *theatre* hewn in the rock (dated to the 4th century B.C.), as well as Roman buildings, baths, etc. are to be seen in Argos. In the area of the modern town, a whole series of important Geometric graves have been discovered during building operations.

The first and fourth National Conventions during the War of Independence of 1821 met at Argos.

THE ARGIVE HERAION

The great sanctuary dedicated to Hera was in antiquity under the supervision of the Argives. The sanctuary is situated at the foot of a hill, near the village Chonika, where there is also an interesting Byzantine church of the 12th century. Life on the site of the Heraion began in the Mycenaean period and continued to the end of antiquity — all relevant finds are exhibited in a room on the upper floor of the

National Archaeological Museum in Athens. Hera, the consort of Zeus, represented eternal youth. The ancients believed that the goddess bathed every year in the waters of the spring of *Kanathos* and regained her virginity. Her union with Zeus symbolized the fertilization of plants, animals and men. Hera was first worshipped in the Argive Heraion, whence her cult spread over the Peloponnese, making her sanctuary one of the most venerated and important in the Hellenic world. The fact that the Argives based their chronology on the years of service of the priestess of Hera attests to the significance of the sanctuary.

Excavations on the site, begun in the 19th century, were conducted by the Americans from 1892 to 1895. In 1925, the Americans again investigated the Mycenaean chamber tombs, and the site was identified as the Mycenaean *Prosymna*. The latest exploration and chronological investigation of the site was carried out in 1952.

The sanctuary occupies three successive terraces, reached by means of a monumental stairway. The temple of the goddess of the Classical age (420 - 410 B.C.) stood in the centre of the second terrace, while on the lower terrace was built a large stoa. The *temple of Hera* was of the Doric order, with an altar in front. The chryselephantine statue of the goddess, a work of Polykleitos, was set up within the sekos of the temple; nearby, stood the statue of Hebe, similarly made of gold and ivory, a work of Naukydes. There was also a *xoanon* of Hera, made of wild pear-tree wood, which the Argives had carried away when they destroyed Tiryns. One of the pediments of the temple was decorated with scenes of the Gigantomachy and the other with a representation of the Sack of Troy. Scenes of the Amazonomachy were depicted on the metopes. Fragments of these sculptures together with architectural members can be seen in the National Archaeological Museum of Athens.

The earlier temple of Hera, dated to Geometric times, was built on the highest terrace. It was destroyed in 425 B.C., through the carelessness of the priestess Chryseis. Two stoas, one of the 7th and one of the 6th century B.C., were erected on the second terrace. Opposite the Classical temple there was a building with five series of columns in the interior; it was probably of the nature of the *Telesterion* of Eleusis. There were also in the sanctuary dwellings for the priestesses, *Roman baths* and, to the west, a *gymnasion*.

Games were performed at the Heraion in the second year of every Olympiad. A hecatomb was offered and the victors received as prizes bronze shields and myrtle wreaths. The Heraion is best visited at dusk, when the setting sun lends it lovely colours.

Museum of Argos

The Museum is on Vasilissis Olgas street and comprises two collections : the one, on display at the Kallergeion, includes works of the plastic arts and finds from the Prehistoric site of Lerna. The second is housed in a new building founded by the French School of Archaeology, and consists of fine clay vases of the Geometric and Archaic periods, bronzes and gold funerary offerings, attractively presented. There are also Mycenaean vases, figurines and other small objects, jewellery, a bronze breastplate, weapons and *obeloi* (the earliest money).

In the courtyard of the Museum the visitor may see under a shed a large mosaic floor with representations of the months and seasons of the year.

Tiryns.
Gallery of the acropolis.

TIRYNS

5 kms. before reaching Nauplia, to the left of the road, stands the Mycenaean *acropolis* of Tiryns, an imposing sight with its remarkably well-preserved Cyclopean walls.

According to legend, the first king of Tiryns, Proitos, had the huge walls built with the help of the Cyclops sent by his kinsman the king of Lycia, Iobates. The site was explored by Schliemann in 1876, but excavations were systematically carried out in 1884 by the German archaeologist Dörpfeld. Excavations were continued till 1928, and some complementary investigations have been undertaken recently by the German Archaeological Institute.

Like Mycenae, the site was occupied from the 3rd millennium B.C. till the invasion of the Dorians. As in Mycenae, life continued through the Geometric and Archaic times, until 468 B.C., when Tiryns was destroyed by the Argives. (Tiryns sent a contingent to the battle of Plataiai).

Tiryns is the birthplace of Herakles. Her great palace on the top of the hill is a representative example of Mycenaean palaces. The vaulted galleries on the interior of the walls are most impressive.

Near the acropolis is the building of the first Agricultural College founded by Capodistria, which today serves as a penal agricultural institution.

Tiryns is indeed one of the most remarkable archaeological sites.

NAUPLIA

Nauplia is one of the most attractive towns in Greece, preserving its local character. It is marked by an atmosphere of distinction, with its fine old houses, shady courtyards with aromatic plants and trees, elegant balconies and picturesque narrow streets. It was, 'till 1834, the first capital of Greece after the Independence and the seat of the first Greek Parliament (Bouleutikon). The city was named Nauplia in antiquity, *Nauplion* in the Byzantine period, *Anapli* later, and *Napoli di Romania* by the Venetians. Two hills rise above the site : *Palamedi* and *Akronauplia* (Its Kale), and the town extends along their north slopes. On the N.W. lies the islet of *Bourdzi,* once the retreat of the public executioners. The Argive plain extends to the north-west.

Nauplia is associated with many legends. It was founded by Nauplios, son of Amymone and Poseidon, as recorded by Pausanias the Periegete. Poseidon fell in love with the nymph Amymone and Nauplios was born of their union. The god, then, rewarded the nymph by revealing to her the spring of Lerna. Another legend cites Nauplios as the father of Palamedes, the hero of the Trojan War. Archaeological finds attest to the tradition of a Prehistoric occupation of the site.

The etymology of Nauplia is related to the word 'naus' (ship). Argos and Nauplia were rival cities in antiquity : the strength of the one was on the land, that of the other on the sea. Hence, the selection of Hera and Poseidon as their patron deities was very appropriate. In the 7th century B.C., Nauplia was a member of the League of Kalauria, to which also belonged Athens, Aigina, Prasiai (now Porto Raphti), Epidauros, Troizen and Hermione, as well as the Boiotian Orchomenos. Poseidon was the patron god of the League and a great temple was dedicated to him at Kalauria.

The ancient history of the city is unknown. In the 2nd century A.D., the site was deserted. Later it was re-inhabited in the Byzantine age, and during the 12th century (in 1149), the *Ayia Moni* with its magnificent Byzantine church was founded near *Pronoia,* the suburb of Nauplia. In front of the doorway of the monastery is the *spring of Kanathos,* where, according to the legend, Hera bathed once a year to regain her virginity. Nauplia remained independent until 1247, and was subsequently occupied by the Franks until 1389. Between 1389 and 1540 it passed into the hands of the Venetians. Conquered by the Turks in 1540, it was recovered by the Venetians in 1686, who held it until 1715. From this date until 1821 it was occupied again by the Turks. Following the Protocol of London, in 1829/30, Nauplia became the capital of the liberated Greek nation. In 1831, the governor Capodistria was assassinated there, and in 1833, Otho, the first king of the Hellenes, disembarked and remained in the city for about a year, until Athens became the capital of the kingdom of Greece.

Akronauplia (Its Kale) is the ancient *acropolis* of Nauplia. Its well-hewn polygonal masonry was re-used in the Mediaeval fortifications. The *Arvanitia,* the coast side of the town, which has a promenade with attractive cafés, commands a fine view. To the N.E. of Palamedi, towards Pronoia, approximately 40 chamber tombs, with square chamber and long dromos were uncovered during excavations by the Greek Archaeological Society. The finds include jewellery made of gold or precious stones and glass, various vessels and vases, clay figurines, most of which are displayed in the National Archaeological Museum of Athens. The site has also yielded Geometric and a few Classical finds. On the precipitous rock of *Palamedi,* the Venetians built a huge *fortress,* which is reached by a climb of 999 steps. A road has recently been engineered leading to the gate of the castle. Visitors enjoy a panoramic view of the plain of Nauplia, the surrounding mountains of the Peloponnese, and the large bay with its islets. On the nearest one, *Bourdzi,* there is a *castle* converted at present into a hotel.

The town of Nauplia has a great number of monuments related to modern Greek history : the first School of Army Cadets, the Bouleutikon, etc.

Museum of Nauplia

The fine edifice on Syntagma Square, which had served as naval depot of the Venetian fleet (built during the second Venetian occupation of 1686 - 1715, as recorded by the inscription in Latin above the central arch of the gallery), has two storeys. Both storeys and the ground-floor have been used by the Greek Archaeological Service since 1955. The ground-floor houses the offices, laboratories and storerooms of the Museum. The two storeys contain the abundant antiquities of the region, which are so essential that the Museum is considered as one of the most important in the world.

Some of the archaeological finds of the Argolid are exhibited in the National Archaeological Museum of Athens, and the rest, those of lesser value, in the Museum of Nauplia. Still, the large and varied pottery collection of the Museum is unique.

The Prehistoric (Mycenaean) collections on the first floor include exhibits : 1) From *Mycenae*: a) a few finds from Schliemann's excavations, b) frescoes, tablets and, mostly, vases from the excavations of the British School of Archaeology, c) vases, a number of objects from the excavation of Grave Circle B, and tablets from the Greek excavations. 2) From *Tiryns*: a) finds from the excavations of the German Archaeological Institute, b) frescoes, vases, and all the finds of the post - war excavations of the Greek Archaeological Society. 3) From *Asine*: finds from the

excavations of the Swedish Institute of Archaeology. 4) From *Dendra* (the ancient *Midea*) : pottery from the excavations of the Swedish Institute of Archaeology. 5) From *Berbati*: pottery and figurines from the excavations of the Swedes. 6) Finds from the surrounding region.

In the second floor are exhibited finds of the Geometric times from Mycenae, Tiryns, Asine and the area around Nauplia.

The early Archaic clay shields, masks and figurines from excavations at Tiryns are noteworthy. Exhibits include vases of Classical and Hellenistic date from excavations at Hermione, a collection of Boiotian ware, a gift of the Episcope Nikandros, and, lastly, a collection of pottery of Attic and other provenance, a gift of Mr. Glymenopoulos.

The Museum of Nauplia is very interesting for it gives an idea of the Prehistoric civilization of the great centres of the Argolid (Mycenae, Tiryns, Asine, Midea) in the Early, Middle and Late Helladic periods. An exhibit of great interest is the unique in the Peloponnese megalithic monument (menhir) found in Midea. Equally interesting are a series of fresco fragments and tablets of Linear B script from the palace of Mycenae, the gravestones from Grave Circle B at Mycenae, part of the entablature crowning the Treasury of Atreus, a splendid bronze cuirass and helmet unearthed during post-war excavations at Dendra (Midea), and many bronze tools, vessels and weapons. Precious jewellery, stone vases and a multitude of Mycenaean figurines complete the picture of the Prehistoric civilization of the Argolid.

ASINE

Asine lies at a distance of 12 kms. from Nauplia. Homer makes a simple mention of the name without giving any information about the site, which is indeed picturesque with its *citadel* standing by the seashore, a majestic solitary castle. No modern building interferes with the ancient ruins. In the citadel there are remains of the Prehistoric and historic times to the end of the Roman age. Excavations on the site, which yielded important finds of Mycenaean date, were carried out by the Swedish Archaeological Expedition under the direction of the then prince Gustav Adolf of Sweden, in 1922, 1924 and 1926.

The strongly fortified acropolis, which had been in use from Prehistoric times, is named at present *Kastraki*. Some parts of the walls —those showing polygonal masonry— were restored in the Hellenistic period. A series of houses at the foot of the citadel date from the Early Helladic to the Hellenistic period. Further west was explored the Mycenaean necropolis, consisting of chamber tombs with a dromos.

The various finds from the site are exhibited in the Museum of Nauplia.

EPIDAUROS

29 kms. from Nauplia and 140 kms. via the new road from Athens, lies the *sanctuary of Asklepios,* famous in antiquity throughout the Hellenic world, both on mainland Greece and overseas.

The ardent quest of man for cures from ailments made him believe in heroes with healing powers. Homer characteristically presents doctors as venerable persons of divine descent.

Asklepios was worshipped in most of the cities of Greece, and several sanctuaries were dedicated to him. He was thought to have been the son of Apollo and

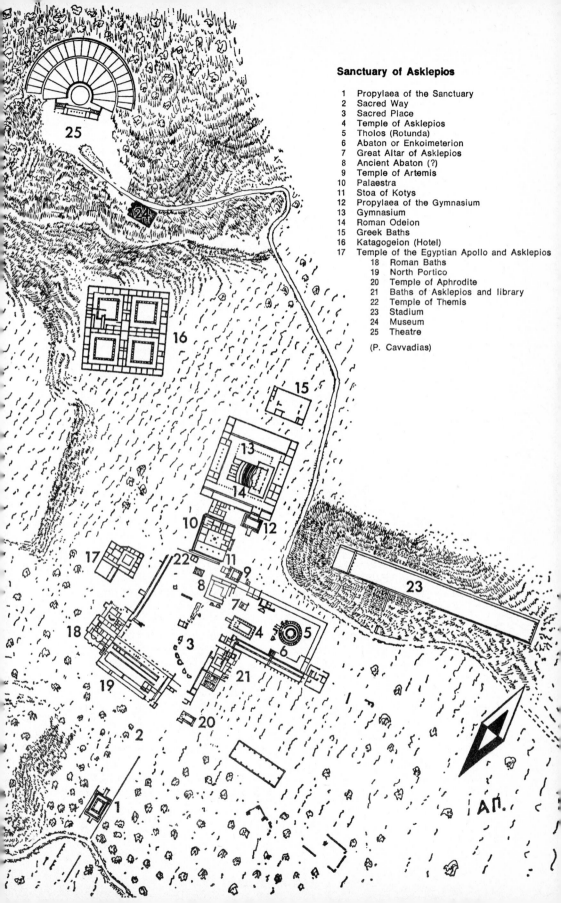

Sanctuary of Asklepios

1   Propylaea of the Sanctuary
2   Sacred Way
3   Sacred Place
4   Temple of Asklepios
5   Tholos (Rotunda)
6   Abaton or Enkoimeterion
7   Great Altar of Asklepios
8   Ancient Abaton (?)
9   Temple of Artemis
10 Palaestra
11 Stoa of Kotys
12 Propylaea of the Gymnasium
13 Gymnasium
14 Roman Odeion
15 Greek Baths
16 Katagogeion (Hotel)
17 Temple of the Egyptian Apollo and Asklepios
18 Roman Baths
19 North Portico
20 Temple of Aphrodite
21 Baths of Asklepios and library
22 Temple of Themis
23 Stadium
24 Museum
25 Theatre

(P. Cavvadias)

Koronis, the daughter of Phlegyas, king of the Lapiths. While Koronis was with child, her father forced her to marry Ischys, son of Elatos. A rook brought the bad news to Apollo, provoking the wrath of the god at the unfaithfulness of Koronis. He turned the rook into a black bird, instead of the white it had been, and killed with his bow Ischys. Artemis, on the other hand, killed with her arrows Koronis. While the young princess lay on the funeral pyre, Hermes took away the child she was carrying, and entrusted him to the care of the Centaur Cheiron. Thus, Asklepios was taught by the Centaur on Mt. Pelion the arts of hunting and medecine. When he grew up he became an illustrious physician. But his success made Pluto protest to Zeus, for his therapies restored to health so many patients that he had upset the balance between the Upper and the Lower World, since the number of the dead was considerably decreasing. So, Zeus struck Asklepios with his thunderbolt and killed him — the tale is recorded by both Hesiod and Pindar. According to a local tradition by the local poet of the 4th century B.C. Isyllos, however, Phlegyas and Koronis were from Epidauros. Isyllos' verses are inscribed on a marble plaque, which is now exhibited in the local Museum. Before the composition of this poem, the Epidaurians believed that Phlegyas, accompanied by his daughter, had visited the Peloponnese with hostile intentions. When Koronis felt the pains of labour, she secretly took refuge on Mt. Titthion, near Epidauros, where she gave birth to Asklepios.

As revealed by the investigations of the Greek Archaeological Society, a cult was first established on the site on Mt. Kynortion, at the foot of which lies Epidauros. A small *temenos of Apollo Maleatas* was founded there. In the late 5th century B.C., the cult was transferred down the valley, in the temenos we see at present, and the hitherto worshipped god Apollo was replaced by Asklepios. Asklepios was married to Hepione and had two sons, Machaon and Podaleirios, to whom Homer attributes medical knowledge. The serpent became the inseparable symbol of Asklepios.

The cult of Asklepios was probably initiated at Trikke (presently Trikala) in Thessaly, whence it spread southwards. Thus, many Asklepieia were founded, which attracted large crowds. But the Asklepieion of Epidauros was the most renowned. Patients arrived there —the moribund and women suffering of hemorrhage were not allowed to enter the peribolos— and after some preliminary offerings, they sacrificed a ram, took the hide and slept on it in a long stoa of the sanctuary, the *Enkoimeterion;* the god made his appearance in their dreams and indicated the way of therapy. Patients who had been cured dedicated rich offerings to Asklepios and, by the 4th century B.C., his temenos was filled with magnificent buildings which were real works of art. The fame of the Asklepieion of Epidauros was not merely the outcome of clever advertisement by the priests, but was also due to the various therapies performed there — the visitor would be interested to see the variety of medical instruments displayed in the local Museum. Cures were achieved through the skill and medical knowledge of the priesthood, and were not restricted to bodily ailment but included psychic disease, successfully treated thanks to the patients' belief in the healing powers of the god and the general atmosphere prevailing in the sanctuary. Patients who had been cured sometimes recorded in inscriptions, the 'iamata', the healing method indicated by the god. Some of these inscriptions have been unearthed during excavations and are now on display in the local Museum.

The sanctuary was plundered by the Roman general Sulla, but it reached a new acme during the Roman period. A Roman officer, Antoninus, built at his expense the Odeum and the Roman baths. The sanctuary survived until the end of the 4th century A.D., when by decree of the Byzantine emperor Theodosius all ancient sanctuaries were closed down.

Excavations on the site were begun by the Greek Archaeological Society in 1881, and in a short while brought to light the monuments of the sanctuary. Entering the temenos through the *Great Propylon,* the visitor faces the main building, the *temple* of the god *Asklepios.* It was a Doric peripteros which included the chryselephantine statue of the seated god, a work of the outstanding sculptor Thrasymedes of Paros. The pediments were decorated with fine sculptured compositions, representing the Sack of Troy (east pediment) and the Amazonomachy (west pediment), works of the sculptors Timotheos, Hektoris and a third one whose name has not been preserved. The splendid sculptures of Epidauros —now exhibited in a separate room of the National Archaeological Museum of Athens— constitute a landmark of that age.

To the north of the temple there was a long and narrow building, open in front like a stoa, built on two levels. This was the *Abaton* or *Enkoimeterion,* where the patients slept; the dreams of the patients were, of course, interpreted by the priests. Opposite the temple stood the most elegant building of the temenos : the *Tholos.* It was a circular building with Doric columns on the exterior and Corinthian columns in the interior, which was adorned with a painting by Pausias, representing Methe holding a glass phiale in her hand. The foundations of this edifice form a labyrinth with three concentric circles. It is believed that this substructure was modelled in the 5th century B.C., when Apollo prevailed as a healer on the sanctuary and Asklepios was just a simple hero. Thus, the underground structure has been interpreted as a place for offering libations to the hero Asklepios; the ritual was continued later, when Asklepios became a great god, venerated and loved by all. The Tholos was built in the 4th century B.C. by the Argive architect and sculptor Polykleitos, grandson of the homonymous sculptor of the 5th century B.C.

Some scholars believe that the strange underground structure of the Tholos served as breeding place for the sacred snakes of the god.

Opposite the Tholos and across the road is the *Stadion,* built before the 4th century B.C. It has a length of 196.45 m. and a width of 23.30 m., and its two ends are rectangular in form, instead of semicircular. Spectators sat on the ground—the few stone seats on both sides were reserved for persons of rank and the judges of the contests. At the north end of the Stadion there was an underground passage leading to the sanctuary. During festivals the sacred procession passed through there and entered the Stadion. This marked the beginning of the Games which were celebrated every four years, nine days after the Isthmian Games.

On the side of the Museum there is another large building with a fine entrance on its N.W. end. This was the *Gymnasion,* which had an internal rectangular court surrounded by a colonnaded stoa. In about A.D. 160, the *Odeion* was built (by Antoninus) in the central part of the Gymnasion; it was a small roofed auditorium for the attendance of lessons, lectures or concerts. Proceeding towards the Museum, the visitor encounters on the right, immediately after the Gymnasion, the *Baths* of the Hellenistic period, and further down, on the left, the *Katagogion* (Hostel), a large building erected in the 3rd century B.C. to accommodate the numerous pilgrims of the sanctuary. The hostel was repaired in A.D. 160, by Antoninus. It was a square building divided into four sections, each overlooking an open interior court surrounded by a colonnade with 19 rooms and a large entrance. This building was the largest of its kind.

Leaving behind the Museum, the visitor reaches the *Theatre*, also a work of Polykleitos the Younger. This is the most remarkable monument of the sanctuary, dated to the mid-4th century B.C. The selection of the location is most successful, and its acoustics are excellent. The theatre can accommodate 15,000 spectators. Its *orchestra* is circular and it is the only one that has survived intact from Greek antiquity. The center of the orchestra, which has a diameter of 20 m., is occupied by the *altar* of Dionysos. Behind the orchestra is the *skene* (stage) flanked by the *paraskenia*, and in front of it the *proskenion* supported by 18 engaged columns. There is a *doorway* on either side, between the scene and the *koilon*, where the spectators sat. The koilon has 55 tiers of seats and is divided into two parts: the upper and the lower, of which the former has 22 sections and the latter 12. The front tier was reserved for persons of rank. The theatre of Epidauros is the finest building of its kind in Greek antiquity. It is still used in our days for performances of ancient drama.

The ruins of the *temple of Artemis* lie northwards of the temple of Asklepios.

Museum of Epidauros

A visit to the local Museum of Epidauros is essential for the better appreciation of the site. With the exception of the theatre, which is preserved in excellent condition, the other splendid monuments of the sacred precinct have only survived in ruins at foundation level. It is therefore difficult for the visitor to restore with his imagination the sight of the temples and buildings of the sanctuary. Nevertheless, the Museum contains all the parts of superstructures discovered during excavations, as well as many restored plans and drawings, which help the visitor visualize the sanctuary as it had been in antiquity. The exquisite sculptures of the temple of Asklepios and the temple of Artemis, together with two sculptured representations of the seated god, are exhibited in the National Archaeological Museum of Athens. Plaster casts of some of these works can be seen in the Museum of Epidauros.

The local Museum offers the visitor an image of the Tholos, the finest building of this type and one of the most splendid edifices of antiquity. Part of the marble wall and samples of the outer Doric and inner Corinthian columns are exhibited there. The coffered marble ceiling is indeed unique, decorated with sculptured flowers : rosettes, acanthuses, etc., producing superb chiaroscuro effects. The metopes from the entablature of the building are adorned on the outer side with exquisite relief rosettes. Fragments of the marble sima of the monument are also preserved, showing spiral tendrils and lionheads.

The architectural elements preserved from the Doric temple of Asklepios are sufficient to permit reconstruction. On the other hand, several sculptures have survived from the west pediment and fewer from the east, decorated with representations of the Amazonomachy and the Sack of Troy, respectively. Some acroteria have also survived from the temples of Asklepios and Artemis.

The Museum includes some very important inscriptions with 'iamata' i.e. records of miraculous cures of patients, who dedicated these votive inscriptions in gratitude for their recovery. Another very significant inscription cites the names of the craftsmen who had worked for the construction of the temple of Asklepios and the Tholos, and records the expenses for the work done and the materials employed.

In addition to the plaster casts of works exhibited in the National Archaeological Museum of Athens, exhibits include some sculptures of the Classical, Helle-

Museum of Epidauros.
Restored part of the Tholos.

nistic and Roman periods, as well as small statues—one of them represents Asklepios as a bearded figure standing and leaning on his staff with the sacred snake coil-
ing around it.

A collection of medical instruments and other bronze objects is particularly
notable. There are also some clay vases and lamps of various periods, though mostly
of the Roman period.

LERNA

A few kilometres outside Argos, on the way to Tripolis, the visitor comes across
a shed (to the left), which shelters a very important circular building of the Early
Helladic period and a fortified peribolos of the same date. Excavations, carried out
on the site by the American School of Classical Studies, have yielded remarkable
discoveries datable to the Neolithic period. An outstanding find is a clay idol representing a steatopygous female figure, which is displayed along with the other movable finds from Lerna in the Kallergeion Museum of Argos.

TRIPOLIS

Tripolis is situated at a distance of 196 kms. from Athens. The city is of great
importance for the history of modern Greece. In the 17th century it became a prosperous commercial and economic centre. The mountains of Arcadia are associated
with many ancient myths. The goat-footed rural god Pan was first worshipped there,
and so was Hermes, who as a child stole the cattle of Apollo and hid them on Pieria.

Tripolis was an important communication and strategic centre during the War
of Independence of 1821.

TEGEA

Tegea is the largest town on the plateau of Arcadia. It was initially formed of
nine agricultural demes united, according to tradition, by Aleos in the 9th century
B.C. Aleos also founded the cult of Athena Alea, performed in the most renowned
sanctuary of Arcadia. It was there that, according to the Peloponnesian legend,
Orestes sought protection when he killed Aigisthos and his own mother Klytaim-
nestra. Pausanias, the Spartan general and victor of the battle of Plataiai (479 B.C.)
sought refuge in this sanctuary. In 550 B.C., a treaty between Lakedaimonians and
Tegeans established the supremacy of Sparta. Tegea participated in the Persian
Wars and was the major rival of Mantineia, the second largest Arcadian city.
The Tegeans were renowned in antiquity as excellent soldiers.

Tegea continued to lead a prosperous life until the 4th century A.D., when it
was ravaged by the Goths under the leadership of Alaric. It was re-inhabited by
the Byzantines and remained, under the name of *Nikli,* as one of the most important
cities of the Peloponnese and the seat of an Episcopate. In 1209, Geoffroi de Villehardouin established a barony there. Subsequently Tegea was totally destroyed
during clashes between the Peloponnesians and the Franks. In 1889 - 1890, and
again in 1902 and 1910, the site was excavated by the French, who uncovered its
ruins. The remains of the old Byzantine church of Tegea have been restored and
some of its sculptures have been built into the walls of the new church. A few hundred
metres away, Greek excavations revealed an Early Christian *basilica* with fine mosaics showing the months of the year, the big rivers and a variety of fish.

The most important monument in Tegea is the *temple of Athena Alea*. Lying to the S.W. of the ancient city, it was the religious centre of the koinon of the Arkadai. The Archaic temple was destroyed by fire in 395 B.C., and was rebuilt and decorated by the illustrious Parian sculptor Skopas (360 - 330 B.C.). The temple was a Doric peripteros, with Corinthian columns in the interior. Several of its architectural members have been built into the walls of local houses; those preserved are of incomparable elegance and beauty. The pediments of the temple were decorated with representations of the hunt of the Calydonian Boar (east pediment) and the duel between Telephos and Achilles in the plain of the river Kaikos at Mysia (west pediment). The foundations of the altar are visible to the east of the temple.

The ancient city was fortified with an oval enceinte (having a perimeter of 5,500 m.). The site of the *agora* and the *temples of Apollo* and *Dionysos,* west of the *theatre,* have been identified.

Museum of Tegea

The Museum is near the temple of Athena Alea and houses the local finds. Exhibits include Prehistoric vases and figurines from Asea and Aïgiorgitika; some fine sculptures from the decoration of the temple of Athena Alea—the acroteria of the temple are of outstanding artistic quality—ceramic products of the Classical age, terracotta figurines of the Hellenistic period and bronze objects of the minor arts.

SPARTA

Sparta is situated at a distance of 260 kms. from Athens and 63 kms. from Tripolis. The modern town with the broad straight streets, large squares, and lemon and orange groves, was founded right after the liberation of Greece following the War of Independence of 1821. Most of the houses are of the Neoclassical style. The actual town is built over the ruins of the famous ancient city, the one of the two great cities of Greek antiquity —the other one being Athens— which shaped the life and destinies of ancient Hellenism. It is situated in the valley of the river Eurotas —whose water now flows scarce— between two high mountains, Taygetos and Parnon.

Traces of life in the area of Sparta date as early as Prehistoric times. The Neolithic settlements found denote that the site has been occupied without interruption since 6000 B.C. Finds dating to both the Neolithic and the Early Helladic periods are similar to those of corresponding dates from other sites of the Peloponnese. Middle and Late Helladic finds are abundant in Lakonia. A whole series of Mycenaean settlements and cemeteries at Sparta, Amyklai, the foot of Taygetos, Stephania, Skala, Molaoi, Neapolis Boion, etc., suggest that the site had been already densely inhabited in those times.

Following the invasion of the Dorians, the new inhabitants of Sparta founded a unique state headed by two kings, with collective upbringing of children, harsh military life in barracks for men (restricted to citizens of Sparta only) and strange marriage customs. All power was concentrated in the hands of the new settlers, the Dorians, while the former inhabitants became the *helots,* forced to labour under the *Spartiates,* with few rights of their own and no political status. The third class of the Spartan society, the *perioikoi,* consisted of tradesmen, artists, craftsmen etc. In Geometric and Archaic times Sparta flourished and became an important mercantile and artistic center, receiving influences from the Cyclades, Ionia, Crete and the East. She subdued successfully two long revolts of the Messenian helots, one in the 8th and one in the 7th century B.C.

This setting changed from the end of the 7th century B.C., as the Spartan constitution became more austere and the Spartans withdrew into a world of their own, avoiding any exchange of ideas and artistic forms with other centers. This reform had been ascribed to Lykourgos, who was believed during Classical times to have been the legislator of the Spartan constitution in the 8th century B.C., with the consent of the Oracle of Delphi, which characterized his system as 'the best'. The reform is now thought to have been due to Chilon of Lakedaimon, one of the Seven Wise Men of Greece. A basic clause of the constitution did not allow intermarriage between Spartiates and helots or perioikoi. And the duty of the pure descendents of the Spartiates was to maintain power in their hands, train themselves to become excellent soldiers and be ready at any time to fight for their homeland. Following the establishment of this legislation, Sparta led a secluded and austere life, and acquired, with the development of the *phalanx,* the best army in Greece. She also founded the Peloponnesian Alliance, which included among its members cities not only of the Peloponnese but of Central Greece as well, perhaps even Athens.

The constitution, which the Pythia had characterized as 'the best', presented a serious drawback, which had dramatic effects on the city with the passing of the centuries. Human losses from constant wars could not be replaced. Thus, after the end of the Persian Wars Sparta suffered from depopulation, which became even more acute after the conclusion of the Peloponnesian War and the conflicts with the Thebans. It was already obvious that this problem would affect the city most seriously, when two Spartan kings, Agis and Kleomenes, made an attempt at a solution by introducing reforms in the 3rd century B.C. Their attempt however was abortive, for the all-powerful Ephors of Sparta failed to understand the spirit of the reforms. Henceforward Sparta barely survived to the end of antiquity, when the natural dissolution of the Greek city-states occurred. She was gradually losing her allies and of necessity becoming more and more self-restricted.

The Spartan constitution was probably hard and harsh on the citizens. More than any other Greek city, however, Sparta provided an unparallelled example of moral, valour and self-sacrifice. And it is in this context that the vision of Sparta has survived in later times.

There exist some indications of flourishing in Sparta during the period of the Roman sway — a fact attested by the splendid mosaic floors of houses uncovered in the course of excavations. The Romans granted autonomy to the koinon of the Free Lakonians, i.e. the coastal centres. In A.D. 396, Sparta was conquered by Alaric, and subsequently suffered for many centuries from various barbaric invasions, as a result of which her inhabitants had to migrate on Mt. Taygetos. The site, inhabited again by the Byzantines, who named it *Lakedaimonia,* was later taken by the Franks who finally settled at Mistra. In 1261, Geoffroi de Villehardouin was forced by Michael Palaiologos to restore to freedom Mistra, Monemvasia and Mani. The site, governed by the Despots of the Palaiologan family for two centuries, was occupied by Mohammed II in 1460, the Venetians in 1669, and again by the Turks in 1715.

With the exception of the attractive landscape with its singular features, the visitor has very little to see in Sparta. Exploration of the site has been prevented by the fact that the modern town overlies the ruins of the ancient city.

Still, a visit is recommended to the acropolis of Sparta, where one may see the *theatre* (of the 2nd century B.C.) and the ruins of the *temenos of Athena Chalkioikos*. The sight of the sparse remains recalls the famous saying of Thucydides : «If some day Sparta were conquered and only her sanctuaries and foundations of public buildings remained, future generations would find it difficult to believe that the fame of the city corresponded to reality». The wall surrounding the site was erected in A.D. 267 and 386, to protect it against the invasion of the Herules and Goths. The wall was later reinforced with towers constructed of re-used material from ancient buildings, to provide better defence against the attacks of the Slavs.

The second great sanctuary of ancient Sparta was dedicated to *Artemis Orthia*, so-named because her xoanon had been found standing, according to the local tradition which ascribes to Sparta the xoanon of Artemis taken by Orestes and Electra from Tauris and transported there instead of Brauron, as cited by the corresponding Attic legend. The Archaic temple of the 6th century B.C. was overlain by the temple of the 2nd century B.C. (All finds from excavations have been transferred to the local Museum). A Roman *amphitheatre* borders the S.E. side of the temple, as if it were a stage. Various ceremonies and flogging tests were initially performed there, replaced later by *contests of endurance*. Cult dances were also performed by dancers wearing masks which they dedicated to the goddess. The amphitheatre was constructed in Roman times to accommodate the spectators of these ceremonies. Excavations at Sparta were carried out by the British School of Archaeology.

Museum of Sparta

It is a local Museum of great interest, for it presents the unique character of the Spartan civilization and its features. The Museum is a building of the Neoclassical style (1875 - 76). The original building (some extensions have been added later) was erected on plans of the architect Hansen, who also made the plans for the Academy of Athens. The Museum has six rooms in all. In the vestibule are exhibited slabs bearing sickles, which were votive offerings of victors dedicated to the sanctuary of Artemis Orthia, with inscriptions recording the names of the victor and his victory, and sometimes also the names of the local archons. Inscriptions are written in the Doric dialect. Artemis Orthia was the goddess of fertility and under this Pre-Hellenic quality she continued to be worshipped in historic times. The earliest stele (No. 1541) belongs to the early 4th century B.C. and has five sickles. Another stele, (No. 1526) showing traces of the once inlaid sickles, carries a representation of the facade of the temple of Artemis Orthia (2nd century B.C.). There are also stelai of Lakonian type —perhaps gravestones— with floral decoration, and the base of a statue of a 'bomonikes' (ephebos who had endured flogging without showing the least sign of pain).

The first room on the right contains some stone works typical of early Lakonian art, a few Archaic inscriptions, as well as a series of stelai with a relief representation of two figures. Some archaeologists interpret these as heroized dead and others as chthonic deities. Noteworthy in the same room is a pyramidal stele bearing reliefs on all four sides, three Archaic statues representing seated figures, and a marble Gorgoneion, probably an acroterion of an ancient temple. The second room (right) includes works associated with the Dioskouroi, the twin sons of Leda from Zeus and Tyndareos, the patron gods of hearths, travellers and seafarers. The Dioskouroi are also represented as twin amphorai or snakes. The third room on the right contains architectural members from the sanctuary of Apollo Amyklaios (among them an excellently preserved capital of composite style), and two stelai from the sanctuary of Athena Chalkioikos on the acropolis of Sparta — one of them (No. 1030), which has been preserved entire, is the votive offering of Anaxibios. In the same room are displayed in separate cases Mycenaean and other Prehistoric pottery, implements and tools, and the finest piece of sculpture of the 'severe style' in Sparta — the torso of the so-named 'Leonidas', a work of great beauty, found near the sanctuary of Athena Chalkioikos. Some Lakonian kylikes are notable finds from the sanctuary of Artemis Orthia.

The first room on the left includes minor votive offerings from Lakonian sanctuaries : masks, lead, clay and bronze objects. Large cases contain a selection of the most important votive offerings from Spartan sanctuaries, which are indeed unique. From the *sanctuary of Artemis Orthia* : lead figurines —similar to present religious ex-votos— dating from the end of the 9th to the 4th century B.C. and representing animals, imaginary creatures, a winged goddess, praying women, warriors, etc. Similar figurines —the best are of the Archaic age, i.e. the 7th and 6th centuries B.C.— have been found in the *sanctuary of Athena Chalkioikos*, the *Menelaion* and the *Amyklaion*. These are believed to have been the dedications of poor helots. Many of them have come from the same mould, where lead was cast and a series of replicas produced. Though they are simple and unpretentious dedications, they are valuable to archaeologists, for they show the development of various artistic types, as well as the foreign (non-Lakonian) influences over the Spartan workshops. Many of these dedications represent deities : Athena in her panoply, Poseidon with his trident, Artemis in various stances, Ares, and the symbols of all the Olympian gods.

The clay masks are of great interest. They have come from the sanctuary of Artemis Orthia and are probably imitations of the wooden masks worn during the performance of sacred dances round the altar of the goddess. Their significance is unknown. There are over a hundred masks in the Museum of Sparta, portraying faces of elderly persons, young men, warriors, realistic figures, satyrs with pointed ears, Medusai, imaginary creatures, or distorted caricaturistic faces. These masks show the possibilities of Lakonian ceramic art in the 7th and 6th century B.C., and are the first attempts at portraiture. There is also a large collection of clay antefixes — these were exported in the 7th century to the entire Peloponnese. Equally important are the Lakonian pithoi with appliqué reliefs showing the remarkable skill of local potters in the 7th and 6th centuries B.C. Another case in the same room contains a few fine bronze statuettes, and the earliest female figurine of Greek art (8th century B.C.), all found in the Menelaion. A small iron rod corroded into many pieces may have been one of the heavy iron coins imposed by the legislation of Lykourgos.

The next room includes Archaising sculpture, Roman copies of famous works, and marble sculptures of later antiquity. A large head shows a striking resemblance with the head of Hera at Olympia. It is dated to the Classical period, though it belongs to an earlier type. Another Archaising head, set up on a herm, is a copy of *Hermes Propylaios*, the famous work of Alkamenes. Among the exhibits there are several works of the Hellenistic period and undecorated funerary stelai. A recent acquisition of the Museum is a collection of finds from the Cave of Alepotrypa at Diros : clay ware, tools and jewellery.

MISTRA

History : Mistra is a Byzantine town of the Peloponnese, lying at a distance of 6 kms. to the N.W. of Sparta. The town is today in ruins but constitutes a valu-

Mistra.
Church of the Pantanassa.

able source of knowledge for the history of art and civilization during the last two centuries of the Byzantine era. The history of Mistra begins in the mid-13th century, when the Franks had conquered the Peloponnese. In 1249, Villehardouin II built a fortress on the eastern slope of Mt. Taygetos, on the hill of Mistra or Myzythra. Following the defeat of the Franks in the battle of Pelagonia (in 1259), the fortress of Mistra was ceded to the Byzantine emperor. In 1262, it became the seat of the Byzantine general and its history, actually starting then, lasted for two centuries. Inhabitants from nearby Lakedaimonia settled around the fortress and this area, called *Chora,* was enclosed by a fortification wall. With the passing of time, another settlement, named *Kato Chora,* was formed outside the wall and similarly surrounded by a fortified circuit.

The administrative system changed in 1308. The generals were made permanent governors, and by the mid-15th century Mistra became the capital of the Peloponnese. Thus, the Despotat of Morea came into being. Wise despots, like Manuel Cantacuzenus, Theodoros II Palaiologos and Constantine XI Palaiologos (subsequently last emperor of Byzantium) established Mistra as the most important center of the Peloponnese, the focus of political and cultural life of the empire as well as the cradle of a revival in the letters and arts. The court of the despots was frequented by artists, scholars and philosophers — George Gemistos Plethon foremost among them. In 1460, Mistra fell to the Turks, but continued to lead an active and prosperous life during the Turkish occupation. The uprising of 1770 is an important event in the history of Mistra. The Turkish occupants of the town were then exterminated, but following the final failure of the attempt, the Turks plundered Mistra for ten consecutive years.

The contribution of Mistra in the War of Independence of 1821 was considerable. In 1825 the town was ravaged by Ibrahim's soldiers and henceforth slowly abandoned. The modern town of Mistra was built at the foot of the hill.

Monuments : There exist in Mistra some of the finest examples of Mediaeval secular architecture, such as palaces, houses, castles, fortification walls, gates, etc., as well as unique monuments of Byzantine religious architecture. The latter include the seven most important churches of Mistra :

1. The *Metropolis — Church of St. Demetrios* (1292) : Originally, this was a three-naved basilica, but later, probably in the 15th century, an upper gallery (gynaikonites) was added as well as a five-domed roof.

2. *Church of the Evangelistria* (late 14th century) : It is of the inscribed cross type.

3. *Church of Sts. Theodoroi* (1296) : It is one of the two churches of the monastic complex of Brontochion and belongs to the octagonal type.

4. *Church of Panaghia Hodegetria — the Aphentiko* (1310) : This is the second in date church of Brontochion. It belongs to the mixed type, which is a fusion of the three-naved basilica (lower part) and the inscribed cross church (upper part). (This composite architectural type is first encountered in Mistra).

5. *Church of St. Sophia* (1350) : It is of the inscribed cross type with two columns.

6. *Church of the Peribleptos* (mid-14th century). It is built next to the rock at the S.E. end of the outer enclosure, which accounts for its irregular shape. It is of the cross type with two columns.

7. *Church of the Pantanassa* (1428). This is the latest building of the Despotat and the most complex in appearance. It is of the composite type mentioned above.

In addition to the unique specimens of Byzantine architecture, Mistra has to show some remarkable wall-paintings of high artistic quality (late 13th to late 15th century). The paintings of the Metropolis reflect old trends and announce new ones. The church of the Aphentiko is decorated with some of the most important works of the 14th century, representing three contemporary but different tendencies in painting of the Palaiologan period. In the church of the Peribleptos the paintings are characterized by idealistic tendencies and deep religious feeling. Finally, in the church of the Pantanassa (15th century) one may admire the last examples of Byzantine art, which prove that even during the last years of its existence, Byzantium had the strength to assimilate artistic elements and produce remarkable works.

MONEMVASIA

Monemvasia is a promontory of hardly one kilometre length, lying at the S.E. end of the Peloponnese, at a distance of 103 kms. from Sparta. It is a forbidding, rocky and waterless site, having the appearance of an island, for the 400 m. long westerly strip of land has been cut off and a stone bridge constructed connecting the remaining part of the promontory with the coast of Laconia. The site owes its name (Monemvasia = single entrance) to the fact that it is only accessible through that bridge from the landward side.

History : The promontory of Monemvasia is to be most probably identified as Pausanias' *Minoa* (*Laconica* 23). It was not inhabited in antiquity, but was used as a refuge by the inhabitants of Laconia and the rest of the Peloponnese during the period of Slav and Avar invasions (A.D. 578 - 582). The chronographer Phrantzes records in his 'Chronicle of the building of Monemvasia' that the fortress was built in the reign of the emperor Maurice (582 - 602), and describes it as «eminent and higher than the clouds». Owing to its important situation —the 'Gibraltar of Greece'— and thanks to its mercantile navy, Monemvasia prospered considerably with the almost exclusive trade and transportation of the famous wine bearing its name. Because of its wealth and prosperity, the site became the target of repeated though ineffective piratic raids, particularly by George Antiocheus, admiral of the Norman king of Sicily, Roger II (1147). In 1248, it was besieged and taken by prince Guillaume II Villehardouin. Following the defeat of Villehardouin at Pelagonia (1259), it was reconquered by the Byzantines in the reign of Michael VIII Palaiologos. It became then the seat of the general and governor of the imperial dominions and enjoyed special privileges.

In 1292, Monemvasia was mercilessly raided by the Catalans under the leadership of the admiral Roger. In late Byzantine times, when the place was governed by local archons, conflicts ensued with the sovereigns of Mistra. In 1394, Paul Mammonas, a member of the local nobility, instigated a revolution against the despot of Mistra, Theodoros Palaiologos. Monemvasia was temporarily occupied a year later by the Turks and finally given to Theodoros Palaiologos. Once more it found itself under Turkish pressure after the fall of Constantinople, but was placed under the protection of Pope Pius II. Later, the town came into the hands of the Venetians until 1540, when it was ceded by them to the Turks, who occupied it until the War of Independence in 1821, with only a brief interlude of Venetian control between 1685 and 1715.

Monuments : The lower town of Monemvasia is reached through the West gate and occupies the S.E. edge of the promontory. It is of later date, for the original town was situated on top of the cliff. On the N.E. edge of the cliff stands the splendid octagonal *church of St. Sophia,* a monument of the 12th century. It was decorated in the interior with rich sculptures and wall-paintings dating from the first half of the 13th century. During the first Venetian occupation a two-storied narthex was added in front of its West side; later the church was converted to a mosque by the Turks. In the lower town is an important church of the domed basilica type, dedicated to *Christ Helkomenos.* It was built during the last years of the first Venetian period (1464 - 1540), on the site of an earlier church of the 12th century. This church, the 'palladion' of Monemvasia, has become famous for the icon kept in it, representing Christ in chains and dating to the 12th century. The present icon of Christ Helkomenos is of much later date. Another remarkable icon is the Crucifixion, dated to the late 14th century, executed by a painter who had probably worked in the church of the Peribleptos at Mistra. Also notable are the domed *church of St. Nicholas* (built in 1703) and the contemporaneous churches of *Panaghia Kretiki* (Myrtidiotissa), *St. Stephanos* and *St. Anna.*

The picturesque houses, most of which belong to the period of the Turkish domination, the various ruined buildings, the surviving walls of the lower town and the acropolis compose a perfect picture of a Mediaeval town.

GERAKI

Geraki is situated approximately 35 kms. from Sparta, on the slope of Mt. Parnon overlooking the green valley of the river Eurotas and beyond it, the austere beauty of Mt. Taygetos. Remains of the Mycenaean period indicate that the site has been inhabited from a very early date. In ancient times, a small commercial centre was developed there under the name of *Geronthrai.* The period of great prosperity began in the 13th century, when the site was named *Gerakion,* probably after the eminent Byzantine family who owned the area. In the years of the Frankish occupation Geraki passed to the baron Guy de Nivelet, but following the defeat of the Franks in the battle of Pelagonia (1259), the Byzantines reconquered the fortress and the site retained its Byzantine character with slight influences from the Frankish rule. Approximately 15 churches have been preserved on the site, the most important being the following :

Church of the *Evangelistria* (in the modern village) : it is of the inscribed cross type with dome and one aisle (12th century), decorated with remarkable wall-paintings of the same date. Church of the *Theophaneia* (at Kastro) : a transverse vault church with wall-paintings of the 12th - 13th century. Church of *St. George* (at Kastro) : a domed basilica with two naves and the later addition of a third nave and narthex, embellished with wall-paintings and a fine relief iconostasis. Church of the *Taxiarchai* (at Kastro): a transverse vaulted church with interesting wall-paintings (13th century). Church of *St. Sozon :* of the composite inscribed cross with dome type, dated to about A.D. 1200. Church of *St. Athanasios* (Cemetery) : of the composite inscribed cross type with wall-paintings datable to about 1300. Church of *Sts. Theodoroi* (in the village): of the transverse vaulted type without decoration. Church of the *Zoodochos Pighi* (at Kastro): of the transverse vaulted type with wall-paintings dated to 1431. Church of *St. John Chrysostom* (in the village) : a domed basilica; Roman inscriptions recording decrees of Diocletian have been employed in the doorway. The entire painted decoration of the church has been preserved, showing the date 1450 on the second layer. Church of *St. Ni-*

cholas (south of Geraki) : a domed basilica with two narthekes and interesting wall-paintings of the end of the 13th century.

MANI

Mani is a highland of grey granite stretching down into the sea to the south of the Peloponnese, swept by winds which bare it of its meager soil. This unhospitable barren land has been inhabited from Prehistoric times, as attested by finds in the caves of *Diros,* particularly *Alepotrypa*. These caves are among the most beautiful and impressive sights ever to be seen. One of them may be visited by boat (on the underground lake) which traverses the dream world of stalactites and stalagmites of fantastic shapes and colours.

The Byzantine emperor and author Constantine Porphyrogenitos has given information regarding the fortress of *Maina* — as he calls it. According to his description, the land is destitute, its only resources being olives, which to this day are the only product worth of mention. The emperor also informs us that the Mainotes were christianized in the 9th century A.D. Present-day investigations however, have revealed on the coast of Mani the existence of basilicas datable to the 6th - 7th century (Kyparissos, basilicas of St. Andrew, St. Peter, of Monastiri). The small church of St. Prokopios is also assigned to a date earlier than the 9th century.

Tiny, single-room churches resembling Prehistoric constructions, built of large stones without mud or bricks, are frequent in Mani. It is difficult to date them precisely, though a date before the 11th century should be assigned to them. Wall-paintings have been preserved in some of them, and one of minute size (2.85 × 5.80), is worthy of particular mention for its wall-paintings are precisely dated by an inscription to A.D. 991/2. From the 11th century onwards we have a great many monuments of interest both for their architectural type and painting decoration.

The prevailing architectural type is the inscribed cross with dome in all its variations (with two columns, four columns, one aisle), though some examples have also survived of the small single-room churches with more carefully constructed ashlar masonry (*St. John* at *Pyrgos Dirou,* etc.). The church of *St. Paul* (near Pyrgos Dirou) is of the free cross type and dates to about A.D. 1000. Many of the churches in Mani belong to the inscribed cross type with two columns, e.g. the church of the *Taxiarches tou Glezou* (near Pyrgos Dirou), the *Sotera tis Gardenitsas* (11th century), which has a typical porch and fine proportions reflecting the Constantinopolitan art, while the wall-paintings in the Prothesis and Diakonikon are of a rather popular character. Among the most remarkable churches are that of *Ayios Strategos* (11th century) in the village Boularioi, for its paintings, of various dates though mostly of the 12th and 13th centuries, have been preserved almost intact. The church of the *Episkopi* (near Kitta), dating to the 12th century, is richly adorned with paintings; their artistic quality is of a high standard and they were probably executed by painters who had come from the Capital. The church of *Sts. Theodoroi* in the village Bambakas is a characteristic example of the architecture of the Helladic school at Mani and the only one of precise date (1075). Finally, the most perfect church at Mani, the church of *St. Barbara* in the village Erimos, is dated to the 12th century. Of the four-columned type are the churches of *Sts. Seryios and Bacchos* at Kitta (12th century), better known as the *Troulloti,* with fine and richly adorned masonry, and the *Blacherna* (12th century). Of the composite four-columned type are the churches of the *Taxiarchai* at Charouda and

St. John at Keria (13th century), the latter of interest because of the ancient reliefs incorporated into the exterior of walls.

Mani played a particularly important role during the period of the Turkish domination. Thanks to its natural fortification and the valour and military training of its inhabitants, the region remained practically independent most of the time, and in the War of Independence of 1821, it became the most important centre of action. The warlike way of life of the inhabitants influenced the type of dwellings, and the traveller who visits Mani will encounter the high rectangular towers —half-ruined and deserted at present— reminiscent of the withdrawn and proud Mainote character.

MEGALOPOLIS

Megalopolis lies at a distance of 34 kms. S.W. of Tripolis. The ancient city, founded by Epameinondas of Thebes in 371 B.C., was the administrative centre of the koinon of the Arcadians. One kilometre outside the modern town are the ruins of the ancient city, not all of which are well-preserved. The most remarkable monument is the *theatre*, which could accommodate 20,000 spectators and was the largest in antiquity. Performances of ancient tragedy are now occasionally given in this theatre. On the west side of the parodos, there is a long rectangular building, the *skenotheke,* for the storage of equipment employed during performances. The stage consisted of the *logeion* (31 m. long and 7 m. wide), which was wooden and movable in the 4th century B.C., replaced by a fixed one built of masonry in the Roman era. Behind the skene, to the north, there is a huge square building, the *Thersilion,* where the representatives of the Arcadian koinon held their meetings. The form of the building reminds that of the Telesterion of Eleusis. Four parallel rows of rectangular piers supported the roof. Various *altars* have been uncovered to the east and west of the Thersilion. The *Stadion* was situated westwards, near the spring and the *sanctuary of Dionysos.* The *sanctuary of Asklepios* extended easwards. A 15-minutes walk after crossing the bridge of the river Helisson leads to the *agora,* with the *sanctuary of Zeus Soter* on the east. The east side of the agora was bounded by a great stoa, the *Myropolis* (perfume market), erected by the tyrant Aristodemos in 250 B.C. The public *Archives* (administrative buildings) were probably on the north side of the agora and occupied also part of the west side with a stoa of 156 m. length, the *Stoa of Philip.*

ANDRITSAINA

Karytaina is visible at some distance on the way from Megalopolis to Andritsaina. Perched on the mountain slope with a well-preserved Frankish *castle,* it presents a most picturesque sight. Crossing the river Alpheios, at a distance of 2 kms., the visitor encounters a stone *bridge* with six arches constructed during the Frankish rule.

Andritsaina, situated 45 kms. west of Megalopolis, was an important town in the 18th century. A remnant of its past glory is the excellent Library, which includes rare editions of the years 1500 - 1550, and a noteworthy *Historic Archive* of the War of Independence. Most of the books of the Library are works of ancient Greek Classics, European literature, archaeology, history etc. Many bear handwritten notes, or dedications and signatures of distinguished men of letters or politicians. The Library also houses a small *Archaeological Collection.*

Temple of Apollo Epikourios at Bassai.

BASSAI: TEMPLE OF APOLLO EPIKOURIOS

The site of the ancient *sanctuary of Apollo* lies 14 kms. from Andritsaina. The scenery is superb with high mountains and deep ravines (Bassai = ravines). The excellently preserved temple is a great surprise to the visitor. It is a Doric peripteros built of local grey limestone. The temple was discovered in the 18th century by foreign travellers, who explored it, found many slabs of the frieze and removed them. They are now in the British Museum. Systematic excavations were undertaken by the Archaeological Society in the early years of our century. This temple is attributed to Iktinos, the architect of the Parthenon on the Acropolis of Athens. There existed on the site an earlier small temple of unknown orientation, of which a few architectural members, particularly of its clay superstructure, have survived. The *temple* we see at present was built in the 5th century B.C., and was necessarily given a N - S orientation adapted to the lie of the ground. In the interior of the temple, along the side walls of the sekos, there were five 'antae' terminating in unusual Ionic semi-columns. A frieze, decorated with representations of an Amazonomachia and other subjects, extended high along all sides of the interior. An Ionic column, standing on the axis of the temple between the sekos and the adyton, was surmounted by a Corinthian capital, the first of this order in Greece. The temple shows a fusion of earlier and later features — its construction is believed to have been completed in about 425 B.C. Discoveries have revealed that the god Apollo, under the attribute *Bassitas,* had been worshipped earlier on the site, as protector from war adventures; in the 5th century B.C., the god was given the attribute *Epikourios* (assistant) and possibly worshipped as saviour from illness. A kouros found at *Phigaleia* (4 kms. from Bassai) is exhibited in the Museum of Olympia. The ancient city of Phigaleia overlooked the narrow wild gorge traversed by the river Neda. Its situation was important and it became a centre for the transport of products from the Arkadian cities to the ports of West Peloponnese and vice versa. Phigaleia was a friend and ally of Messene and an opponent of Sparta. The Phigaleians founded at their expense the temple of Apollo Epikourios and were responsible for its administration. Remains of *walls* are visible on the site of the ancient city; these had a perimeter of approximately 4 kms. and were equipped with round and square towers at intervals. Ruins of the *agora* and temples have also been unearthed.

KALAMATA

The present capital of the Nome of Messenia, Kalamata, has an age-long history, the beginnings of which are traceable to old legends of a remote past. It most probably occupies the site of Homeric *Pharai*. It lies at a distance of 292 kms. (via Tripolis) from Athens. There is an interesting old castle, built by Geoffroi de Villehardouin on the site of the ancient acropolis. From the period of the Messenian Wars (8th, 7th and 5th centuries B.C.) to the War of Independence of 1821, the town and its surrounding area suffered successive occupations by Greek and foreign conquerors: the Spartans, Macedonians, Romans, Franks, Goths, Avars and Turks, and became free only after the naval battle of Navarino. It was at Kalamata, however, that the War of Independence was declared on the 23rd March 1821, in the old church of the Sts. Apostles.

Museum of Kalamata

The Archaeological Museum of the town is worth a visit. Exhibits include: stone implements and ware dating from the Neolithic period to the Mycenaean age, found during excavations at Malthi; a series of vases and figurines of the Mycenaean age uncovered in the course of excavations at Karpophora; a collection of pottery from Protogeometric and Geometric to Hellenistic times, and small sculpture. Exhibits from the sanctuary of Poseidon at Akovitika include an important Archaic inscription and a small bronze kouros, found before the excavations on the site. Architectural members, sculptures, inscriptions and an interesting mosaic floor are on display in the basement of the Museum. There is also a notable collection of Post-Byzantine icons, and relics of the war of Independence, all gifts of eminent native families, as well as an important collection of ancient, Byzantine and Venetian coins.

Another place of interest in Kalamata is the *Gallery* on Aristomenous Street, where approximately 350 paintings of Greek and foreign artists are exhibited, as well as the Kyriakos *Historic Gallery.*

MESSENE

55 kms. from Megalopolis (via Meligala), the modern village Mavrommati stands at the foot of Mt. Ithome (Voulkano) and includes a small part of the ancient city. Epameinondas, the famous Theban general who defeated the Spartans and founded Megalopolis, also built Messene (in 369 B.C.) and fortified its impregnable acropolis, to serve as a threat against eventual Spartan schemes.

The *walls* of Messene, constructed of local limestone, and particularly the *Arkadian Gate* (north gate), are of the most imposing fortifications of historic times to be seen on Greek territory. The wall is well-preserved and equipped with towers at intervals. From the summit of Mt. Ithome (1 ½ hour from Mavrommati) one may enjoy a splendid view and visit the 14th century *Monastery of Voulkano* with its very old katholikon and interesting wall - paintings of the 17th century. This site was occupied in antiquity by the *sanctuary of Zeus Ithomatas.*

The *sanctuary of Artemis Laphria* is situated southwards of the summit of Mt. Ithome. Beyond the *temple* is the *Spring of Klepsydra.* Excavations by the Greek Archaeological Society, still continued every year under the direction of Professor A. Orlandos, have uncovered the centre of the ancient city, the so-called *agora,* with the temples and other buildings, particularly the *Synedrion,* known from ancient sources. The *temple of Asklepios* occupied the centre of the area which was surrounded by stoas and yielded several interesting statues, inscriptions and architectural members.

PYLOS

Pylos is situated 160 kms. from Tripolis. The modern town was built in 1829, around the Venetian fortress, and its name has become familiar from the naval battle of *Navarino* (20th October 1827), the outcome of which was of decisive importance for the final liberation of the Greek nation. A memorial in the town honours the three foreign admirals who destroyed the Turkish fleet. The castle *(Palaiokastro)* is an attractive sight. The hill is the site of ancient *Koryphasion* and commands a superb view of one of the most beautiful seashores in Greece, Voïdokoilia, with its golden sandy beach. The site has been explored by Professor Sp. Marinatos. Legend has it that Hermes led there the oxen he had stolen from Apollo and hid them in a cave. At the bay of Navarino, on the south end of the harbour, stands another castle, parts of which are very well-preserved.

In the bay of Navarino lies the island of *Sphakteria,* known from the fierce battle between the Spartans and Athenians in 425 B.C., during which the Spartan soldiers were taken captives.

Museum of Pylos

The local Museum (Antonopouleion), recently arranged, is quite interesting. One of its rooms contains remarkable clay vases, gold vessels and jewellery, and many other minor objects of Mycenaean date. Among the exhibits there are also ceramic and glass products of the Hellenistic period found during excavations by the Greek Archaeological Service at *Tsopani Rachi,* and two interesting bronze statues of the Roman age, which are believed to represent the Dioskouroi. An entire room houses the remarkable Réné Puaux Collection of engravings.

KORONE

Korone lies on the coast of the Messenian Gulf, at a distance of 52 kms. from Kalamata. The site was given this name in the Middle Ages, when refugees from the village Korone, which is farther north, migrated there. The fine Byzantine *castle* of the small town commands a spectacular view to the sea and the opposite coasts of Mani. The town flourished in Mediaeval times, when it became the most important commercial port of Western Peloponnese. Following the fate of the whole nation, it underwent successive occupations. The greatest part of the castle preserved at present was built by the Turks in the 16th century, and was fortified with bastions. The south end of the castle is Venetian, while the Byzantine wall has been preserved to a considerable extent along the east side. There exist also ruins of fortification walls.

METHONE

Methone, named in antiquity *Mothone,* lies southwards of Pylos on the coast to the Ionian Sea, at a distance of 348 kms. from Athens and 15 kms. south of Navarino. It was one of the most important harbours of the Peloponnese in Mediaeval times, and was consequently occupied by the Venetians. Methone and Korone were said to have been «the two eyes of Venice», for the occupation of these two promontories afforded the Venetians control over the Ionian Sea and the Mediterranean in general. The great Venetian *fortress,* which is very well - preserved, has built - in relief plaques showing the Lion of St. Mark and other Venetian escutcheons.

The site of Methone is of strategic importance and served in antiquity as an outpost for the defence of the inland. Its Mediaeval name was *Mothon* and its fortress, built by the Crusaders and the Venetians, is a characteristic example of Mediaeval fortifications. It stands on a promontory and the crenellation rises high above the usually rough sea. Its landward side was protected by a wide moat, crossed by an arched bridge which leads to the monumental *Gateway.* On the edge of the promontory is the *Sea Gate* and the causeway connecting the fortress with an islet that had been fortified by the Turks. This causeway overlies the mole of the

ancient harbour. The Spartans used Methone as a stronghold during the Peloponnesian War, conducting successfully their defence from there. Methone attained its greatest peak in the Middle Ages, when it became the most important
naval base between Europe and the Holy Lands. The town was built within the
walls of the citadel and was renowned for its wine trade and silk industry.

ANCIENT PYLOS - CHORA TRIPHYLIAS

The site (210 kms. from Patras and 140 kms. from Tripolis), including the village and the surrounding area, has been explored with remarkable results by Professor Sp. Marinatos and the American School of Classical Studies. 18 kms. north
of the modern town of Pylos, a great Mycenaean palace was uncovered on the
hill of *Ano Englianos*. This is, according to the American archaeologists who conducted the excavations, the *Palace of Nestor*. The study of this two-storied building
with its two annexes and the countless finds it has yielded contributed to the advance of Mycenology. Hundreds of tablets inscribed in Linear B script (deciphered by Ventris) led to important conclusions, the most outstanding being that
the Linear B is a very ancient form of Greek, considerably earlier than the age
of Homer. The Palace had a guard-room, a waiting-room, and the hall of the
throne adorned with a circular monumental hearth in the center and superb frescoes
on the walls. It also included long corridors, the queen's quarters and a bath. A
large building to the north served for the storage of wine or other liquid products
— about 40 large pithoi stood there in a row. Remnants of a stone staircase
suggest the existence of a second storey in the great palace.

The earlier building is similarly important and the whole complex with its
tholos tomb is most impressive. The movable finds are exhibited in the Museum
of Chora. Excavations were conducted by the American archaeologist Carl Blegen.
In addition to the other data brought to light, the most remarkable find was a great
number of Linear B tablets, which were deciphered by Michael Ventris in collaboration with John Chadwick; this is one of the most outstanding discoveries. The
palace also yielded many kylikes, several large storage jars and other vases. Most
of the walls of the three buildings of the palatial complex have been preserved to
a height of 1 m. All the columns supporting the roof were wooden. The date of
destruction of the palace coincides with that of other Mycenaean palaces on mainland Greece. Eastwards of the central compound, there were some buildings which
served as workshops — one of them was intended for the repair of chariots, as excavation data have revealed.

The tablets and most precious finds of the palace are displayed in the
Mycenaean room of the National Archaeological Museum of Athens. (Excavations,
begun in 1939, were interrupted by the outbreak of the Second World War, and
resumed after the War). The palace was destroyed by fire in circa 1200 B.C. Preliminary investigations indicate that the Mycenaean city extended below the hill
of Englianos, from which one has a splendid view of the landscape as far as the
sea. Professor Sp. Marinatos has investigated a great number of tholos and chamber
tombs over an extensive area of Messenia; his finds are of outstanding value and
singular importance for the history of those tombs on mainland Greece. In view
of the important and rich finds that have come to light during excavations, the
village *Kakovatos* Triphylias was thought by some archaeologists to have been
the site of Nestor's Pylos.

Museum of Chora

A visit to this Museum is essential after the acquaintance of the archaeological site. Finds from excavations on the hill of Ano Englianos are finely displayed. The palace frescoes are exquisite. Exhibits include abundant clay ware, gold jewellery, and other movable finds. Gold objects and other finds from Professor Marinatos' excavations at *Volimidia* and *Peristeria* are also exhibited in the Museum.

PYRGOS

Pyrgos is situated at a distance of 321 kms. from Athens. Before reaching the last bifurcation of the road, the visitor encounters on the right, very near the sea and amidst a wood of eucalyptus and oak trees, the old *Monastery of Panaghia Skaphidiotissa*, with two very unusual towers. The Miramare hotel compound is on the beach. Those of the old Neoclassical buildings preserved in the town of Pyrgos are noteworthy.

12 kms. from Pyrgos, at Ayios Andreas on the shore of *Katakolo* are the engulfed ruins of ancient *Pheia*. On the right stands the ancient *acropolis* of Pheia (Pontikokastro). From the age of Pausanias, the ancient traveller of the 2nd century A.D., the area of Elis has been considered as the richest in Greece after Macedonia and Thessaly. Elis was very active and flourishing in the Classical period. South of Pyrgos is the radioactive Spa of Kaiapha, famous since antiquity.

30 kms. from Pyrgos the road diverges to Kyllene, from where there is a ferry - boat connection with Zakynthos. *Kyllene* was the harbour of ancient Elis. In the period of the Frankish occupation it was named *Glarentza*. Near Kyllene is the *Moni Vlachernon*, a fine Byzantine monastery, and 5 kms. farther, *Chlemoutsi* with its imposing Frankish *castle,* built by Geoffroi de Villehardouin in 1219. Farther still, is the *Kyllene Spa,* a thermal establishment amidst a eucalyptus grove, recommended for asthma cures.

ANCIENT ELIS

At a distance of 12 kms. from Pyrgos, lay Elis, the capital of the prosperous region of Elis. Ancient ruins exist over an extensive area, which has not been entirely explored yet. Excavations on the site were carried out by the Austrian Archaeological Institute and in recent years by the Greek Archaeological Society. So far, excavations have revealed the *theatre* and some clusters of houses of Roman and Hellenistic times. Monuments of earlier periods have not been uncovered yet, for excavations have not reached lower levels. Pausanias the Periegete records that Elis had been embellished with fine buildings and many works of art. The Eleans were entrusted with the administration of the Olympic Games and the sanctuary of Olympian Zeus. Elis was very rich thanks to her fertile soil and became an important centre from the 8th century B.C. At that time and until the third decade of the 5th century B.C., no city-state was formed, but several komai existed under a central administration. Owing to the influence of the Athenian Themistokles, the synoecism took place in circa 471/470 B.C., and Elis began to have expansionary tendencies towards nearby territories. By reason of the Olympic Games, which were to some extent organized by the Eleans, Elis was regarded as a sacred city and excluded from the internal strifes of the ancients. Although the Spartans had been annoyed when the synoecism occurred, they did not exert pressure on Elis but rather aimed at having a friendly influence over her so that in the event of economic difficulties they might seek assistance from the rich city, which, moreover, administered the riches of the sanctuary of Olympian Zeus.

Like the rest of the Peloponnese, Elis suffered successive invasions. The plundering of the sanctuary of Olympian Zeus by the Goths was a great disaster. Later, the region became the 'apple of discord' between the Palaiologues and the Frankish princes.

ANCIENT OLYMPIA

Olympia occupies a small part of the valley lying on the right bank of the river Alpheios, at the point of confluence with Kladeos, its tributary flowing from the north.

In historic times the area was never permanently inhabited, but was just a holy place, destined for the worship of gods, filled with temples, altars and sacred precincts. It was never autonomous, but depended from one of the strong neighbouring cities: Pisa, at first, and, later, Elis. The main *Sanctuary of Olympia*, which included the temples of the gods and the temeni of the old local heroes, was named *Altis*, i.e. grove. This area was quadrilateral, measuring approximately 200 m. from west to east and 160 m. from north to south.

Our knowledge regarding the earliest foundation of the Sanctuary does not derive from history but from tradition associated with that remote past. The site had been undoubtedly inhabited in Prehistoric times. Older excavations revealed between the Heraion, Metroon and Pelopion, the existence of oblong apsidal dwellings assigned to an earlier than the Late Helladic period. Without gaining particular importance or fame, the settlement prospered considerably in the Mycenaean age, as evinced by the discovery of an extensive Mycenaean cemetery in the area of the new Museum and a number of isolated graves in the surrounding area.

The first cult on the site was that of *Ge,* the goddess Earth. Her sanctuary is supposed to have stood by a chasm on the slope of Mt. Kronion, north of the Heraion. *Rea,* the mother of the gods, was also worshipped there, in the *Idaion Antron* at the foot of Mt. Kronion.

The *Pelopion,* a temenos situated between the temples of Hera and Zeus, included the tomb of Pelops, the local hero to whom tradition ascribes the initiation, or at least the revival, of the Olympic Games. Legend has it that Pelops came from Phrygia, contested with the king of Pisatis Oinomaos in a chariot-race, and received as a victor's prize the king's daughter Hippodameia and the kingdom. The preparation for this contest forms the subject of the representation on the east pediment of the temple of Zeus. Beneath the tomb of Pelops, excavations uncovered an empty grave dated to the end of the 2nd millennium B.C., showing the first clear traces of cult. The earlier finds are datable to about 1100 B.C., and they are mostly bronze or clay human and animal figurines, as well as bronze tripods which were prizes won in the funeral contests held in honour of the hero. Some historians suggest that the Olympic Games performed in later times had evolved from these earlier contests held in honour of Pelops.

In 776 B.C., when the Sanctuary was under the control of the Eleans, their king Iphitos, whom legend cites as a descendent of Oxylos, reorganized the games and replaced the chariot-races with a foot - race of one stadion (192.27 m). The first recorded victor of this race was Koroibos of Elis. Henceforth, the Olympic Games were held every quinquennium and the Olympiads were used as the basis of chronology, starting from 776 B.C.

In historic times Zeus superseded the local hero Pelops and dominated over the Sanctuary. The fame and influence of the Sanctuary grew and it became a Panhellenic political, cultural and religious centre.

The oldest building in the Altis was the *temple of Hera,* dated to the mid-7th century B.C., or, according to another view, to the late 8th century B.C. Tradition speaks of a first temple built by the Skilluntians in 1096 B.C., but the evidence of the sherds and bronze objects found beneath the original foundation of the temple contradicts such an early chronology. The first temple (an apteros) was destroyed by fire, and replaced by the second (a peripteros) in about 600 B.C. The temple housed later the famous Hermes of Praxiteles.

At about the same age were built the *Prytaneion* and the *Bouleuterion.* The *Prytaneion* stood N.W. of the Heraion, and contained the hearth with the ever-burning flame. The ruins we see at present are of the Roman age and hardly give a picture of the building which was contemporary with the second Heraion. The *Bouleuterion,* which was adjacent to the south peribolos of the Altis, was a complex consisting of two similar oblong apsidal buildings dated to the 6th and 5th centuries B.C., respectively. The Olympic Boule, which was responsible for the financial administration and the general supervision of the Sanctuary sat in the Bouleuterion.

The cult continued for a long time to be centred around the altar of Zeus and the tomb of Pelops. The *altar of Zeus* was situated east of the Pelopion and is assigned to very ancient times — according to tradition it had been founded by Herakles Idaios. Pausanias describes it as a mound of 22 feet height. The tomb of Pelops was enclosed for the first time by a peribolos.

The *Treasuries,* dedicated by various cities to the Sanctuary of Olympia, were erected at the foot of Mt. Kronion. The first *Stadion* was constructed in 550 B.C.

Meanwhile, after struggles against their neighbours the Pisatans, the Eleans secured domination over the Sanctuary, and a splendid era began for Olympia. The *temple of Zeus,* a Doric peripteros with a peristyle of 6 × 13 columns, was built in 456 B.C. by the Elean architect Libon. A local conchiferous stone was employed for the construction of the lower parts of the temple, while its sculptures were originally carved in Parian marble — Pentelian marble was later used in replacing three figures of the west pediment. The location on which the temple of Zeus was erected has preserved traces of earlier cult datable to the beginnings of the 1st millennium B.C., but has revealed no traces of older foundations. Immediately after the construction of the temple, the *Stadion* was relocated a little farther to the east, though still within the sacred Altis, as contests maintained their sacred character. Later, the Stadion was removed outside the sacred Altis and modelled with inclined banks so as to accommodate spectators. In the Hellenistic period it was given access to the Altis through a vaulted entrance — the *Krypte* — with an imposing propylon on the side of the sacred precinct. The *altar of Demeter Chamyne* was recently uncovered on the north bank of the Stadion, and the *Bema of the Hellanodikai* to the right.

The Sanctuary assumed its final form in the 4th century B.C. following the foundation of new temples, secular buildings and stoas. The sacred Altis was then enclosed by a peribolos along the west and south sides, while the terrace of the Treasuries formed a natural boundary on the north. The Sanctuary was bounded on the east by the Stoa of Echo and the so-called Southeast building. The *Stoa of Echo,* also named *Stoa Poikile* because of the wall-paintings dec-

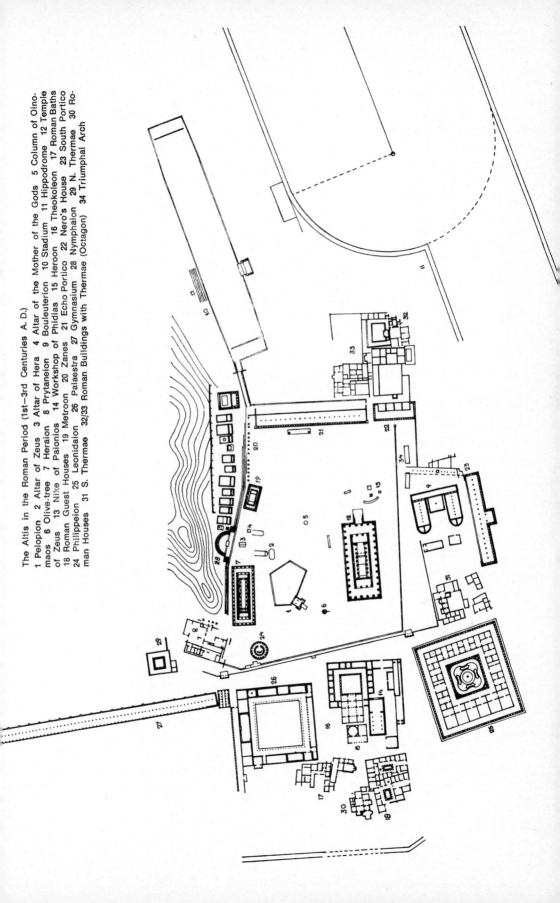

The Altis in the Roman Period (1st—3rd Centuries A. D.)

1 Pelopion 2 Altar of Zeus 3 Altar of Hera 4 Altar of the Mother of the Gods 5 Column of Oinomaos 6 Olive-tree 7 Heraion 8 Prytaneion 9 Bouleuterion 10 Stadium 11 Hippodrome 12 Temple
of Zeus 13 Nike of Paionios 14 Workshop of Phidias 15 Heroon 16 Theokoleon 17 Roman Baths
18 Roman Guest Houses 19 Metroon 20 Zanes 21 Echo Portico 22 Nero's House 23 South Portico
24 Phillippeion 25 Leonidaion 26 Palaestra 27 Gymnasium 28 Nymphaion 29 N. Thermae 30 Roman Houses 31 S. Thermae 32/33 Roman Buildings with Thermae (Octagon) 34 Triumphal Arch

orating its inner wall, was 98 m. in length and 12.50 m. in width, and had two colonnades, of which the outer was Doric and the inner Ionic.

The so-called *South Stoa* was built in the 4th century B.C., outside the sacred precinct, on the side of the river Alpheios. The *Metroon* and the *Philippeion* were also built at that age, i.e. the 4th century B.C. The *Metroon* stood east of the Heraion and was a small Doric temple, measuring 20.67 × 10.62 m., with a peristyle of 6 × 11 columns — the existence of an inner colonnade is uncertain. The cult of the Mother of the gods had been long established on the site, associated with the cult of Ge.

The *Philippeion,* southwest of the Heraion, was a circular building with a conical roof. Its construction is believed to have begun in the age of Philip, after the battle of Chaironeia, i.e. after 338 B.C., and to have been completed by Alexander the Great, who set up the five chryselephantine plastic 'images' of members of his family, all made by the celebrated sculptor Leochares.

The southwest end of the site was occupied by the *Leonidaion,* a secular building erected at the expense of Leonidas of Naxos, which served as hostel. North of the Leonidaion stood the *Theekoleon,* which served as residence for the permanent priests.

Excavations uncovered on the site of the Early Christian basilica built in later times, the so-called *Workshop of Pheidias.* Clay moulds, fragments of ivory and obsidian, various tools, and a broken small clay jug bearing the inscription ΦΕΙΔΙΟ ΕΙΜΙ, i.e. I belong to Pheidias, a truly moving find, attest to the fact that this had been the workshop where the famous sculptor worked with his assistants for the making of the chryselephantine statue of Zeus. The building had approximately the same measurements as the sekos of the temple of Zeus and its interior was divided by two colonnades into three aisles. The statue under construction could have been set up there.

West of the workshop of Pheidias lie the ruined foundations of extensive buildings, apparently hostels, assigned to the 1st and 2nd century A.D. North of the Theekoleon, outside of the sacred Altis to the west, have survived the remains of the *Gymnasion* and the *Palaistra.* The *Gymnasion,* as named by Pausanias, was a complex of installations serving for the training of athletes. So far, only the east side of the Gymnasion has been studied. The external wall was built of rectangular poros stones and supported with external buttresses. In the interior, a stoa where runners practiced had a colonnade of 66 columns. The *Palaistra* was a square building, each side measuring 66.75 m. In the interior there was a square court surrounded by a Doric colonnade. The main entrance was from the northwest corner, where there was a porch of 4 Doric columns. The building, dated to 200 B.C., was intended for the training of athletes in wrestling, boxing and jumping.

On the southwest corner of the Altis lie the foundations of the so-called *house of Nero,* erected on the site of the *Prytaneion of the Pisatans* and the *shrine of Hestia.* The Prytaneion of the Pisatans had declined following the domination of the Eleans over the Sanctuary.

An older Π - shaped *Stoa,* supposed to have been erected in the early 4th century B.C., was adjacent to the Stoa of Echo.

The so-called *Nymphaion,* west of the terrace of the Treasuries, was built by Herodes Atticus between A.D. 156 and 160, and served as water reservoir: water was conducted from the springs in the area of the modern village Miraka to Olympia, where it was stored in the reservoir and distributed to various parts

Ancient Olympia.
East side of the Gymnasion.

of the Altis — a process which replaced watering by wells. The Nymphaion consisted of a rectangular basin enclosed by a circular peripteral building. Behind the water reservoir rose a semi-circular apse, of 16.62 m. diameter, with inner niches containing statues of members of the family of Herodes Atticus. This building was dedicated to the Sanctuary of Olympia by Herodes Atticus in honour of his wife Regilla, who had served for a year as priestess of Demeter Chamyne.

The Olympic Games

The Olympic Games were held every quinquennium, after the summer solstice at the time of full moon. Duration of the games was initially restricted to one day, but was later gradually extended to more, in view of the fact that originally the games comprised only the foot-race of one stadion, while more contests were added later: the *diaulos* (foot-race of two stadia) in 724 B.C., the *dolichos* (foot-race of 24 stadia) in 720 B.C., the *pentathlon* (running, wrestling, spear- and discus-throwing, and jumping) and *pale* (wrestling) in 708 B.C., the *pygme* (boxing) in 688 B.C., the *tethrippon* (four-horse chariot racing) in 680 B.C., then the *pankration* (combination of wrestling and boxing), the contests of boys, etc. Participation to the games was reserved only to the free Greeks. Later, the right to participate was also granted to the Romans. Slaves were excluded from participation but were allowed to attend the performance. Women were strictly forbidden attendance, with the sole exception of the priestess of Demeter Chamyne.

The games were administered and judged by the *Hellanodikai,* who were appointed by lot well in advance of the Olympic festival. Originally there was only one Hellanodikes, but more were added later until their number reached twelve. The first day of the games was devoted to the gods: sacrifices were performed and athletes took their oath. Fines were imposed to athletes who did not observe the regulations. The money collected from such fines was employed to set up within the Sanctuary bronze statues of Zeus, the *Zanes.*

Victors were crowned by the elder of the Hellanodikai with the *kotinos,* a branch of the secred wild olive planted at the opisthodomos of the temple of Zeus. The names of victors were inscribed on stones and immortalized by great poets and artists. After their third victory Olympic athletes were granted the right to set up a statue of themselves, not larger than lifesize, at Olympia. From the 5th century B.C., prizes were displayed on a magnificent chryselephantine table made by Kolotes, a pupil of Pheidias, and placed within the Heraion.

Museum of Olympia.
Head of Antinoos.

Museum of Olympia

The entire archaeological yield of the sacred enclosure of the Altis and of the neighbourhood of Olympia, as well as a selection of objects excavated by Greek archaeologists in the area of ancient Elis, will eventually find a permanent home in the recently inaugurated museum at Olympia. The sculptures which are still housed in the old museum founded by Andreas Syngros, including the pediments and metopes of the Temple of Zeus, the Nike of Paionios and the Hermes of Praxiteles, are due to be transferred to the new museum where two empty halls have been reserved for them.

Of all Greek sanctuaries Olympia is the one in which bronze votive offerings prevail. Apart from a variety of these bronze objects, weapons and ex-votos, architectural fragments from the treasuries and other sacred edifices are exhibited in the museum. The bronze objects were gifts offered as tokens of gratitude to the god for having granted the donor victory in some athletic or martial contest. In this connection, it is interesting to note that Pausanias, in his *Description of Greece*, devotes a whole book to the enumeration of offerings contained in the sanctuary at Delphi. Writing of Olympia, he is obliged to extend the corresponding account to two books.

In the entrance hall of the museum, which is one of the richest in the country, the visitor will find a recently completed model rendered to scale of all the buildings in the Altis and its periphery. Bases of statues of Olympic victors, made by great artists, are also displayed here.

The central hall, which forms the main axis of the museum, is reserved for the display of the sculptures from the two pediments of the Temple of Zeus. Paionios' Nike will be placed at the end of the hall. The east pediment depicts the preparations for the famous chariot race between Pelops and Oinomaos, a legend of great significance in the mythology of Olympia. In the centre stands the dominating upright figure of Zeus, invisible to mortals, «the father of men and gods», in the words of the Homeric phrase, flanked by the two royal couples : on the one hand, Oinomaos and Sterope, doomed to be defeated, on the other, Pelops and Hippodameia, the future victors. On either side of the two contestants are palace attendants and the two chariots. The two angles of the pediment are filled with beautifully rendered personifications of the two local rivers, the Alpheios and the Kladeos, depicted as two reclining youths with marvellously flowing lines. To the right (facing the spectator) is the striking figure of the aged palace seer. The dramatic events that are fated to follow, entailing the death of Oinomaos and the rise of a new royal dynasty at Olympia, seem to be dumbly reflected in the old man's profoundly meditative expression.

The west pediment represents the battle of the Centaurs and the Lapiths. The scene is dominated by the figure of Apollo, who is also invisible to mortals, his right arm outstretched in an imperious gesture, as he watches the combat, determined that justice shall be done and victory be awarded to the righteous. Whereas the figures in the east pediment are seemingly static, those in the west pediment are convulsed with movement. Both pediments, like the twelve metopes of the Temple of Zeus depicting the Labours of Heracles, are masterpieces of the late severe style. The figure of Apollo, the upper part of which is preserved intact, is one of the supreme sculptural achievements of the period.

Museum of Olympia.
Clay group of Zeus carrying off Ganymedes.

At the end of the hall Paionios' beautiful Nike will be exhibited in a small four-sided alcove. The work, a masterpiece of the second half of the 5th century B.C., once stood on the top of a triangular pillar, 9 m. high, and the goddess must have given the spectator the impression of floating down to earth from heaven. The same hall will contain the tools found in Pheidias' workshop: the clay moulds, typical specimens of implements used in the modelling of the great chryselephantine statue of Zeus, including Pheidias' cup.

Clay and bronze objects of the Neolithic to the early Geometric periods are admirably displayed in show-cases in the first hall (left). The Mycenaean objects were brought to light in the course of excavations carried out in the vicinity of the new Museum and in other neighbouring localities. A sturdy bronze Geometric horse of fairly large dimensions, an outstanding work of a period in which the Greeks had not yet mastered the technique of casting bronze, is placed in the centre of the hall. There are also — as well as in the immediately following hall — clay and bronze objects of the Geometric and Archaic periods: figurines of animals which constituted either individual votive gifts or adornments to handles of cauldrons which were placed on tripods presented as awards to Olympic victors in the earliest times. Other exhibits include figures of helmeted men holding javelins in their raised right hand; more helmeted figures with arms uplifted, which are thought to represent the god granting victory to an athlete. Until the beginning of the Classical period the god was generally depicted as a martial deity. For the first time Pheidias, in his magnificent chryselephantine statue, represented Zeus as the god of peace.

The contents of the second hall are chiefly confined to armour. The helmets (of varying provenance), breast plates, greaves, shields, for the most part lavishly decorated, were, as suggested by the votive inscriptions, the spoils of victorious battles, dated from Geometric to early Archaic times. Interesting exhibits of historic significance in this category are displayed in the fourth room: two helmets, on one of which is engraved the name of Miltiades, the victor of Marathon; the other is undoubtedly a Persian helmet from the spoils captured in the Persian Wars. Both are dedicated to Zeus. Victors often made votive gifts of bronze cauldrons, most of which have not been preserved intact. Protomes of griffins, sirens, bulls and lions once adorning large bronze cauldrons which constituted formal votive offerings presented to the god of the Sanctuary, have been preserved in large quantities. From the same period to the mid - 5th century B.C. are dated the numerous statuettes of gods, heroes, victorious athletes, mythological figures, large and small animals, etc. A large *head of Hera* is a particularly fine work, believed to have belonged to the cult statue in the temple of the goddess. The work of a Lakonian sculptor, it is dated to the 6th century B.C. An enormous central *acroterion* of clay from the Heraion, displayed along the axis of the hall, is very impessive. In the third hall there is an imposing piece of pedimental sculpture, depicting a *Gigantomachia* (battle between the gods and giants), from the Treasury of the Megarians. The fourth hall contains works of the 'severe style' and Classical masterpieces: clay groups, such as those of *Zeus and Ganymedes,* a *Silenos with a Mainad,* and the figure of a warrior, very finely executed. All these sculptures bear traces of the lavish use of paint.

Various sculptures by unknown artists are exhibited in the other halls. A special hall is reserved for the celebrated *Hermes of Praxiteles* (4th century B.C.). The god is represented bearing the infant Dionysos to Mt. Nysa, where the future god of wine, whose mother Semele was dead, would be brought up by the Nymphs. Hermes is depicted as a handsome young man, with an expression of profound and dreamy serenity. The so-called Kouros of Phigaleia, some fine inscriptions, and sculptures from the Exedra of Herodes Atticus are also on display. An unusual exhibit is the enormous stone which bears an inscription in Archaic letters stating that Bybon raised it in one hand. This hall (the eighth) contains in general objects associated with the Olympic Games: votive offerings of Olympic victors, bases of their statues, as well as alteres, stlengides, diskoi, and other such clay or bronze minor objects of various periods.

Leaving the Museum and its unique collection, the visitor who has time on his hands would do well to climb the hill of Kronion or the opposite one of Drouva in order to obtain a superb view of the Alpheios valley.

Olympia also possesses a *Museum of the Olympic Games* which houses various relics from the Olympic Games held in 1896 and 1906 in Greece, and other collections.

From Olympia, too, one has the opportunity of visiting the Ladon Dam; after crossing a beautiful tract of wooded land, the traveller would reach Vytina and Tripolis.

THE NORTH-WEST PELOPONNESE

Beyond Pyrgos the traveller reaches *Amalias*, the second largest town in the province of Eleia, whence it is only ten minutes drive to the coastline of *Kouroutas*, one of the finest and widest stretches of sandy beach in the country. 72 kms south of Patras lies *Gastouni*, an extremely important commercial center during the Middle Ages and the Turkish occupation. The old *Church of the Dormition of the Virgin* (of Roman Catholic rite in Venetian times) is of great architectural interest.

Farther to the north (60 kms south of Patras) the road crosses through *Andravida*. Now an insignificant place, it was, during the 13th century, the capital of the Frankish *Principality of Achaia* and the seat of a papal bishop. Here assembled the High Court of the Principality, a kind of parliament composed of twelve Frankish barons of the Morea, several feudal chieftains of lower rank and high dignitaries of the Roman Catholic Church. The sanctuary of the *Church of St. Sophia*, a Roman Catholic cathedral until the 15th century, recalls the city's one-time prosperity. It is also worthwhile visiting the *burial place of the Frankish Princes of Achaia* and the *Church of St. James*.

The coastline of the Peloponnese as far as Patras is very beautiful. Beyond *Kato Achaia* (23 kms south-west of Patras), probably the site of ancient Dyme, numerous excursions can be made into the heart of *Mt. Erymanthos*. From Kato Achaia the traveller may also obtain a fine view towards *Cape Papa*, otherwise Araxos, where there are fisheries in the adjacent lagoon of Papa. It was at Kato Achaia that the Frankish knights landed in 1205 and organised the military campaign to conquer the Peloponnese.

Passing through the beautiful coastal villages of *Tsoukaleika* (13 kms south of Patras), *Vrachneika* (12 kms south of Patras), *Mintilogli* (9 kms south of Patras) and the magnificent beach of *Ities*, one reaches Patras.

PATRAS

The city, which lies 220 kms west of Athens, has a very ancient history, having been inhabited in prehistoric times. Today it is an important industrial, commercial and administrative center. Ferry boats from Italian and other Mediterranean ports are constantly entering its busy harbour; others, bound for Cephalonia and Brindisi (via Corfu) also sail from here.

The history of Patras is a turbulent one, its inhabitants having taken part in all the wars of antiquity. The city was conquered successively by Macedonians, Romans, Franks, Venetians and, finally, along with the rest of the country, by the Turks. Patras played a major part in the War of Independence which broke out in 1821, and in the course of which it was totally destroyed. A few excavations undertaken in the area have revealed beautiful mosaic pavements of the Roman period, some statues and other sculptures.The present city was built during the Presidency of Ioannis Capodistria. The town plan is noteworthy, with large wide squares and porticoed streets. The atmosphere of the city's former ascendancy is still reflected in some streets and the architectural style of certain houses. For a long time Patras flourished economically, thanks to its thriving trade in currants. The town climbs the gentle slopes of an elegantly shaped pine-clad hill, on the summit of which the Villehardouins built the Frankish castle on the site of the ancient acropolis. Behind it rises *Mt. Panachaikon*. In one of the city's finest squares, that of *Psila Alonia*, whence there are magnificent views of the sun setting in the Ionian Sea, is a statue of *Germanos, Bishop of Patras*, hero of the uprising of 1821. The ancient Roman *Odeum*, in which theatrical performances are now held and concerts given, is situated in Ayios Georgios Square. Other sites worth visiting are the old *Monastery of the Yerokomion*, the *Roman aqueduct, King George's I square* and the *Municipal Theatre*. The *Church of Ayios Andreas*, scene of the martyrdom of St. Andrew, patron saint of the city, is situated near the waterfront. Recent excavations have revealed the foundations of an Early Christian basilica. The modern church possesses the saint's skull which is placed in a gold reliquary. Until recently this famous relic was kept at St. Peter's in Rome. Pope Paul VI returned it to Patras.

It was at Patras that Lord Byron landed when he came to Greece in 1824.

Museum of Patras

The museum is housed in a pleasant old two-storey building in Maisonos Street, just off Olga Square. In it are displayed objects found in Patras, in its vicinity and in the province of Achaia.

The most interesting exhibit on the ground floor is a Roman mosaic pavement of the 2nd century B.C., in which scenes of musical, theatrical and athletic competitions are depicted. There are also two beautiful marble portraits, various bronze and gold ornaments and a few Byzantine sculptures. The marble objects belong, for the most part, to the Roman period, few to the Archaic and Classical. The copy of Phidias' chryselephantine statue of Athena in the Parthenon is especially noteworthy.

Prehistoric vases of the Early and Middle Helladic and Mycenaean periods are beautifully displayed in show-cases. Among the bronze vessels, jewellery and weapons are some important bronze greaves found at Kallithea (Achaia).

The sculptured pediments excavated at Skillus are also exhibited in the Museum.

R H I O N

7 kms east of Patras lies Rhion, with its charming Venetian castle —the *Castle of the Morea*— restored during the Turkish period. From Rhion ferry boats cross

to Antirrhion on the opposite coast of mainland Greece, where lies another castle —the *Castle of Roumeli*— also restored by Sultan Bayazit.

AIGHION

From a commercial and industrial point-of-view Aighion, which lies 41 kms east of Patras and 93 kms west of Corinth, is the second most important town in Achaia. It is also a centre for the export of currants. From Aighion the traveller can cross the channel to Galaxidi on the mainland or to *Itea*, the port of Delphi. Although Aighion was an important place in antiquity, little is known of its history. In 146 B.C. it was captured by the Romans. Pausanias, in his *Description of Greece*, praises the city's springs. The *Church of the Panayia i Trypiti*, built into a cave at the entrance to the town (coming from Patras) is worth noticing. The *Monastery of the Taxiarches*, with its famous rosegarden, its splendid Library and important ecclesiastical embroideries, is also worth visiting.

It was at Aighion in January 1821 that the notables of Achaia and Kalavryta assembled, together with the valiant Papaphlessas, a hero of the War of Independence, and decided on the outbreak of hostilities against the Turks.

DIAKOPHTO

Diakophto lies 40 kms east of Patras. From here one can travel by rack and pinion railway up the beautiful and grandiose Buraikos gorge to Kalavryta and Megaspileon. A road linking Diakophto with both these places of pilgrimage has recently been completed.

Megaspileon was once a place of especial significance; the monastery, however, was burnt in 1934 and subsequently rebuilt. A seven-storey monastic edifice clings to the bare face of a sheer cliff. A cave situated behind the church has given its name to the monastery (the *mega spileon*, the great cave). The monastery was originally founded on an abrupt vertical rock. According to a local tradition, in A.D. 342 a shepherdess found an icon of the Virgin ascribed to the brush of St. Luke in the cave. From Megaspileon the traveller may climb up to the *Source of the Styx* near the summit of Mt. Chelmos. In antiquity it was believed that if the gods swore an oath in the waters of the Styx they never broke their word. The treasury of the monastery possesses a fine collection of Christian (including saints') relics, Byzantine Gospels with enamel-decorated covers and a miraculous icon of the Virgin. The 4th century founders of the monastery were two brothers from Thessaloniki, Symeon and Theodore. Apart from its collection of relics, the monastery possesses another aspect of especial significance to Greeks, being profoundly associated with the national conscience, for the community of monks played a major role during the period of the Turkish occupation and the subsequent War of Independence. A determined defence of the holy place was believed to result invariably in a successful outcome. Its impregnable position on this vertical rock of Mt. Chelmos in fact prevented the monastery from falling to the Turks. The buildings have actually been destroyed by fire more than once and subsequently restored or rebuilt. Of the original foundation, two fountains, some cannons and other relics of the past remain. In 1943 the Germans set fire to the monastery and killed its inmates.

KALAVRYTA

The terminus of the rack and pinion railway is Kalavryta (22 kms south of Megaspileon), famous for its springs and streams, to which it owes its name. In order to reach Kalavryta from Diakophto the traveller crosses a beautiful valley of great scenic variety, green with tall bracken. Road and rail repeatedly cross each other, and the little train rattles across bridges, enabling the passengers to obtain magnificent views of the surrounding country.

The small town spreads across a slope of Mt. Chelmos among fir trees. At one hour's distance is situated the *Kastro tis Orias*, one of the most romantic mediaeval castles, which recalls the days of prosperity of the Frankish and Venetian periods. The role played by Kalavryta during the War of Independence was of great importance: even more so when the War of Independence broke out in 1821. There are remains of three ruined towers from which the inhabitants besieged the Turks. Kalavryta was burnt twice during the course of the war : in 1826 and 1827. In 1943 the German occupation forces massacred the male inhabitants and burnt the town. A large cross, eight metres high, raised above the collective tomb of the martyred men, serves as a reminder of this savage deed.

The *Monastery of Ayia Lavra* is situated 7 kms north-west of Kalavryta. Like Megaspileon and Kalavryta, it is profoundly associated with the turbulent days of the War of Independence. Here, on the 25th March 1821, Germanos, Bishop of Patras, raised the standard of revolt, using the *vellum* which separated the sanctuary from the main body of the church as a banner. The act was a symbolic one, for it marked the opening round of the War of Independence. The monastery was founded by St. Athanasios, founder also of the Monastery of the Great Lavra; in 1585 it was burnt by the Turks but refounded in 1600. Its fate, however, was destined to be a tragic one. In 1826 it was reduced to ashes by Ibrahim Pasha. Only the Katholikon was spared. In 1943 it was burnt again: this time by the Germans. In 1947 it was once more rebuilt. A majestic *memorial to the heroes of the War of Independence* has been raised on a hill nearby.

A *Museum of the War of Independence* has been founded by the monastic authorities. It contains relics of the uprising and a fine library. Among the relics is the skull of St. Alexios.

SIKYON

87 kms west of *Corinth* lies *Rizomilos*, whence a road to the right leads to the site of what is believed to have been ancient *Helike*, capital of the Achaian Confederacy. According to a local tradition, a group of Ionians from Asia Minor came to Helike in 373 B.C. to ask for a copy of the beautiful statue of Poseidon. The inhabitants of Helike refused to comply and went so far as to drive the Ionians out of the city without even permitting them to sacrifice to Poseidon. For this display of hybris, Poseidon, the Earth-Shaker, flew into a rage and caused a tidal wave to engulf Helike which was wiped off the face of the earth. Professor Spyridon Marinatos, equipped with all the technical means now available to archaeologists, has recently undertaken to locate the site of Helike. Should he suceed, the achievement will be one of immense importance, for the entire town will be revealed in the state in which it was when inundated in the 4th century B.C.

Proceeding eastwards towards Corinth, the traveller may take a turning to the left which will soon bring him to the magnificent beach of *Xylokastro* shaded by great umbrella pines. From Xylokastro an asphalt road mounts up to *Trikala* (1300 m. high), a lovely summer resort, shaded by plane, pine and fir trees. Trikala is also the starting-point for a number of excursions popular with mountain-climbers, and one of which leads to the *Cave of Hermes* where are impressive stalactites. From Kiato, 120 kms east of Patras, an asphalt road leads to the site of *Sikyon*, one of the most important city states of antiquity, full of mythological traditions. In the 6th century B.C. the city was ruled by the powerful tyrant, Kleisthenes. In the Archaic and Classical periods it was a great artistic center, famous for its paintings, sculptures and pottery. Excavations undertaken by Professor Orlandos have revealed part of the ancient town, including the *Roman baths* (3rd-2nd centuries B.C.) in which the local museum is now housed, a theatre with a beautiful view towards Corinth, where theatrical performances are given, a remarkable monumental *fountain,* a gymnasium, remains of a *temple of Artemis* and (a little to the south) an Early Christian basilica. At Sikyon there was also a temple of Athena, in which oil gushed forth at the instigation of the goddess as a token of her gratitude for the honour paid to her by the Sikyonians.

Museum of Sikyon

As already observed, the museum is housed in the Roman baths within the perimeter of the ancient city. Of the Archaic and Classical periods, when Sicyon was at the height of its power, only a few sculptures remain. Most of the exhibits are of the Hellenistic and Roman eras. A section of the brick superstructure of the Temple of Artemis survives. There are also vases and idols of different periods and a magnificent mosaic pavement of the 4th century B.C. In the entrance hall there are some scanty sculptures of the Early Christian and Byzantine periods.

STYMPHALIA

A good road, 41 kms long, ascends from Kiato to Stymphalia, now called *Kionia.* The valley is fertile and springs gush forth all around. The legendary Stymphalian Birds, killed by Heracles, are supposed to have haunted the banks of the lake. During the 2nd century B.C. the Emperor Hadrian built an aqueduct which supplied Nemea and Corinth with water.

At the 56th kilometre the road reaches the beautiful mountain village of *Kastania* (900 m. high) among fir trees. Twelve kilometres beyond Kastania the motor road comes to an end at *Goura* (950m. high), also situated among fir trees, whence the traveller can climb the snow-covered slopes of Mt. Ziria, passing the «Kastro tis Orias», and reach, at a high altitude, the site of ancient *Pheneos*, where the climate is wonderfully bracing. Excavations undertaken during recent years at Pheneos have revealed an ancient house with a mosaic pavement and part of a large «acrolith» statue.

CENTRAL GREECE

THEBES

Thebes (73 kms north-west of Athens via Eleusis, Mandra and Kaza, 83 kms via the Athens - Lamia highway) was one of the most celebrated cities of ancient Greece, and its fame was equally great in the prehistoric and historic eras. According to mythological tradition, the city was founded by Kadmos. The fate of its royal house, which included Oedipus, Jocasta, Antigone, Ismene, Eteokles and Polyneikes, inspired some of the outstanding masterpieces of the great Athenian dramatic authors of the Classical age. Recent excavations have revealed Thebes to have been an important commercial center during the Mycenaean period, with large palaces in which the kings established workshops for the production of signet-rings and cylinder-seals of precious and semi-precious stones.

Rivalry between Thebes, which was defended by walls with seven gates, and the other great Boiotian city, *Orchomenos,* was endemic. At various times during antiquity it was the seat of the *Panboiotian League.* Ruled by an aristocracy, Thebes sided with Sparta in the Peloponnesian War. At a later period (first half of the 4th century B.C.), under the leadership of *Epameinondas* and *Pelopidas,* allied with the Athenians, the Thebans were defeated at the battle of Chaironeia by Philip II of Macedonia. In 336 B.C. they revolted against Macedonian rule, and the city was attacked and razed to the ground by Alexander. Only the house of Pindar was spared. In 316 B.C. the city was rebuilt, but it never regained its former power. In 87 B.C. it was again destroyed —by the Roman general Sulla this time. Complete decay set in. Only in Byzantine times did the city undergo a revival, thanks to its industry in silken fabrics. It then became the headquarters of the Byzantine military governor of Greece. In 1205 it was captured by the Franks who made it the capital of the *Duchy of Athens and Thebes* under Othon de la Roche. Although visited by a further holocaust at the time of the Catalan onrush in 1311, parts of the mediaeval tower of the Dukes of Athens survive. After the Turkish conquest of the country, the town passed into oblivion.

Museum of Thebes

The museum, one of the most important in provincial Greece, is situated on the outskirts of the town in I. Threpsiades Street (named after the archaeologist who supervised the display of the exhibits in the museum). The garden is littered with numerous inscriptions which were found not only in and around the town but all over Boiotia. A mosaic pavement is displayed in a shed situated between the front of the museum and a workshop. Fragments ranging from prehistoric times to the Roman period and a series of noteworthy Early Christian and Byzantine carvings are exhibited in the entrance hall.

Four halls follow. In the first sculptures of the late Geometric and Archaic periods predominate. The beautiful Ptoion kouros, placed along the main axis of the hall, is very impressive. There are also a number of typically Boiotian funerary stelai. Pottery ranging from the prehistoric to the Archaic periods, both from large necropoles in the vicinity and from all over Boiotia, are displayed in the second hall.

Unique funerary stelai found at *Thebes* and *Tanagra* are exhibited in the third hall : rare specimens, both as regards design and representation, of the Classical period. A fully armed warrior, wearing a helmet, breastplate and greaves, and holding an extended javelin, is depicted in combat with an invisible opponent. This remarkable representation has been finely incised and granulated on black stone of local provenance. All traces of paint have vanished. Beautiful sculptures of the Hellenistic and Roman periods fill the rest of the hall. An impressive ensemble of statues discovered in the course of excavations carried out at the *Sanctuary of Artemis at Aulis* should be noted.

The fourth hall contains a series of Mycenaean painted sarcophagi of clay with unusual representations discovered in the course of the excavation of the large necropolis of Tanagra. Of major interest too are the objects from the Kadmeion —the lavishly decorated leg of an ivory throne, the wonderful signet-rings composed of precious stones with beautiful representations and numerous highly finished objects of the minor arts. The large stirrup jars inscribed with Linear B script from the Kadmeion also merit careful attention.

GLA - PTOION

Two fascinating archaeological sites may be easily visited from Thebes. The one is the acropolis of *Gla*, where a Mycenaean palace and an edifice believed to have been an agora have been identified. A beautiful view is obtained from the Mycenaean acropolis which is encircled by strong walls pierced by imposing gateways. The second site is the *Sanctuary of Apollo at Ptoion* whence came a series of Archaic sculptures (kouroi) now exhibited at Thebes and in the Archaeological Museum at Athens. The landmark for the traveller anxious to visit the sanctuary is the village of *Perdikovrysi*.

LEVADEIA

Beyond Thebes, a branch road at the 78th kilometer from Athens leads to *Thespiai* (13 kms) where there are ruins of a Byzantine castle and an *altar of the Muses*. Here, it was believed in antiquity, *Pindar* lay down to rest one day. On falling asleep, he was besieged by a swarm of bees that alighted on his lips and filled his mouth with wax. Consequently, his poems possessed a quality as sweet as that of honey.

At the 199th kilometre from Athens the traveller enters Levadeia, a charming town full of verdure and running water. It is a lively place, the local centre of the cotton trade. Throughout its long history, Levadeia underwent turbulent times, its natural wealth attracting the attention of a succession of conquerors : Romans, Franks, Ali Pasha himself, who inflicted much suffering on the inhabitants, and, of course, the Turks, who conquered the town in 1394 and subsequently made it the capital of Roumeli. For a long time it was the largest town after Athens.

The *Oracle of Trophonios*, so celebrated in antiquity that it attracted the most distinguished consultants, both Greek and foreign, including Croesus, King of Lydia, is believed to have been situated near a place now called «Nera» (Waters), where numerous rivulets pour their waters into the main stream of the *Herkyna*. The site of the oracle was on the left bank. Pausanias gives a detailed account of the sanctuary and of the method of consultation which involved a period of exacting preparation. Consultants had to fast and drink from the waters of *Lethe* in order that they might forget all that they had known in the past. The oracular chamber was situated in an underground pit which the consultant entered by descending a movable wooden ladder. It is believed that the oracle's therapeutic qualities were mainly confined to the cure of mental ailments, for consultants seem to have been afflicted with psychological shakings that might well be compared to what we nowadays call «shock». The exact position of the site of the oracle is uncertain. It may have been on the side of the hill of Ayios Elias or on its summit now crowned by a mediaeval tower. A fine view is obtained from the acropolis of Levadia with its crenellated ramparts.

HOSIOS LOUKAS, PHOKIS

The monastery can be reached by taking the road from Levadeia to Delphi. Turn left at the fork, 154 kms from Levadeia. The setting is unforgettable. *Hosios*

Loukas of Stiris, in whose memory the monastery was founded, died in the middle of the 10th century (946 or 949 A.D.).

The monastery was founded in the 11th century, the Katholikon built in 1020 A.D. This is decorated inside with wonderful mosaics on a gold backround of the highest quality. There are two large icons, one of the Virgin and one of Christ, beautifully executed by Michael Damaskinos, the teacher of El Greco. The architecture of the building is also interesting, for it is one of the most important Byzantine monuments surviving from the 11th century.

The dome, wich was destroyed by fire in 1659, has been covered with frescoes. The small church to the north of the Katholikon is older and has carved panels.

In the garden of the monastery Bishop Esaiah of *Salona* (Amphissa) blessed the weapons of the local military leaders before the beginning of the War of Independence in 1821.

The crypt of the Katholikon has some very interesting painted decoration.

DELPHI

Proceeding from Levadeia towards Delphi, one reaches Arachova (157 kms from Athens) a very picturesque village with a flourishing handicraft of woollen and embroidered goods, blankets, carpets etc., executed in folklore patterns. On the heights of Parnassos, above the village, is the *Corycian cave* dedicated to Pan and the Nymphs, recently excavated by the French Archaeological School. It has many galleries and chambers filled with stalactites and stalagmites.

On arriving at the village of Delphi the first thing the traveller encounters is the *Sanctuary of Athena Pronaia* which lies to the left of the road on a small area of level ground on the downward slope of the hill. The local inhabitants call it *Marmaria*. From Mycenaean times it was a place of worship of a female deity, the protectress of women. Athena replaced this goddess in historical times.

Descending to the terrace below the visitor first comes across a temple dedicated to the goddess built of local limestone, dating from the 4th century B.C. It was fronted by six columns; on its left side, continuous with the temple, there was a building consisting of two rooms and an ante-chamber which is thought to have been the house of the priestesses of the goddess.

East of this temple there is the *Tholos*, a circular building with an outer Doric colonnade, built entirely of marble. Its original function is unknown. It also was founded in the 4th century and is considered to be one of the most beautiful of ancient Greek buildings. The columns of the inner colonnade are of the Corinthian order. The cornice was decorated on the outside with metopes carved in relief which represented a battle of the Amazons *(Amazonomachia)*. Such as survive are to be found in the local museum.

East of the Tholos are two small *Treasuries*, one Ionic (that of Marseilles) and one Doric. The former was built between 535 and 530 B.C., the latter in 490-460 B.C.

In front of the Treasuries, and standing at an angle to them, are the remains of a rectangular *altar*.

Further east is the last building of importance in the Sanctuary, the older temple of Athena, a peripteral temple of tufa in the Doric style. It was founded at the beginning of the 5th century B.C., but was destroyed by a rock-fall from the Phaidriades in 373 B.C. and abandoned. In 1905 more rocks fell. These can still be discerned today. East of the temple are the remainings of three altars. To the north,

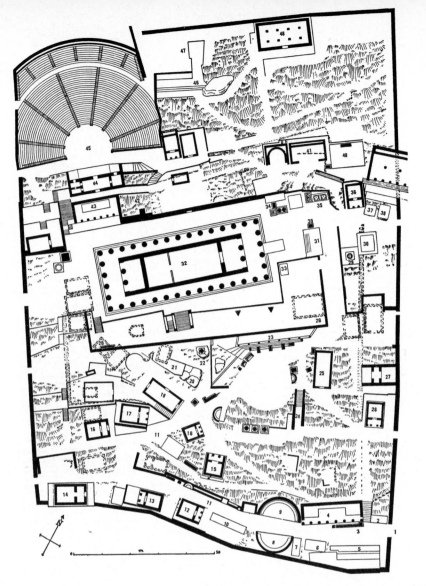

PLAN OF THE SANCTUARY TO APOLLO AT DELPHI (CIRCA 150 B.C.)

1. Main Entrance - 2. The Bull of Kerkyra - 3. Memorial Arcade - 4. Spartan Admirals - 5. Votive Offering of the Athenians of Marathon - 6.-9. Votive Offerings of the Argives: 6. The Seven against Thebes - 7. The Trojan Horse - 8. The Epigons - 9. The Kings of Argos - 10. Base of the Tarentines - 11. The Sacred Way - 12.-18. Treasure Houses: 12. Sicyonian-13. Siphnian-14. Theban - 15. Aeolian(anonymus)- 16. Potidean - 17. Athenian 18. Cnidian - 19. Council House (bouleuterion) - 20. Sibylline Rock - 21. Gaia's Shrine - 22. The Sphinx of Naxos - 23. Hall of the Athenians - 24. Steps - 25. Treasure Houses of the Corinthians and 26. The Cyrenes - 27. Prytaneum (Hall of Assembly for Prytanes - chief officials) - 28. Polygonal Wall - 29. Plataean Tripod - 30. Rhodian Chariot - 31. Altar of Chios -32. The Temple of Apollo - 33. Pillar of Aemilius Paullus - 34. Pillar of King Prusia - 35. Tripods of the Deinomenides - 36. Acanthian Treasure House (?) - 37. Statue of King Attalos - 38. Statue of King Eumenes - 39. Pillar of King Eumenes - 40. Shrine of Neoptolemos - 41. Votive Offering of Daochos - 42. Site where the Charioteer was found - 43. Votive Offering of Krateros: Alexander hunting - 44. Proscenium - 45. Theatre - 46. Hall and Passage Way - 47. Spring of Kassotis - 48 Cnidian Hall of Assembly (lesche).

in a small walled sanctuary, are two small buildings held to be the shrine of the local hero, *Phylakos*.

The Gymnasion

On the terrace immediately above is located the *Gymnasion*. Constructed in the 4th century B.C. and repaired in Roman times, it was an indispensable establishment for the young men of the area who wished to exercise, and for the training of the athletes who took part in the *Pythian Games*. The gymnasion is constructed on two levels. On the upper level stood the *Xystos*, or covered portico, where it was possible to practise in bad weather. Next to this was the *Paradromis*, an uncovered track used when the weather permitted open-air exercise.

On the terrace between the xystos and the Sanctuary of Athena was the *palaistra*, a building where athletes trained in wrestling. As was customary in antiquity, it was divided into several compartments. On the west side a round pool served for the hot baths. On the retaining wall which divides the two levels of the gymnasion it is still possible to distinguish the marks where the *taps* for water were placed.

Kastalia

The setting of Delphi is one of the most striking in the world. Two massive rocks, the *Phaidriades*, dominate the scene. In ancient times they were called *Hyampeia* and *Nauplia* (now *Phlembouko* and *Rhodini* respectively). At their base, where they join to form a narrow gorge, emerges the water of the sacred spring of *Kastalia*. This water was used for the purification of the temple and for the lustrations of the pilgrims.

The older original Kastalian fountain entirely of marble, stands next to the road towards Arachova. Its floor is below the present ground level. Further up is the later Kastalian Spring, which was carved out of the cliff-face and had a monumental façade. The water run from the mouths of seven lion-headed spouts which have not survived.

The Sacred Precinct of Apollo

This is perhaps the most impressive of all ancient Greek sanctuaries. The different buildings were raised on successive terraces, compelling the visitor continually to ascend and presenting him at many points with wonderfully constructed walls which are really nothing less than retaining walls that prevent the earth of the upper level from sliding down.

The precinct is completely enclosed by a surrounding wall containing various gates and posterns. The main entrance in antiquity was the one used today.

The sanctuary at Delphi, dedicated to the worship of Apollo, was one of the largest and most important spiritual, artistic and religious centers in the ancient world. Here Apollo was worshipped as the god of the golden «rule», as the presiding deity in charge of human activity. At his command men were forbidden to exceed what was proper, nor could they transgress in any respect the canons of moderation. For such transgression was accounted hybris, which might be defined as the disregard for the harmony marked out by the Gods as the limit of human action. In its rôle as an oracle the sanctuary offered signal service to the cause of the civilisation and pacification of the Greeks in the archaic period, a phase of great political conflict and antagonism.

According to the myth, the god arrived there and set up his sanctuary by killing the serpent, *Pytho*, the ancient guardian of the shrine of Mother Earth. For this act of bloodshed that is, Apollo of his own free will, imposed on himself the punishment of serving as a slave to Admetos, King of Pherai, for seven years. By his example he demonstrated the means whereby man might achieve remission of the crime of murder, how he might achieve sublimity of mind and awareness of the nature of his actions.

The oracle also played an important part in the second wave of colonisation, directing the states who sought its advice where they should send their colonists. Pythian Apollo is a civilising deity, a god of harmony and of music.

The will of the god was expressed through the words of the Pythian priestess who presided the oracle in the Adyton (Holy of Holies) of the temple. The priestess, seated on a tripod and chewing laurel leaves, was enveloped in the fumes rising from a cleft in the rock below her and uttered inarticulate cries, by means of which the questions of the faithful were answered. Originally her utterances were in verse, later in prose. Priests assisted in the interpretation of the oracles to the pilgrims.

In the early period games were held in Apollo's honour every eight years. About the 6th century B.C. the program was changed. The games were held every five years and athletic contests, horse and chariot races were added to the original musical contests. Athletes came from the whole of mainland Greece and from Magna Graecia for the Games, while Greek cities, and even foreign rulers, on various occasions sent precious gifts to the god.

The buildings and different monuments in the Sanctuary spread out on either side of the Sacred way, which has two loops. Ex-voto offerings from the Argives, the Athenians, Lacedaimonians, and Arcadians can be seen immediately beyond the main gate, just within the Sanctuary. There follow many treasuries, the rich gifts of the different Greek cities and islands, such as those of Siphnos, Sikyon, Athens and Corinth.

At the apex of the first loop is the reconstructed *Athenian treasury*, the ruins of the *Bouleuterion* (the Senate House of the Delphic Council) and three strange rocks — the *Rock of the Sibyl*, another stone which supported the base for the *Naxian Sphinx*, and *Leto's Stone*, from which it was believed Leto encouraged the young Apollo to kill the Pytho with the words — ἴε παῖ! («Go, my son!»).

The *Stoa of the Athenians* follows. Here were set up in 478 B.C. the spoils of the various naval victories from the Persian Wars.

Behind the Stoa is the famous *polygonal wall* which is covered with inscribed decrees, *psephismata*, or resolutions of the Athenian parliament. The second loop is dominated by the *Tripod of the Plataians*. It was crowned by a golden cauldron supported by three entwined serpents in bronze. It was dedicated by the Greeks after their victory over the Persians at Plataiai. To the left is a beautiful *altar* to Apollo, offered by the island of *Chios*, as its inscription records. The Chians defrayed the expenses for it and received as their reward the privilege of priority of access to the oracle. All around are the pedestals of other ex-voto offerings.

In the S.E. corner of the temple precinct is the base of the high column erected by the Roman general, *Aemilius Paulus*, to commemorate his victory over the Greeks at Pydna in 168 B.C.

The temple of Apollo was raised in the 4th century B.C. on the same site as two preceding temples. The first of these was destroyed by fire in the 6th century, while the second was destroyed by an earthquake in 373 B.C. The later temple was erected from the proceeds of a Panhellenic fund. It is in the Doric style, peripteral in plan.

In the prodomos there was an altar on which a flame burned constantly for the salvation of the whole of Greece. The Adyton was in the temple proper, but below ground. It was here that a golden statue of the god Apollo stood. Behind the cella, or main section of the temple, was the opisthodomos.

In the north-west corner of the precinct is a large rectangular niche which held a group of bronze statues by Lysippos and Leochares. It depicted the lion-hunt in which Krateros saved the life of Alexander the Great when he was in danger of being killed.

Ascending the stairs the visitor reaches the *Theatre*, which is marvellously preserved. It was built in the 4th century B.C., repaired in 159 B.C. at the expense of Eumenes II, King of Pergamon. It held 5,000 spectators. To the east of the theatre is the *Lesche of Knidos* (rest-house or hostel). Inside there were at one time the famous paintings of Polygnotos of Thasos, which depicted the descent of Odysseus into the Underworld, inspired from that passage in the Odyssey called the «Nekyia».

On leaving the theatre, the visitor comes upon the *Kernaian spring* and, after a further brief climb, reaches the *Stadion*. It is the best preserved structure of its kind and is 177.55 meters long. It was built in the 5th century B.C. The tiers on the north side were constructed in the second century A.D. at the expense of Herodes Atticus. The starting and finishing points can still be discerned.

Museum of Delphi

The museum has ten halls and an ante-hall. It is one of the most interesting local museums in Greece, full of exquisite works of art.

In the ante-hall there is a marble omphalos, or navel-stone, of the 3rd century B.C. A large continuous relief forms the remains of the proscenium frieze of the theatre of Delphi. It was carved in the era of the Roman occupation and depicts the Labours of Heracles.

The first hall contains three bronze shields, the head of a griffin which decorated a bronze tripod, and a bronze cauldron on a marble base which consists of three female figures. The most beautiful work in this hall is a small bronze archaic statuette of a young man of the 7th century.

In the large hall to the right the dominant exhibits are the sculptures from the *Treasury of Siphnos*. They belong to the frieze and pediment of the building. The pediment depicts the struggle of Apollo and Heracles for the tripod. The frieze, a work of outstanding power, a council of the Gods and scenes from the Trojan War. On the west wall there is displayed a *Gigantomachia*, or battle of the Gods and the Giants, the *Judgement of Paris* and a rape of women from some mythological account. One of the chief works in the room is the *Sphinx of Naxos*, a work of exceptional sensitivity. It was consecrated by the people of Naxos in 570 - 560 B.C. To the left of the Sphinx is the statue of a woman, one of the two Caryatids who supported the façade of the treasury of Siphnos. The head on the right belongs to a Caryatid from an unknown treasury (dated to approximately 540 B.C.).

In the third small hall the commanding exhibit is that of two archaic kouroi from Argos; these are representations of Kleobis and Biton and date from the end of the 7th or the beginning of the 6th century B.C. There are also on display five metopes from the treasury of Sikyon, very fine works of sculpture which illustrate the high standard of the art of Sikyon in the mid-6th century B.C.

These metopes represent the Rape of Europa, the theft of cattle by the Dioscuri, the Calydonian Boar and episodes from the quest of the Golden Fleece.

In the fourth hall there is a display of 24 metopes from the Treasury of the Athenians. It was built of Parian marble and the metopes depict the Labours of Theseus and of Heracles.

In the two following halls there are exhibited the two pediments from the second temple of Apollo. The west pediment, now in a very fragmentary condition, depicted a representation of a Gigantomachia, the east the advent of Apollo to Delphi in the company of his mother and sister. This temple and its decorations were executed under the direction of the Alcmeonidai, a wealthy and noble Athenian family.

In the next hall there is a very fine funerary relief of an athlete (460 B.C.) and other fragments. Another entire hall is given over to a reconstruction of a part of of the cornice of the Tholos from the Sanctuary of Athena Pronaia. On the walls to the right and left are fragments of sculpture from the decoration of the building, Doric capitals from the external colonnade and a re-assembled Corinthian column from the interior of the Tholos.

The next hall is dominated by the famous *Column of the Dancing Girls*. Three female statues are set on the summit of a very high column. It is an Athenian ex-voto of about 332-322 B.C. There is a fine statue of an old philosopher in the N.E. corner of the hall (about 280-270 B.C.). Six large interesting statues, copies of originals by Lysippos, belong to the *ex-voto of Daochos II*, tetrarch of Thessaly, who had them set up in memory and honour of his family.

The hall containing the bronze *Charioteer*, a work outstanding for its restrained and severe style, attracts the greatest attention of visitors to the museum. The charioteer is depicted in the act of making his triumphal circuit of the stadion. It was presented to the sanctuary by the tyrant Polyzalos, who was victorious in the chariot-race at the Pythian Games in 478 or 474 B.C. It is perhaps the work of Pythagoras of Samos, an important sculptor of the period. Part of the base for the group survives, with its dedicatory inscription, and in the display-cases set into the wall there is the hand of a statue of the charioteer's small slave and all that has been preserved of the team of horses.

In the last hall is displayed the statue of *Antinoos*, the Emperor Hadrian's favourite. There is a headless herm, which depicted Plutarch, a priest of Apollo and the well-known author of the *Parallel Lives*. A very attractive exhibit is that of a statue of a small boy holding a goose and a fine head of the 2nd century B.C. Finally there is a statue of a graceful young girl and a very fine head, believed to be a portrait of Plutarch (50-125 A.D.). Pottery, bronze objects and a mass of other works of the minor arts are displayed in show-cases in this hall.

ORCHOMENOS

For the archaeologist and traveller versed in Greek history this is an area steeped in associations. There are the many cities and localities such as Thisbe (5 kms from Thebes), the *Vale of the Muses* on Mt. Helikon, *Thespiai*, *Haliartos* (25 kms from Levadeia), *Vassilika* (23 kms from Levadeia site of the famous battle against the Turks on August 26th, 1821), *Distomon* (24 kms from Levadeia), site of the battle against the Turks under the generalship of Karaiskakis. In June, 1944, the Germans burned the village, after executing its 223 inhabitants. All these places and many more played their part in the history of antiquity and of later times.

A fork to the right, 126 kms from Athens and 13 kms from Levadeia, leads to the village of *Skripou*, the ancient *Orchomenos*. This was an important Boiotian

Orchomenos, Boiotia.
The byzantine church of Skripou.

city, famed for its rivalry with *Thebes*. Excavations carried out there have uncovered finds from the Neolithic period. This is the Minyan Orchomenos of antiquity, seat of a distinctive race, the *Minyans*, who, as the ancient Greeks believed, had come from Thessaly and carried out drainage operations for the reclamation of Lake Kopais, with the aim of making the land fit for cultivation. The impressive fortifications of the acropolis of Gla (see page 91) are also of Minyan construction. The present-day traveller to Orchomenos can visit the Mycenaean tholos tomb, called the Tomb of Minyas. It has a rectangular burial chamber and fine decoration. Remains of an archaic temple belonging to the middle Helladic settlement have been preserved, as also those of a larger temple of *Asklepios*.

Beyond the temple of Asklepios are the ruins of the city founded by Philip II of Macedon and Alexander the Great. The original city had been destroyed by the Thebans in 349 B.C. On the western extremity of the city is the small, four-sided acropolis, at one time defended by strong fortifications. The walls that survive to the present day are of the 4th century B.C.

The most important sight, apart from the Tomb of Minyas, is the famous Byzantine *Convent of Skripou*. It is a domed church, dedicated to the «Dormition of theVirgin», of the 8th or 9th century A.D. Fragments of ancient columns and inscriptions, chiefly from the Byzantine period, have been incorporated in the walls of the church. The church is believed to have been built on the site of the temple of the *Three Graces* (the Charites) who were worshipped here and held to be the daughters of Eteokles. Mysteries were held in their honour in antiquity, called the *Charisia* or *Charitesia*.

AULIS: THE TEMPLE OF ARTEMIS

Aulis is easily accessible from Chalcis, lying at a distance of 19 kms south of the city on the mainland facing Euboia. The site is 70 kms from Athens. Excavations have uncovered the *Temple of Artemis*. The statues now in the museum at Thebes were discovered here. Various buildings include a potter's workshop of a later date and an ancient spring. The acropolis, dating from Mycenaean times, spreads out impressively before the traveller, while further inland, and opposite the Mycenaean acropolis, is the Classical one.

CHAIRONEIA

Chaironeia is 144 kms north of Athens. It is the northernmost city in Boiotia. In the battle that took place here in 338 B.C. between the Macedonians on one hand and the Boiotian and Athenian forces on the other, Philip II of Macedon was victorious, thus sealing the fate of those Greeks who opposed his rule. There is a statue that commemorates the battle, called the *Lion of Chaironeia*, which was set up over the graves of the fallen, as guardian of the dead. It was restored in 1902 - 1904 at the expense of the Greek Archaeological Society. The remains of the *theatre* are preserved in the modern city, on the slopes of the acropolis. Chaironeia was the birthplace of Plutarch.

Museum of Chaironeia

The museum houses important ceramics of the prehistoric period, dating from the Neolithic period to the end of the Mycenaean era. There are also displayed inscriptions and vases from the classical period and from the period of Roman conquest, as well as armour and jewellery.

The Tanagra Collection

Antiquarians should not miss visiting this collection which consists of works from the Archaic period to the Byzantine era. It includes sculptures, architectural fragments, ceramics and inscriptions.

KAMENA VOURLA

Kamena Vourla has some famous radio-active springs and the climate is dry and healthy. Near Loutropolis, and very near Mylo Koniaviti, there are some other springs containing sodium hydrochloride and the *Springs of Aphrodite*, which are very beneficial for the skin.

THERMOPYLAI

The *Pass of Thermopylai* is 26 kms distant from Kamena Vourla. The shape of the land has been changed by the retreat of the shoreline, so what was once a narrow defile between the mountains and the sea, is now a fairly broad strip of land. The pass was a major obstacle to foreign invaders. There were times when the Greeks successfully repelled the invaders and other times when they were forced to sacrifice their lives fruitlessly in its defence. The Greeks, however, always offered fierce and courageous resistance at this point; against the Persians in 480 B.C., against the Gauls in 279 B.C., the Romans in 191 B.C., the Goths in A.D. 395, the Crusaders in A.D. 1205 and the Germans in 1941. The most memorable stand of all was that of the king of Sparta, Leonidas, against the Persians, which failed only because of the treachery of Ephialtes. The heroic self-sacrifice of the 300 Spartans and the 1,000 citizens of Thespiai has entered into European legend. Professor Spyros Marinatos has excavated the site and found spear-heads dating from this battle which are now displayed in the National Archaeological Museum, in the hall of archaic small scale bronze implements.

A fork at the 182nd km, at *Kato Bralo,* leads to *Gravia* where, in the War of Independence, Odysseus Androutsos conducted a heroic defence at the inn of the village with only a few soldiers.

LAMIA

Lamia is a very picturesque city, built on a slope, 120 meters above sea level. History of the city was eventful both in ancient and modern times. In 1204 it became the seat of a Frankish barony. Later the Catalans captured it and later still it fell to the Turks. It was the last city to be taken from the Turks in 1832. Its Kastro, or castle, is of particular interest. Near the city is the *Alamana Bridge*, scene of the tragic death of the revolutionary hero *Athanasios Diakos*. On being charged by the Turks who had captured him to disavow his religion, he refused and was consequently roasted alive.

The *Archaeological Collection* is housed in the local Library. It contains ceramics of the Mycenaean and all the historic periods of antiquity, as well as works of the Roman period. The chief exhibits are the sculptures from *Echinos,* which date from the 4th century B.C. There are also inscriptions of the Hellenic, Hellenistic and Roman periods. The *Kounoupis Collection* (a private collection housed at 17 Myronos Street) includes ancient vases and sculptures, folk-art jewellery of later centuries and weapons. In another private collection, that of G. Platis, there are vases and small idols of the classical period.

THESSALY

Thessaly is of importance both for its classical remains and for its rôle in pre-Hellenic history. At *Halmyros*, 95 kms north of Lamia along the National Road, there is the ancient acropolis of *Halos*, with the remains of walls and towers. The local museum, which is housed in the neo-classical building of the Philarchaios Hetaireia (the Society of Friends of Antiquity) there are prehistoric finds and sculptures as well as ancient and early Christian ceramics.

To the north of Halmyros, after turning right off the National Road towards Volos, are located the ruins of *Phthiotic Thebes* (nowadays called Nea Anchialos). Near by is the site of the ancient Pyrasos, the port of Phthiotic Thebes. The town was destroyed in 217 B.C. by invaders, while in early Christian times it became once more an important city. Early Christian basilicas with beautiful mosaics have been discovered here, as well as architectural sculptures and a large four-sided building, which was perhaps an episcopal palace. In the *Archaeological Collection* there are several architectural fragments, sculptures and a notable collection of ceramics, as well as gold jewellery of the Roman era. In ancient times *Pyrasos* was the site of the Sacred Grove and temple of Demeter.

PAGASAI AND DEMETRIAS

Further along the road towards Volos, where a promontory juts out into the sea, stood the two cities of Pagasai and Demetrias. Objects of the Neolithic period have been discovered in both places. In 353 B.C. the city of Pagasai was captured by Philip II of Macedon. In 293, Demetrios Poliorketes built a second city, which he named Demetrias after himself. This second city incorporated the older one, so that the combined settlement had two citadels. After the destruction of Phthiotic Thebes in 217, the city became a busy and active port for the export of products of the fertile Thessalian plain.

Of the acropolis of Pagasai there remain 27 towers and some walls. Pagasai reached its peak in the 5th century B.C. Of Demetrias, apart from the surviving walls with their 76 towers, it is still possible to see the ancient *theatre* of the city and the Roman aqueduct. Excavations revealed the existence of scores of painted funerary stelai which illustrate in the most conclusive manner the high standard of ancient Greek painting. They are now in the *Volos* Museum.

VOLOS

The Mycenaean acropolis is situated on the hill now called *Palia*. This was the ancient *Iolkos*, the legendary city ruled over by Peleus who had usurped the throne of his nephew, Jason. Some years ago excavations were carried out and revealed a small part of a Mycenaean palace. Facing the shore, where the ancient shipyards were located, traces of Mycenaean culture were found, among which were some very interesting vases. The site is identified with that of ancient *Neleia*. The inhabitants of Iolkos were famous ship-builders in antiquity. According to the famous myth, they built the Argo, and it was from their harbour that the vessel sailed, carrying Jason and the Argonauts, in search of the Golden Fleece. Mt. Pelion, which is richly wooded, provided plentiful material for their requirements.

The modern city of Volos was founded in the 16th century and after its liberation from the Turks and its re-union with the rest of Greece in 1881, it underwent considerable expansion.

Leaving Volos and re-joining the Highway, the traveller comes upon two very important citadels of the Neolithic period. These are Dimini, where there are several large bee-hive tombs and an acropolis ringed round with several series of walls, and, nearer to Larissa, Sesklo, which is the oldest Neolithic acropolis in Europe. It is expertly planned with successive surrounding walls and interesting buildings.

Dimini and Sesklo were explored for the first time by the famous archaeologist, Christos Tsountas. Rich finds from both sites coming from the original excavations are set in the hall of the National Archaeological Museum, specially given over to the finds from the first prehistoric period. They include vases, idols and implements of stone and clay. In recent times confirmatory excavations have been carried out; they have been helpful in the definitive classification of the different phases of the Neolithic period. Excavations at Sesklo and in surrounding regions have shown how densely populated Thessaly was in the Neolithic period and have even revealed traces of occupation from the Palaeolithic period. The relevant finds are housed in the museums of *Larissa* and *Volos*.

Many sites of great archaeological interest have been discovered in the vicinity of Volos. In addition, lying at the foot of Mt. Pelion, a locality rich in mythological associations, a visit to the city affords the traveller with a unique experience.

On the sea-front at Volos there is a church decorated by the painter, G. Gounaropoulos.

Athanasakis Archaeological Museum of Volos

The museum is situated on Athanasakis Street. It consists of four halls and an ante-hall. In the ante-hall there are maps, diagrams and a large collection of objects of the Palaeolithic period. In the north hall are representative examples from the Neolithic period. These are methodically set out with many explanatory diagrams. Apart from the Palaeolithic objects much interest will be aroused by the movable finds of the Mesolithic period (small stone implements) and by the finds of the first phase of the Neolithic period, which goes under the name of the Preceramic phase, because men had not then learned how to model clay. There is an interesting collection of fossilized bones. The variety of the small idols of the Neolithic period is remarkable. There are vases, idols and implements of bone and stone of the Neolithic period and the Bronze Age.

In the second hall, to the left as the visitor enters, there are ceramics of the Geometric period, bronze objects (tools and weapons) of the Archaic period and valuable gold jewellery from Geometric, Archaic and Classical tombs.

In the first hall to the right the display is dominated by an impressive variety of *painted stelai* from Pagasai and Demetrias. Finally, in the last hall on the right there is a display of sculptures of exceptional interest. They are of Thessalian workmanship and date from both Archaic and Classical times. The funerary stelai of the classical period are interesting on account of their distinctive style.

The museum also houses a large and well arranged collection of coins of various periods.

The private collection of *K. Makris* possesses fine works of regional folk art.

MT. PELION

The beautiful mountain is thickly wooded with oak, chestnut, plane, walnut, cypress and poplar trees. There are apple - tree orchards and abundant streams. The wonderful aspect of this area stirred the imagination of the ancient Greeks and they created a whole series of myths associated with it. The most famous is that of the *Centaur Cheiron*, tutor of the great heroes of mythology. A visit to Mt. Pelion will particularly appeal to the traveller with an interest in traditional architecture and the popular minor arts, including painting and sculpture. In the 18th century Mt. Pelion became a refuge for all those Greeks who abandoned their towns and villages in order to escape from Turkish oppression. They were so enterprising that in time they founded 24 villages and succeeded in persuading the Turks to grant them special privileges. *Zagora* and *Milies* became the most important centers of learning in Thessaly. Local folk art flourished and has survived to this day (the interior walls of many mansions in the villages are frescoed by *Theophilos*, the early 20th century folklore artist). The carvings on the fountain in the central square of Makrinitsa are noteworthy. Similar carvings are to be found throughout the area. The *Kondos house* at *Ano-Volos*, the walls of which are frescoed by Theophilos, is destined to become a Museum of Popular Art. There are also paintings by Theophilos at the *Velentza bakery* at *Alli Meria*. At *Makrinitsa* there is an interesting *Church of the Panayia*, founded in 1222, the inner and outer walls of which are lavishly decorated with folk-art reliefs. There are fine frescoes in the chapels of Ayios Nikolaos and Ayioi Pandes (dependencies of the church). At Makrinitsa too there is a *Museum of Pelion Popular Art*. The old way of life led by the archons (village notables) can be vividly recaptured at *Zagora*, a center of learning in the 17th and 18th centuries, where the arts and literature flourished. The school where Righas Pheraios, the national martyr, Anthimos Gazis and other intellectuals taught in the days of the Turkish oppression, is still preserved under the name of the *Ellinomouseio* (the Greek Museum). It has a splendid library with rare books and manuscripts. The *Churches of Ayios Georghios* and *Ayia Kyriaki* possess iconostases which are outstanding examples of popular art (at Ayia Kyriaki there are also frescoes). The three-naved Church of Ayia Marina in the village of *Kissos* (altitude 550 m.) where Righas Pheraios taught, is entirely frescoed by the folklore artist *Pagonis*. Both Yanni and Thanasi Pagonis (father and son) were born at *Drakeia* (altitude 500 m.), a village in Western Pelion, where they frescoed the walls of many houses and the *Church of Ayios Georghios* (they also frescoed houses in other villages). The *archons'* houses at Drakeia have woodcarved ceilings and doors with multicoloured glass panes. At *Milies* (altitude 350 m.), birthplace of Anthimos Gazis, writer and warrior, traces of that brilliant period during the Turkish occupation when the village was a center of learning, still survive. There is a splendid library and a beautifully carved iconostasis in the Church of the Taxiarches (the Archangels). In Eastern Pelion, *Tsangarades*, nestling among oak, plane and chestnut woods, there are many old mansions which recall the days of affluence. Beautiful woodcarved iconostases adorn the sanctuaries of the 18th century *Churches of Ayia Paraskevi, Ayios Georghios, Ayia Kyriaki* and *the Taxiarches*. At *Trikeri*, a fishing village on the tip of the Magnesian peninsula and at *Ayia Kyriaki* there are old mansions with elaborate woodcarving and lavish interior decoration. Many picturesque customs are preserved during Holy Week and on May 1st.

LARISSA

The town is built on both banks of the Peneius which is spanned by a Byzantine bridge with twelve arches. Storks nest on the roofs of houses. All this area, which played an important role in antiquity and later periods, has been inhabited uninterruptedly from prehistoric times to the present day. When ruled by the Aleuadai, literature and the arts flourished, and the city attracted the attention of intellectuals, including Gorgias, Hippokrates and Pindar. During the Russo-Turkish war it suffered terribly at the hands of unruly bands of *zeibeks*. There has not been much in the way of archaeological excavation, but traces of an ancient *theatre* and *odeum* survive.

Museum of Larissa

The museum, housed in the Turkish mosque (2. 31st Augoustou Street), possesses a noteworthy collection of Palaeolithic objects and of the Preceramic period found in the course of excavations undertaken by the German Archaeological Institute, including a Neolithic *menhir* and funerary stelai of the Archaic and Classical periods. Three private collections — those of G. Gourgiotis, H. Katsigras and D. Tloupas — contain nacre and other objects of the minor arts, paintings by Greek artists and neolithic idols and tools.

AMBELAKIA

Ambelakia, situated 34 kms north-east of Larissa on a slope of Mt. Ossa at an altitude of 600 m., entered the limelight in the 17th and 18th centuries, when the first co-operative in Greece was established there. As a result of the export of cotton and silk goods, the locality enjoyed great economic prosperity which in turn encouraged an intellectual movement. Schools, at which eminent men of letters taught, were founded and performances of ancient tragedy were given every Sunday free of charge to the public. The Ambelakia co-operative was the first step along the long road that ultimately led to the establishment of social insurance, and the poor of Ambelakia had access to free medical treatment offered by highly qualified doctors. The village was destroyed by Ali Pasha in 1821. Its decline, however, was due to the failure of the Bank of Vienna, where the inhabitants' assets had been deposited.Of the days of prosperity, all that remains are the mansions of the *Schwartz* family, one of which is decorated with wall paintings and woodcarvings and is open to the public.

Numerous excursions on and around the Mt. Olympos and Mt. Ossa country can be made from Ambelakia.

ELASSON

The town was the first to be recaptured by the Greek army in the Balkan War of 1912. The *ravine of Petra* is one of the most majestic in the region, with the *Monastery of Petra,* founded by the Emperor Andronikos II Pàlaiologos in about 1300, situated among venerable oak forests. At the exit of the ravine an abrupt rock is crowned by an ancient Macedonian fort.

A collection of archaeological objects is housed in a Moslem Mosque in Elasson. The collection includes architectural fragments and Hellenistic and Roman inscriptions. There are fine Byzantine icons in the Treasury of the *Monastery of Ayia Triada (Sparmou)*.

The most important monument in the area is the *Monastery of the Olympiotissa*, a Byzantine foundation of the 13th century. There are Byzantine and post-Byzantine icons and woodcarvings in the treasury. The door leading into the Katholikon, dated to 1296 or 1305, is very finely executed. The monastery also possesses gold - threaded embroideries, ecclesiastical objects and some Byzantine architectural fragments.

METEORA

History: On the N.W. side of the Thessalian plain, near the foot of the mountain range of Chasia, at a distance of 9 kms. from Kalambaka, a cluster of precipitous grey rocks rising to a great height offer a unique awe-inspiring sight. On top of these rocks a splendid monastic community was developed in the 14th century. We do not know when monks and anchorites retreated there first, but we are informed by literary sources that the beginning of the history of Meteora was marked by the foundation of the *skete* of Doupiani Neilou. Later, numerous and rich monasteries were built by prominent men with the help of Byzantine and other rulers. In the second half of the 15th century the community was nearly destroyed as a result of dissensions and disputes among the monks for reasons of land property and administration. Fortunately, however, the wise hierarchs of Thessaly and the long period of peace that had prevailed, saved the monastic community. New monasteries were built (Monasteries of Varlaam, Roussanou) and old ones were restored (Monastery of the Transfiguration). Libraries and schools of copyists were also founded in the mid-16th century. With the passing of time however, taxes, disputes, poverty, and more generally the decline of monasticism led to decay. Finally, during the Second World War (1941 - 1944) the monasteries suffered extensive damage.

Monuments: Only two of the earliest katholika founded in the 14th century have survived : the katholikon of the *Monastery of Hypapanti* (1366), which had been carved out of the rock, and the small *Byzantine chapel,* which is the sanctuary of the *Monastery of the Great Meteoron.* Most of the surviving monasteries are of the post-Byzantine age, the main ones being the following : 1. The *Monastery of Ayia Trias* (1476). 2. The *Monastery of Varlaam* (1518). 3. The *Monastery of the Transfiguration* (1544). 4. The *Monastery of Ayios Stephanos* (15th century) repaired in 1798. 5. The *Monastery of Ayios Nikolaos Anapafsa*. 6. The *Monastery of Roussanou.* Each monastery is a whole compound consisting of the katholikon, refectory, hearth, hospital for the sick and the aged (a unique example of this kind is to be found in the Monastery of Varlaam), storerooms, cisterns, cells, guest-rooms, and the 'brizonion'. The architecture of the katholika and other buildings is admirable. Most of these katholika are of the Athonite cross type and preserve the tradition of Byzantine architecture with their lofty dimensions, well-constructed domes, etc.

The painting decoration of the Monasteries is of great interest. The visitor has the opportunity to admire good examples of works by two of the outstanding representatives of the Cretan School — Theophanes the Cretan (in the Monastery of Ayios Nikolaos Anapafsa) and Phrangos Katelanos (in the katholikon of the Monastery of Varlaam). In the Monastery of the Transfiguration there are examples of the art of the Macedonian school, as modelled after the fall of Constantinople.

The Libraries of the Monasteries include codices, documents and rare books, and the sacristies contain icons, objects of the minor arts, liturgical vessels, vestments and Gospels.

EUBOIA

CHALCIS

Chalcis, capital of Euboia, the largest Greek island after Crete, lies at a distance of 36 kms from Thebes, 70 from Athens. From the most ancient times the history of Euboia is full of interest. Archaeological research has not, however, yet been carried out on a thoroughly systematic basis, and only scanty evidence has so far been added to the few references made by ancient writers. In the historical era there were four large cities : *Chalcis, Eretria, Aidepsos* and *Kyme*. Ancient remains of the Mycenaean and Geometric periods have been discovered by the British School of Archaeology at the village of *Lefkandi*, near Chalcis. Throughout Euboia the traveller will encounter Byzantine remains. In antiquity Chalcis was a city of importance : an importance which acquired even more significance in the Archaic period. The first great war in which, according to Thucydides, all the Greeks took part, was fought between *Chalcis* and *Eretria* for the possession of the fertile *Lelantian plain*. In the course of the second great wave of Greek colonisation, the Chalcidians founded colonies in the Chalcidice, Italy and Sicily. The city was a busy commercial centre, specialising in the manufacture of small bronze objects (as its name implies, *chalkos* meaning copper in Greek), in weapons and handicrafts. In the Christian era, Sultan Mehmet II laid a memorable siege to the town in 1470. Across the strait, a hill on the mainland shore was crowned by the Fort of *Karababa*. In the town itself there was a Venetian castle. Few architectural traces of those stirring times survive, and it is only from old engravings that one is able to obtain an impression of the picturesqueness of the town in the last century. Excavations undertaken in recent years have brought to light Hellenistic mosaic pavements and ruins of ancient houses.

Museum of Chalcis

The museum houses in a neo-classical building founded in the last century at 21, Eleutherios Venizelos Avenue; it consists of an entrance and two halls. Ceramics, chiefly of the Protogeometric period, are displayed in show-cases in the hall to the left, where is also a superb funerary statue of a seated woman. In the entrance hall there are sculptures of the Hellenistic and Roman periods. The statue of a Roman Emperor was found at Aidepsos. The chief glory of the museum, however, are the sculptures from the west pediment of the *Temple of Apollo Daphnephoros* at Eretria, in which the rape of Antiope by Theseus is depicted — a real masterpiece, full of delicacy and softness. Carved architectural elements, inscriptions and small funerary stelai are displayed in the court.

Visits to the Early Christian Church of Ayia Paraskevi and the Turkish mosque, where there is a collection of Byzantine objects including mosaic pavements, carvings and ceramics (both Early Christian and Byzantine), will be found rewarding. Venetian doorways and Turkish reliefs are encountered in different parts of the town. There are also the two forts and the «house» of Malios.

ERETRIA

Eretria is still known as Nea Psara, because it served as a refuge to the inhabitants of the island of Psara which was destroyed by the Turks during the War of Independence. Recent excavations have revealed that Eretria was inhabited during the Mycenaean period (for the momentous war between Eretria and Chalcis for possession of the *Lelantian plain*, see p. 104). The modern town is built on the foundations of the antique one. Traces of ancient buildings are often encountered in the courtyards and paving stones of contemporary houses. Preliminary excavation of a *Sanctuary of Demeter Thesmophoros*, situated on the acropolis of the ancient city, has begun in recent years. On the slopes of the acropolis hill is a fairly well preserved ancient theatre in which the works of the classical dramatists are now performed. The underground passage which led to the center of the orchestra, used for the apparition of the gods by means of a mechanical device is a special feature of the theatre. A temple of Dionysos has been identified beside the theatre; some way beyond it is the *Temple of Apollo Daphnephoros*, whence came the superb pediments and sculptures now in the museum at Chalcis, and a Prytaneion.

Museum of Eretria

The museum, which consists of a large hall and a roofed shed, is situated near the excavation field. Among its contents is the fine prehistoric pottery discovered at Lefkandi. Archaic, Classical and Hellenistic pottery is displayed in other show-cases. The noteworthy Panathenaic amphorai found in the course of recent excavations will in time be exhibited here. Some of the funerary inscriptions are worth noting. In the shed there are sculptures of the Classical and Hellenistic periods.

AIDEPSOS

The city was a flourishing one in antiquity, well known in the 4th century B.C., as mentioned by Aristotle, for its hot springs. During the Roman period it became a fashionable summer resort to which visitors came to take the waters. Among these —in the year 83 B.C.— was Sulla, the Roman general, who suffered from gout. Other distinguished visitors, in search of relief for their ailments, included the Macedonian king Antigonos (in the 3rd century B.C.) and, at a much later period, the Emperor Hadrian.

In the early Byzantine period the hot springs were still functioning, but after the 11th century we have no further textual reference to the town until 1814, when it was destroyed by the Turks. When Turkey and Greece agreed on the exchange of Euboia for Samos, the spa began to function again.

North - east of Aidepsos, at a place called Elia, is the *Monastery of Ayios Georgios* (eight kilometres from the village) with beautiful frescoes, ecclesiastical objects, reliquaries and vestments in the treasury.

The *Archaeological Collection of Aidepsos* (Roman carvings and inscriptions) is housed in a storeroom in the town hall.

KYME

No archaeological research has been undertaken at Kyme, which is a picturesque little town with a distinguished past, for it was from here that the first Greek colonists sailed for Italy, where they founded Naples and Cumae. The alphabet of the Kymeans, similar to that of the Chalcidians, was thus introduced into Central Italy where it formed the basis of the Latin alphabet. The Byzantine *Monastery of the Soter* is situated near Kyme.

Minor archaeological collections are to be found at the Ghiokaleion Foundation at Karystos (Hellenistic and Roman reliefs and pottery), in the Town Hall at Istiaia (Hellenistic pottery and Roman architectural fragments) and in the parish hall at Oreoi (Classical and Hellenistic pottery). A recently discovered sculpture of a bull has been placed in the main square of Oreoi.

THE NORTHERN SPORADES

PEFKI

Pefki is a lovely pine - clad sandy seashore on the northern tip of Euboia opposite the entrance to the Pagasitic Gulf, whence boats sail for the *Northern Sporades*: *Skiathos*, *Skopelos* and *Alonnesos*. *Skyros* is reached by ferry boat from Kyme. All these islands have an ancient history and their remotest past is known chiefly from inscriptions and the texts of ancient writers. Many localities still preserve their ancient place names.

SKIATHOS

The island, which is of incomparable beauty, has been immortalised by the great modern writer, Alexandros Papadiamandis. In antiquity Skiathos formed part of the Athenian maritime hegemony. In Hellenistic times it was incorporated in the Macedonian Empire. Later it suffered from numerous foreign invasions. During the Frankish occupation (until 1454), it formed part of the fief of the Guise. Later it came under the rule of the Venetians who fortified the Bourdzi and the castle. In 1538 it underwent the terror of a visitation of Haireddin Barbarossa. In the 17th century it was a refuge for patriot insurrectionnaries from the Pelion area and Macedonia. When the country was liberated from the Turks the inhabitants abandoned the Kastro and settled in the present Chora. Apart from Papadiamandis, who sung the praises of the island's natural beauty, Skiathos produced another important writer in the person of Alexandros Moraitidis.

Papadiamantis' house, converted into a museum filled with souvenirs and relics of the great writer, is a place of pilgrimage for Greek visitors to the island. The 14th century castle is also worth visiting. Formerly there were eighty churches on the island. Of these only eight survive, one of which, the *Church of Christ*, has been made well known by the writings of Papadiamandis. The *Monastery of the Panayia Ikonistria* (or Kounistria) has an interesting woodcarved iconostasis and Byzantine icons. The *Monastery of the Evangelistria* is also not without interest.

SKOPELOS

This thickly wooded island has a large number of churches with beautiful icons and an individual style of architecture, both as regards the interior disposition and the woodcarved ceilings of the old houses of the island archons (notables). There are twelve monasteries with interesting relics. In antiquity Skopelos was known as

Skyros.
View of the acropolis and the village below.

Peparethos, founded by Staphylos. Like the rest of the country, the island suffered from successive invasions. During the War of Independence it was the headquarters of the chieftains, Nikotsaras and Yannis Stathas.

ALONNESOS

The interior of the island is particularly attractive. There are three villages. Recent excavations on neighbouring uninhabited islets have revealed traces of life in the prehistoric era. A recently salvaged vessel, shipwrecked off the coast, contained among other fine objects, a quantity of ceramics of Byzantine manufacture.

SKYROS

The island is full of mythological associations of the remotest past. Theseus was buried here. Tradition has it that Kimon later removed the hero's bones to Athens and buried them in the Theseion which was founded for this purpose. Here too Achilles was brought up in the closest secrecy among the daughters of Lykomedes in order that he might escape the terrible fate that his mother Thetis had predicted for him. But Odysseus came to Skyros and persuaded Achilles to join the rest of the Greeks in the Trojan War. There are traces of life during the Stone Age, but systematic archaeological research has not yet been undertaken. Mycenaean tombs and pottery of the Mycenaean,Geometric, Archaic and Classical periods have been discovered. The scenery is of unique picturesqueness and the visitor would do well to walk across the length and breadth of the island. The architectural style of the houses retains local island traditions. The interiors of the houses are also distinctive. The 10th century *Church* of *Ayios Georgios* and the Venetian castle built on the site of the ancient acropolis are worth visiting.

There is a *Museum of Popular Arts and Handicrafts*. Some fine Archaic, Classical and Roman sculptures are displayed in the court of the *Archaeological Museum*. Objects found in the scanty excavations carried out so far are displayed in show-cases in the first hall: for the most part pottery of the Mycenaean and Roman periods. The second hall is set aside for the exhibition of furniture and handicrafts of local origin.

AITOLO - AKARNANIA

The journey from *Naupaktos*, crowned by its fine castle, to *Amphilochia* is across beautiful country. The road passes through *Misolonghi*, the «sacred city» of modern Greece, profoundly associated with the epic exploits of the War of Independence and, in particular, with the heroic exodus of the besieged inhabitants on 11th April, 1826. The history of all this country is fully recorded from the Geometric period onwards. A detailed account of earlier times is lacking. During the Turkish occupation the entire area was a well organised centre of resistance and the combats waged by patriots were both fierce and decisive.

The archaeological sites, few but important, include the *Sanctuary of Artemis Laphria* at *Kalydon*, *Oiniadai* (now called Lessini), *Thermos*, overlooking Lake Trichonis, and *Stratos*.

There are fine frescoes and a beautifully embroidered shroud (epitaphios) in the *Church of the Panayia* at *Aitolikon* (12 kms north of Misolonghi), site of the trial of Karaiskakis and of two sessions of the regional National Assembly (a kind of parliament of mainland Greece during the War of Independence).

THERMOS

The ruins of the ancient site, which was the seat of the Aitolian League, lie 22 kms east of Agrinion. Polybius, the ancient historian, calls it «the acropolis of the Aitolians». Representatives of the Panaitolian Assembly met here once a year. The *Temple of Apollo Thermios* was remarkable for its painted entablature, and the surviving fragments are representative of the architecture of the Archaic period, the decoration of the entablature, like that of the Temple of Artemis Laphria at Kalydon, being highly distinctive —a typical example of Corinthian monumental sculpture— with heads of Satyrs and Gorgons and figures of unusually large proportions, all lavishly painted, disposed on the *sima*. The metopes of clay were also painted. Corinth, which maintained commercial relations with its colonies in Italy and, above all, Southern Italy (Syracuse was the oldest Corinthian colony), had every reason to wish to exercise control over Aitolo-Akarnania in order that its merchant vessels plying the Corinthian Gulf and Ionian Sea might make use of the harbours along the Aitolo - Akarnanian coast. The impressive sculptures and clay objects discovered on the site of the temple have been removed to the National Archaeological Museum in Athens, where they are displayed beside other finds from all over Greece (with the exception of Attica). A stoa, 170m. long, still survives at Thermos. The local *Museum* contains a collection of pottery dated from the Mycenean, the archaic and Hellenistic periods. There are also painted clay metopes, inscriptions and architectural fragments. Statue bases found here have been removed to the *Museum at Agrinion* (Stoa Papastratos). Other exhibits in the latter include finds from all over Aitolo - Akarnania, among which are a large collection of prehistoric arrow - heads, sculptures (mainly funerary reliefs and inscribed stelai from Astakos), vases, idols, architectural fragments, inscriptions and bronze objects of the minor arts.

STRATOS

The most important ancient site near Agrinion is *Stratos*. The city spread across four low hills enclosed within a vast enceinte of fortifications. There are ruins of an ancient *theatre* and a notable 4th century B.C. Doric *temple of Zeus*.

EPIROS

From an archaeological point-of-view, the most impressive sites are those of *Arta, Nikopolis*, the *Oracle of the Dead* at *Thesprotian Ephyra* and *Dodona*. There are also traces of life in the Palaeolithic age: particularly near Ioannina. During successive periods of antiquity and the Middle Ages the history of Epiros was an eventful one. The War of Independence brought out all the qualities of the inhabitants, whose noble exploits set an example to all Greeks.

The landscape of Epiros —high mountains, deep valleys, dense forests, abundant streams— is unique, its beauty unlikely ever to be forgotten by the visitor. Ancient ruins lie scattered beside humble post - Byzantine chapels, Byzantine monasteries and other monuments are perched on seemingly inaccessible sites. The impact made on the traveller is tremendous. In *Ioannina* and *Arta* the discerning traveller will be fascinated by the old houses of the *archons*, both as regards their exterior architecture and interior disposition. Of particular interest too are the lavish wood-carved iconostases of Epirot churches.

ARTA

A tour of the town may well begin at the beautiful 17th century *bridge* which spans the Arachthos and inspired an anonymous poet to compose an immortal folksong. The Mediaeval *castle* is particularly interesting. Arta was the capital of Pyrrhos, king of Epiros, in antiquity, of the Despots of Epiros in the Middle Ages. Beneath the modern town lies *Ambrakia,* the ancient colony of Corinth.

The 13th century *Church of the Parigoritissa,* a most careful study of which has been made by Professor A. Orlandos, is unique both in its dimensions and architectural style. An *Archaeological Collection* housed in the Refectory of the Monastery includes mosaics, funerary stelai, inscribed bases, and the remarkable late Archaic capital found in the town, as well as a few funerary offerings from graves dating to various periods, and clay figurines from the excavation of the *Cave of the Nymphs* at Koudounotrypa.

The 13th and 14th (respectively) century *Churches of St. Theodora* and *St. Basil* merit the closest attention. The *Monastery of Kato Panayia,* situated in an idyllic setting, is also a 13th century foundation. 4 kms. north of the town, in another lovely setting, is the *Monastery of Vlachernai,* where the visitor may view the tomb of the Despot Michael II Angelos.

An exploration of the Tzoumerka region, with its picturesque and historical villages, is extremely worthwhile.

NIKOPOLIS

At *Preveza,* the Venetian *castle,* which commands a superb view, as well as various churches and old mansions are worth visiting.

The magnificent ruins of Nikopolis, covering the Roman and Early Christian periods, lie 7 kms. north-east of Preveza. The city was founded by Augustus to commemorate his victory (when still Octavian) over Antony's fleet at the battle of Actium (31 B.C.). It was consequently named Nikopolis, the 'city of victory'. The city enjoyed great prosperity and, according to the evidence of ancient writers, the population numbered 300,000 in A.D. 293, when it was the capital of Epiros. St. Paul the Apostle preached the Christian faith here. In the 11th century the city was destroyed by the Bulgars, and decline set in. Ruined houses, churches, a *gymnasium,* a *theatre* with twenty five rows of seats in the koilon, an *agora,* a *stadium,* and an impressive *aqueduct* which carried water from the river Louros to the city, are scattered all over the vast site. The Roman *odeum,* in which performances are now held, has been restored. Two necropoles extend beyond the city walls. In the Early Christian period Nikopolis was a city of considerable importance. Four large *basilicas* with beautiful mosaic floors have been identified. The most splendid one decorates the floor of the *Basilica of Dumetius* (5th century A.D.). Birds, flowers, animals, fish, hunters, fishermen, etc., are depicted in a wonderfully harmonious composition which consists of one hundred and fifty representations.

The *Museum* of Nikopolis contains sculptures, funerary monuments, statues, sarcophagi, architectural members and inscriptions, glassware from graves, various minor objects, and a collection of lamps and local coins.

Near Kamarina, is the *Monastery of Zalongo,* a sacred pilgrimage for Greeks because of its associations with the tragic dance performed by the women of Souli, who fell one by one off a steep cliff rather than risk capture by the Turks.

THE ORACLE OF THE DEAD

The oracular seat is situated at Ephyra in Thesprotia. The *Acheron,* whose source lies in the mountains of Suli and waters the whole area, winding in endless sinuo-

Ioannina.
Mosque of the Kastro.

sities, flows past. Very often the stream disappears into profound gullies, only to emerge into the open a little farther on. The wild and awe - inspiring setting led the ancient Greeks to believe the river to be that of Hades, the entrance into which was the *Acherousian Lake*. The excavations carried out by the Greek Archaeological Service on the summit of a hill beside the Church of Ayios Ioannis have resulted in the identification of an entire building with passages, numerous chambers and underground cells, in which the oracular pronouncements are believed to have been made. Apparitions of the souls of the dead (whose emergence was aided by a mechanical device composed of chains found in the course of the excavations) answered the questions put by consultants. The oracle was already established in Homeric times. Hither came Odysseus to seek advice from the soul of Teiresias the seer and, at a later date, an emissary of Periander, Tyrant of Corinth, to consult Melissa, the king's wife who had died very young. The edifices with large doors are of the Hellenistic period. Consequently, it is impossible for us to form a reconstruction of the architectural disposition of the oracle in the earliest times. The site is extremely impressive and unlikely to be easily forgotten by the visitor.

IOANNINA

The town is situated at a distance of 459 kms north - west of Athens on the banks of a lake of the same name at an altitude of 470 m. Mountains crowd round on all sides. The exact date of the town's foundations is uncertain. It may have been in 527-528 A.D. during the reign of the Emperor Justinian. Other sources suggest the 8th century. What is certain is that by the 10th century the town's prosperity was assured. It was evidently named after a monastery of Ayios Ioannis Prodromos (St. John the Baptist). From 1738 onwards in the time of Ali Pasha (who had temporarily succeeded in establishing his independence of the Sultan), Ioannina reached the peak of prosperity and consuls of the three Great Powers of the period, England, France and Russia, were accredited to Ali's court. The town became a haven of civilization, with good schools where Greek, French and Latin were taught. In Ali's army, famed for its martial prowess, many Greeks, including Karaiskakis, acquired a military training which was to serve them well later in the bloody battles of the War of Independence. The fact that Ali Pasha maintained relations with European countries enabled the Greek population to make contacts with France, Italy and, in particular, Venice. The minor arts of the goldsmith, woodcarver and weaver flourished. The city had a Turkish *citadel*, on the highest tower of which the martyr George was killed by the Turks. Outside the castle, near the mosque, was Ali Pasha's palace. To the left of the entrance to the *Fetiye Mosque* were the tombs of Ali's family.

The Cathedral is particularly interesting. It possesses a superb woodcarved iconostasis and a side chapel with the tomb of the martyred George. The old mansion of the Misios family is worth visiting. On the green and wooded islet on the lake, reached by motor boat, is the historic *Monastery of Ayios Panteleimon*, where Ali Pasha was assassinated. Two of the monastic cells have been converted into a museum of the pre - War of Independence period which contains textiles, lithographs manuscripts and photographs.

Museum of Ioannina

The Museum, situated in the Ano Plateia (Upper Square) near the Municipal Gardens, houses finds from the whole area of Epiros. Exhibits, displayed in the five rooms and the corridor of the Museum, include a characteristic collection of Palaeolithic bone and stone tools (from the Caves of Asprochaliko and Kastritsa), Bronze Age pottery, weapons and jewellery. There is also a fine collection of bronze implements and minor objects and a number of bronze figurines chiefly from the Sanctuary at Dodona. The bronze tablets inscribed with the queries of pilgrims to the Oracle are of particular interest. A restored part of the door of the Bouleuterion of Dodona is also on display. The finds from the latest excavations in Epiros (at Monodendri, Vitsa, Zagorion, the Oracle of the Dead and other sites) presented here, are dated from the Geometric to the Hellenistic

Ioannina.
Stalactites and stalagmites from the Cave of Perama.

and Roman times. Classical and Hellenistic pottery and various sculptures are exhibited in the second room, which also contains jewellery, inscriptions, a finely arrayed collection of coins, Byzantine and Post-Byzantine architectural sculpture, a few Post-Byzantine icons, and specimens of metalwork and silverware.

The third and fifth room house a gallery of 19th and 20th century works of Greek painters and sculptors. The Collection has been donated by the Society of 'The Friends of Ioannina'.

The *Municipal Museum,* within the precinct of Aslan Pasha in the Kastro, possesses collections of embroideries, textiles, silverware, woodcarvings and weapons.

The Philosophical School of Ioannina has founded a *Museum of Popular Arts* and an *Archive* in the University grounds. Exhibits include textliles, embroideries, ceramics, woodcarvings, silverware, metalwork, musical instruments, religious objects, etc.

The visitor with time on his hands and a sense of natural curiosity would greatly enjoy a visit to the *Cave of Ioannina* (at *Perama,* near the town), where nature has created an endless variety of patterns with stalactites and stalagmites of incomparable beauty.

DODONA

The site is situated 22 kms south of Ioannina. The setting, over which towers the lofty range of Tomaron, is one of great wildness.

The origins of the Dodonian cult are lost in the mists of prehistory. The excavations carried out by K. Karapanos in 1874 (before the liberation of Epiros from the Turks) brought to light stone axes, blades of flint-stone, vases decorated with crude reliefs —all of which suggest that the cult was fully established as far back as the Early Helladic Age (if not earlier). During the Middle Helladic Age, Dodona seems to have come under two influences: one from the north, related to the worship of Zeus in association with the oak tree, the other from the south related with the cult of Ge (Earth). At the beginning of the Middle Helladic Age the Helloi (or Selloi), a branch of the Thesprotians, who were Hellenes and had settled in Epiros, was established at Dodona. Here, as elsewhere throughout Epiros and the Pindos country, there are also Mycenaean remains. The inhabitants of the Mycenaean period in Epiros were for the most part migratory cattle-breeders. Every autumn they led their herds to more temperate coastal areas, to the plain of Epiros, to Thessaly, the Spercheios valley and Aitolo-Akarnania. They thus came into contact with other people with whom they exchanged goods and ideas and were subject to new artistic influences. At about the time of the Trojan War migrations of peoples spread across the country, in Epiros, as well as in Eastern and Central Greece. *The Molossians,* a Hellenic race, settled in Epiros and the *Thesprotians* descended into Thessaly. Some Thesprotians, however, remained at Dodona.

Among these new Hellenic peoples were the Helli who dwelt in the plain around Ioannina and produced handmade pottery decorated with Geometric patterns, specimens of which have also been found on the plateau of Korytsa, in Aitolia and the Kastoria basin. From the 7th to the end of the 5th century B.C. Dodona was ruled by the Thesprotians. The history of the earlier period (12th century to 730 - 700 B.C.) is very obscure and full of blanks as regards the whole of Epiros, where systematical archaeological research has yet to be undertaken. During that period there was no contact with Central and Southern Greece. Piracy was rife, and cattle-breeders did not risk venturing far afield. Moreover, no merchants from Southern Greece visited the Epirot coast. The inhabitants, however, maintained contact with the north, whence they obtained raw materials. Objects of northern provenance have been found, not only in the Sanctuary of Dodona, but also in the heart of the Pindos country. The same circumstances apply to the period of the Turkish occupation, when it was found easier to maintain contacts with the Balkan countries than with Central Greece.

Some of the tripods, figurines, jewellery and bronze weapons discovered at Dodona have been dated to the late 8th century B.C. The implication is clear: security had now been restored in Greece. The first colonists from Elis settled along the Epirot coast during the period 730 - 700 B.C. After them came settlers from Corinth in the 7th century B.C. The number of votive offerings in the sanctuary increased considerably. But no change, as regards either the general, political or cultural history of Epiros up to the late 5th century B.C., can be deduced from the discoveries made at Dodona. As formerly, the inhabitants dwelt in open villages. While the men looked after the herds, the women tilled the soil, made clothes and pottery, built the huts and of course prepared the meals (this way of life has been preserved intact by the Sarakatsans of the Pindos mountains). Hereditary kings, in whose hands were concentrated all the reins of power — military, political and religious — ruled over the cities, in spite of the continued predominance of the Molossians in the sanctuary. Certain changes did, however, take place during the reign of the pro-Athenian King Tharypas (423/2-385 B.C.). Walled cities with a geometric town-planning, Kassope, Ammotopos, etc., were founded and impressive public buildings raised. Administration was modernised and the archons and the senate were elected annually. The Attic alphabet and script were introduced and an expansionist policy affecting the west coast, from which many of the earlier inhabitants were driven out, was adopted. On Molossian initiative, the first political confederacy, the Molossian State (early 4th century - 330/325 B.C.), in which originally four Epirot races (at a later date fifteen) participated, was formed. The sanctuary of Dodona now came under Molossian domination. An edifice, the Sacred House, destined solely for the worship of Zeus, was raised for the first time. Within the precinct, the sacred oak tree, surrounded by tripods had formerly been the centre of worship. Now the god received the praises of the faithful in his own temple, his terrestrial abode. Quarters for priests, officials and representatives of the Molossian State were soon established. In the meantime, Olympias, who was a Molossian, married Philip II of Macedon. After the latter's assassination, Dodona was not forgotten either by his widow or his son, Alexander the Great, and it was decided that the sanctuary, together with five others of panhelenic status, should be financed from Macedonian funds. A peribolos of ashlar masonry then replaced the tripods surmounted by cauldrons in front of the first temple of Zeus.

After 232 B.C., when a democratic form of government was established, a Bouleuterion (senate house) for assemblies of representatives of the Epirot alliance was built. During the reign of Pyrrhos (297 - 272 B.C.) Dodona was considerably embellished, the sanctuary underwent architectural restoration, the temple of Zeus was refashioned, a monumental theatre was built and the entire precinct was surrounded by stoas, including a temple of Heracles.

The State of the Epirots also established its headquarters at Dodona after 232 B.C. In 219 B.C. the Aitolians, under the leadership of Dorimachos, invaded Epiros and plundered the sanctuary. The stoas were burnt, many votive offerings destroyed and the Sacred House (that is to say, the temple and the holy oak tree), scene of the

birth of many Epirot agreements and decrees, demolished. It was rebuilt immediately afterwards —this time with the spoils of the war which the Epirots and Macedonians waged against the Aitolians.

The peak period in the sanctuary's history is 232 - 168 B.C. The Sacred House
became a monumental edifice. The *Bouleuterion* and the temples of *Dione, Themis,
Heracles* and *Aphrodite* were rebuilt. The *theatre*, to which a stone proskenion
with 17 Ionic half - columns was added, was repaired. A large *stadion* built of stone,
in which were held spectacular celebrations of the *Naia* in honour of Zeus, was erected in front of the tower - like buttresses of the theatre. The sanctuary was once
more filled with votive offerings. After 170 B.C., when the Roman armies had become an important factor in the Greek scene, the Epirot breeds began to split up;
some espoused the Roman cause. After the defeat of Perseus, the Macedonian
king, at the battle of Pydna (168 B.C.), the Romans turned their attention to the
Epirots which were compelled to come to terms with the conquerors. But the Romans
were not content with mere submission. By order of Aemilius Paulus, the victorious
Roman general, 70 Epirot towns and villages were razed to the ground and 150,000
young men and women carried off into captivity. Evidence obtained from the excavations suggests that it must have been at about this time that the sanctuary was
burnt. Some edifices (the theatre and Bouleuterion and probably some temples)
had, however, been roughly repaired by 148 B.C. The Romans also permitted the
minting of bronze coins to cover the needs of the area. In 86 B.C. the sanctuary
was once more plundered — this time by the Thracians of Mithridates.

By the end of the 1st century B.C. the sanctuary was almost deserted, and the
once large cities of Epiros were reduced to decaying villages. After the battle of
Actium (31 B.C.) Augustus obliged the inhabitants to emigrate to the new city of
Nikopolis which he had founded on the Ambracian Gulf. The Emperor however
showed some interest in the sanctuary itself, and the theatre was transformed into
an arena for Roman circus-games. In the 2nd century A.D. Pausanias refers to the
sanctuary of Zeus and the oak tree «sacred to the god». In A.D. 132 Dodona was
visited by Hadrian and undoubtedly profited from the Emperor's public-spirited
munificence. Until the mid-3rd century B.C. the Naia continued to be celebrated
in honour of Zeus. In A.D. 362 the oracle was still functioning and was consulted
by Julian the Apostate before embarking on his campaign against the Persians.
At the end of the 4th century Dodona, like all the other sanctuaries in Greece,
was closed by an edict issued by the Emperor Theodosius the Great.

In the very late 4th century Dodona became the seat of a Christian diocese
and a large *three - naved basilica* was built out of ancient materials lying about the
site. A *second basilica* was erected soon after. At the time of the great barbarian
invasions Dodona was abandoned, probably in 562. Some Vandal coins of the 5th
and 6th centuries were found in the course of the excavations. Earthquakes, heavy
rainfalls and the silt carried down by torrents finally combined to cover up the
ruins of the sanctuary.

Excavations carried out by the Greek Archaeological Service are still under way.

The *Naia* were celebrated every four years in honour of Zeus Naios. It is not
known when the festival was founded, certainly not before the 3rd century B.C.
On the evidence of the *Odyssey*, the oracles were originally delivered by the rustling
of the wind through the leaves of the sacred oak tree. Another form of consultation was by means of interpreting the flight and cooing of doves that nested in
the foliage of the sacred oak. At a later period, the god's wish was divined by the
interpretation of the echo produced by the wind whistling in the cauldrons that

crowned the tripods around the tree. Still later, the oracles were interpreted by the sound produced by a bronze vessel presented to the sanctuary by the Corcyreans. In the earliest times questions were put by word of mouth. In about the 6th century B.C. they were inscribed on the surface of a metal leaf with a jagged instrument. The answers were delivered orally; sometimes, but more seldom, they were inscribed on the reverse of the metal leaf on which the question had been scratched on the obverse. Some of these oracular inscriptions survive. The questions vary from purely personal and family problems to queries made by cities or groups of people. Some specimens are preserved in the first hall (left) of the museum at Ioannina, others in the Karapanos hall at the National Archaeological Museum, Athens.

The following is a selection of some of the questions :

Shall the winter be a heavy one ?

The city of the Chaonians asks whether the sanctuary of Athena Polias should be transferred to another locality.

Am I the father of the child to which my wife has given birth ?

Who has stolen my money ?

METSOVO

The mountain village of Metsovo, 58 kms east of Ioannina, is superbly situated at an altitude of 1030 m., among the fir forests of the Pindos. The village enjoyed its period of greatest prosperity during the Turkish occupation when the inhabitants offered hospitality to an exiled Turkish Grand Vizir. On being reinstated at Constantinople, the Vizir showed his gratitude to the people of Metsovo by granting them special privileges. At that time this large village was both a cultural center and a refuge for Christians who had been obliged to abandon their homes in the cities. Metsovo is not only renowned for its scenic beauty. It is even more famous for its handicrafts and house - furnishings —textiles, embroideries, woodcarvings— for which there is always a great demand. Specimens of Metsovo folklore art are to be found in the Tositsa house, a *Museum of Popular Art*, which contains furniture, embroideries, various valuable objects and ornaments from other old mansions dated to the period 1650 - 1850. The «Foundation» itself was financed by the bequest of Tositsa, the site of the museum being the family's residence of the donor. Metsovo is indeed the birthplace of several eminent public benefactors who have always cared for the well - being of their native village.

The *Church of Ayios Demetrios* and the little *Monastery of the Panayia* are noteworthy. From Metsovo the traveller can proceed by cable railway towards Karakoli where there are ski-fields (season : December - April).

In and around the *Gorge of the Vikos* are the famous *Zagorochoria*, 45 villages which acquired semi - autonomy during the Turkish occupation. Their economy was a flourishing one, and learning was encouraged. The Zagorochoria are the birthplace of many national benefactors.

THE IONIAN ISLANDS

. All seven islands are remarkable for their beautiful landscape, fertility and colourful atmosphere. Cephalonia is the largest; next in size is Corfu, most famous of all. Everything about the seven islands (Corfu, Paxoi, Leukas, Cephalonia, Ithaka, Zante and Kythera) is likely to attract the traveller. Many mediaeval castles are preserved and monasteries are dotted all over the countryside.

Life existed on these islands from the earliest times. In the Palaeolithic Age

Corfu, where remains of this period have been found, formed part of the mainland of Epiros. As a result of their geographical position, nearly all the islands achieved maritime prosperity; and they soon became great mercantile and cultural centers. Several memorable episodes in the *Odyssey* are associated with Corfu and Ithaka. In the opinion of the most cautious scholars, Corfu may well be the ancient Scheria, the kingdom of Alkinoos, whose daughter, Nausikaa, encountered the shipwrecked Odysseus on the shore and offered him the hospitality of her father's palace. Ithaka is the native country of Odysseus and Penelope. The islands experienced all the misfortunes that befell the motherland : foreign invasion, plunder and numerous other disasters. But they had the good fortune to escape Turkish occupation. After the Roman period, the islands formed part of the Byzantine Empire. They were then successively occupied by Venetians, Genoese, Russians and, during the Napoleonic Wars, by the French who, after 1814, ceded them to Britain. In 1864 they were united with the motherland.

Cephalonia, Corfu and, to a certain extent, Zante experienced a great intellectual upsurge in the latter part of their history. It was on Zacynthian soil that *Dionysios Solomos*, the poet and author of the national anthem (set to music by *N. Mantzaros* of Corfu), was born. The larger islands possess an old musical tradition. They have long established philharmonic orchestras (the one in Corfu was founded in 1840) and several choral ensembles. Innumerable wandering serenaders enliven the night with their melodious songs in various parts of the islands. *Kythera*, the so-called seventh island, removed in distance from the main group, tends to belong geographically to the Peloponnese, whose history it shared.

CORFU

From Palaeolithic times life has continued uninterruptedly on the island. The fact that no Mycenaean remains have so far been discovered tends to make the identification of the island with Homeric Scheria rather more difficult to accept. In antiquity and during the Roman period the island was called Corcyra. In mediaeval times it became Koryfo or Corfu, so-called because of the two castles that were built on the summits (Greek: koryfes) of two hills in the town.

The island was first inhabited by Illyrians, many of whom, however, settled elsewere so that when the Greeks colonized Corfu, the Illyrians formed only part of the population. The first Greeks to land on Corcyrean soil were *Eretrians*, the great seafarers of the early Hellenic world, in the second half of the 8th century B.C. The locality in which they settled is not known.

In 734 B.C. a group of Corinthians, under the leadership of Chersikrates, a member of the family of the Bacchiadai, founded a colony on the island, with a view to securing (and dominating) all maritime communications between Corinth and Sicily and Southern Italy. The Corinthians settled on the peninsula south of the modern town (between Anemomylos and Kanoni) which was known in mediaeval times as *Palaiopolis*. There were two harbours : Hyllaikos (on the lagoon of Chalkiopoulos) and Alkinoos near the modern Anemomylos. In 664 B.C. Corcyra threw off the Corinthian yoke, after a great naval battle mentioned by Thucydides. At the end of the 7th century B.C. Corinthian rule was reestablished under Periander. A period of great architectural activity was ushered in and distinguished Corinthian artists were employed. Temples and other large edifices were raised and prosperity continued until the 6th century B.C.

In 585 B.C. the Corcyreans recovered their independence, minted their own

Corfu.
The islet of Pontikonesi.

coins and strengthened their fleet. In 229 B.C. the Illyrians made a devastating raid on the island, after which it passed into Roman hands. In the 1st century B.C. A-grippa plundered the island, and the sufferings of the inhabitants were only miti-gated at a later date by the favours granted them by the Emperor Tiberius. *Kassope*, founded by King Pyrrhos in the north east part of the island, flourished under Ro-man rule. In the 2nd century A.D. large buildings, baths, heroes' tombs and stoas were built and a new currency was put into circulation.

The Christian faith was preached by SS. Jason and Sosipater, pupils of St. Paul, in memory of whom a basilica was dedicated in the 12th century on the Pa-laiopolis peninsula. The inhabitants suffered the persecutions undergone by the Christians throughout the Empire and the toll of casualties was great. Then came the terrible shock of the Gothic invasions. Many of the city's monuments were destroyed and the fortified position was transferred to the present-day *Palaion Phrourion* (the Old Fort). Henceforward the city was called Korypho or Koryphai.

After sharing the fate of the rest of Greece and undergoing successive periods of foreign occupation (except the Turkish), Corfu, together with the other Ionian Islands, was reunited to Greece in 1864.

Various historical epochs are represented in the modern town, with its two castles, mediaeval alleys, tall Venetian houses, Byzantine churches, the 16th century walls of the *Castle of San Marco* or *Neokastro*, to which additions were made by the French and British. The six-storeyed house in which Edward Lear stayed for a while is till preserved. It was in Corfu that Shakespeare set the scene of Prospero's Cell in *The Tempest*, and the beauty of the island greatly attracted the Empress Elizabeth of Austria. On the waterfront rise the tall proud mansions of the Corfiot aristocracy, of which the most imposing is the one in which Ioannis Capodistria, the first ruler of liberated Greece, was born. Beside it are the neo-classical edifices. The most beautiful of these is the *Palace*, built in Regency style by the British. Originally the Lord High Commissioner's residence, it was converted in 1864 into a palace of the Kings of Greece. It now houses the Municipal Library and a fine collection of Oriental works of art. The palace dominates the wide expanse of the *Spianada* (Esplanade) which is dotted with commemorative statues. There are several picturesque porticoed streets of which the finest is the *Liston*.

Below the ruined castle of San Salvatore was the tomb of Menekrates (from the Archaic necropolis of the 7th century B.C.). Ruins of a magnificent sanctuary of Hera and other ancient edifices have been discovered within the park of the Palace of Mon Repos. Kanoni, named after a French cannon which stood here, and Pondi-konisi (Mouse Island) inspired Boecklin among other artists, to paint «The Island of the Dead». A causeway, below the Kanoni restaurant, leads to the *Monastery of Vlachernai*. Near Mandouki is the *Monastery of the Platytera* which contains the tombs of Ioannis Capodistria and Photis Tzavellas, a hero of the War of In-dependence, a collection of various relics and icons painted by the post - Byzantine artists, Poulakis, Tzanes and Kandounis. In 1891 the *Achilleion* was built in the Florentine Renaissance style on the initiative of the Empress Elizabeth on the slopes of Mt. Ayioi Deka. All the rooms are preserved in the state in which the Kaiser Wilhelm II, who purchased the palace and subsequently spent his holidays there, left them. Achilles, being his favourite hero, the Kaiser commissioned the interior walls to be frescoed with the exploits of the leader of the Myrmidons and had sta-tues of him raised in the park, whence there is a panoramic view of the island.

The temple of Artemis, to which the large west pediment now in the Archaeo-logical Museum belongs, is situated near the lagoon of Chalkiopoulos. The Cathedral possesses a large collection of 15th century icons. The relics of St. Spyridon, the miraculous patron saint of the island, in whose honour litanies and impressive ceremonies are held four times a year, are kept in the *Church of St. Spyridon*, the dome of which is frescoed by the well-known painter Panayotis Doxaras (late 17th century). The Venetian castles in the town are worth visiting. One was originally Byzantine, probably 6th century. In the 16th century the Venetians enlarged it; at the same time they repaired the older castle, to which the French and British made further additions. The *town hall*, founded between 1663 and 1690, later served as a club for the Venetian aristocracy. The building itself and its decoration is of exceptional interest. The island is full of beauty spots : *Peleka*, with its spectacular sunsets, Glyphada, Hermones, with its lovely wood-fringed beach, Palaiokastritsa, where the family of the Angeli, Despots of Epiros, built a castle, the ruins of which still survive on the summit of a steep mountain.

Archaeological Museum of Corfu

The museum, situated at Garitsa, consists of a ground floor and one storey with four halls. It possesses a fine collection of works, some of which are indeed outstanding masterpieces, displayed with great care, expert knowledge and good taste. Chief among these is the magnificent Archaic funerary monument, known as the *Lion of Menekrates*. In another hall are displayed the sculptures of the west pediment of the Temple of Artemis, in which the Gorgon is depicted in the center, flanked by her offspring, Chrysaor (left) and Pegasos (right) and other figures. The next hall contains the remarkable objects discovered in the excavations at Mon Repos. Other exhibits include fine inscriptions, architectural fragments of the Archaic period, Protocorinthian and Corinthian pottery, idols, bronzes and many other objects. There are also beautiful sculptured heads and coins. The objects displayed in the museum occupy a very special place in the history of Archaic art in so far as that they constitute oustanding examples of the great Corinthian school of sculpture, none of which survive at Corinth, the city itself having been totally destroyed at the time of the Roman conquest.

Apart from the Archaeological Museum, Corfu possesses an important *Collection of Chinese and Japanese works of art* (donated by Gregorios Manos, see p. 180) which includes some 8,000 beautifully and lavishly wrought Chinese objects covering an enormously wide range — from the Neolithic period to the 19th century. In view of the provenance of the exhibits, this museum is one of exceptional importance in Greece. Other exhibits consist of works of the minor arts, paintings, theatrical masks, weapons, porcelain and stone, bronze and clay objects.

Museum of Solomos

The museum is situated at the *Mouraghio*. The poet's house, destroyed in the course of an Italian air raid in 1940, was rebuilt in 1962 - 65. The museum contains relics and souvenirs of the poet assembled by the Society of Corfiot Studies, to which the museum belongs.

The Byzantine Collection

The collection is housed in the Palace. It includes 11th and 13th century frescoes from a local chapel, superb Byzantine and post-Byzantine icons and some carvings and a mosaic floor from the Palaiopolis basilica. The *Ecclesiastical Museum*, in the Monastery of the Pantokrator possesses a noteworthy collection of icons from the Cathedral. In the *Historical Museum*, housed in a building dated to 1824 (formerly the Nomarchy's offices), are displayed historical relics, 17th-19th century paintings and objects of the popular arts. The private *collection of R. Evelpides* consists of ancient pottery, idols and coins, all of which were found in the course of excavations carried out within the property of the Evelpides family.

PAXOI

The island has a beautiful landscape, as yet unspoiled by modern man. There is only one village: the port at which vessels anchor.

LEUKAS

The history of Leukas is similar to that of the other Ionian Islands. Crowned by a high mountain (1120 m.), the island is not without gentle plains and enchanting shores. The whole place seems to bask in the sunshine of its natural beauty. Separated from Aitolo-Akarnania by a narrow isthmus (100 m), the island served as a refuge for *klephts* and *armatoloi* (bands of patriots) driven out of Epiros and other parts of Western Greece during the War of Independence. The German archaeologist Doerpfeld undertook excavations at *Nydri* (the finds are housed in a small local museum) which he believed to be the site of Homeric Ithaka.

The tourist trade has developed rapidly, and annual literary and artistic events include lectures, recitations, popular dances, exhibitions of handicrafts, etc. There are Venetian churches and large old mansions. The 13th century *Castle* (Santa Maura) is situated at the end of a lovely beach, and the bay of Vlycho, near Nydri, is of exceptional beauty.

In antiquity there was a temple of Apollo on the site of the present lighthouse, near the vertical rocks of Cape Leukatas. This is presuned to be the site of the *Leucates Leap* (69 m. above the sea) from which alleged criminals were obliged to cast themselves into the watery deep below. If they survived they were deemed clear of the charges brought against them. The whole procedure was a kind of substitute for a legal trial. From here too unhappy lovers would leap to their death, as indeed did Sappho, the great lyric poetess of antiquity driven desperate by her unfortunate love for Phaon. In the *Church of Ayios Demetrios* there are icons by Doxaras (18th century).

CEPHALONIA

The scenic beauty of the island is unforgettable. There are lofty mountains, the highest, Mt. Ainos, being about 1600 m. Dense forests and, on the whole, lush vegetation cover the hillsides. The inhabitants are renowned for their ingenuity and humour, those of Lixouri and the area around it for their cultural accomplishments.

According to a local tradition, Kephalos, who gave his name to the island, was its first king. Homer says Cephalonia formed part of the dominion of Odysseus. In antiquity there were four large cities: *Krane* (opposite Argostoli),

Leukas.
Local costumes.

Pale (2 kms distant from Lixouri), *Same* (the ancient capital situated near the modern little town of the same name), where there are ancient ruins, and *Pronnaioi* (near the village of Markopoulo in the south-east). Thorough excavations have not yet been carried out. Consequently there are gaps in the island's history. The fact that the island was inhabited during the Mycenaean period has been verified by the discovery of a Mycenaean necropolis, where over eighty tombs were excavated, near *Mazarakata*, of another one at *Kokkolata* just outside Argostoli and of remains of settlements at *Metaxata* and *Kondoyenata* in the Lixouri area. Necropoles of a later date and houses of the Roman period with fine mosaic floors, etc., have also been discovered. Cephalonia experienced the same fate and was occupied by the same conquerors as the other islands. In 1823 Lord Byron landed here and stayed for a while at Metaxata. Many distinguished personalities in the world of art and literature of the post-liberation period were of Cephalonian origin. The maritime village of *Assos* is a paradise of beauty — the views unforgettable. The *Livatho* region is considered to be the area from which the best sailors come. It is also the birthplace of several great national benefactors. In the church at *Kallighata* there is a superb iconostasis, and in the *Monastery of Ayios Andreas* at *Peratata* an ancient relic: the left foot of St. Andrew. Various collections of icons, wall paintings, woodcarvings, vestments and ecclesiastical embroideries of the post-Byzantine period from various churches destroyed in the earthquake of 1953 have been assembled in the monastery. The icons by Poulakis on the woodcarved iconostasis constitute one of the strangest works in post-Byzantine art because of the variety of foreign influence that they reveal. It is worth visiting *Ayios Georgios*, site of the old capital of the island, abandoned in 1757. There are mediaeval walls, underground passages — and, above all, beautiful views. On the shore of Argostoli are the remarkable *katavothres* (deep subterranean channels). At Mazarakata, a little above the ancient necropolis, is the 16th century *Monastery of Ayios Gerassimos*, patron saint of Cephalonia. Throughout the island there are beautiful beaches, one of which is Plati Yalo, near Lixouri.

Museums of Cephalonia

The *Archaeological museum* of Argostoli houses a rich collection of Mycenaean pottery, weapons and small objects discovered in the course of the local excavations. There are also Geometric and Archaic vases and idols and Hellenistic sculptures. A bronze head is very impressive.

The *Historical and Archaeological museum* is on the ground floor of the Koryalenios Public Library, has 17th-19th century icons, Venetian carvings, ecclesiastical vestments, textiles, woodcarvings, metal objects, lithographs, maps and photographs.

The Church of the Evangelistria (on the Castle of Ayios Georgios) and the Episcopal Collection of Cephalonia (housed in the bishop's palace) also possess post-Byzantine icons and vestments. Finally, in the Archaeological Collection at *Lixouri* (housed in the 19th century building of the Iakovateios Library) there are Classical and Hellenistic pottery and numerous fine icons.

ITHAKA

Home of the wily Odysseus, famous for its mythological traditions, the island suffered the same fate as the other Ionian Islands. In 1797 the French raised it to the rank of a capital with administrative control over Leukas, Cephalonia, Preveza and Vonitsa. In 1864 it was united with Greece. The fact that the island has countless bays and anchorages and that the landscape is remarkably similar to the one described by Homer in the *Odyssey* seems to confirm the traditional account of it as the capital of Odysseus' maritime kingdom. *Vathy*, in the middle of the island, would be the ancient Phorkys, to which the Phaeacians brought Odysseus, the *Rock of Koraka* and *Marathia* the pigsties of Eumaios, the spring of *Pera Pighadi* that of Arethusa, *Porto Andreas* (in the southern part of the island), the spot where Telemachos landed at the end of his journey from Pylos. On *Mt. Aëtos,* rising above the isthmus, there is a 7th century B.C. Archaic acropolis, locally known as the *Castle of Odysseus*. The cave of *Marmarospilia*, which has stalactites and could be identified with the Cave of the Nymphs of the *Odyssey*, is situated above the Gulf of Vathy, whence it commands a magnificent view of the island. Close by Perachorio is the site of a 16th century town. *Stavros* is believed to have beeen the domain of Laërtes.

Archaeological Museum of Ithaka

In the museum at Vathy are displayed Protocorinthian and Corinthian pottery and bronze objects from the excavations of *Mt. Aëtos.* At *Stavros* there are prehistoric remains. Excavations undertaken by the British School of Archaeology have brought to light Early Helladic and Mycenaean objects and beautiful bronze tripods.

ZANTE (ZAKYNTHOS)

The Venetians called the island «fioro di Levante»». Numerous houses and churches, remarkable both for their beauty and contents, were destroyed in the disastrous earthquake of 1953. Zante's history is similar to that of the other Ionian Islands. Its musical and cultural tradition has been maintained and, when the town was rebuilt after the 1953 earthquake, an attempt was made to preserve the old style of architecture. Both in antiquity and in mediaeval times the great maritime powers sought to occupy the island. The Venetian occupation lasted from 1485 to 1797. After the Italians came the French, the Russians and, in 1810, the British. Throughout the Turkish occupation the island was a refuge for persecuted Greeks from the rest of the country. Greek history proudly records the struggles waged by Zakynthian patriots for the reunion of the Ionian Islands with the motherland. From the historic *hill of Strani*, Dionysios Solomos, the national poet, gazing at the opposite coast of oppressed Greece, was inspired to write his «Hymn to Liberty». During the 18th and 19th centuries Zante experienced a tremendous cultural upsurge. Apart from Solomos, Andreas Kalvos, A. Matesis and Ugo Foscolo were born here.

The modern town is spread out along the east coast of the island below a hill (108 m. high) crowned by a mediaeval castle. The whole countryside is a limitless garden. The relics of St. Dionysios, patron saint of the island, are preserved in the Cathedral.

Byzantine Museum of Zante

The museum was rebuilt after the 1953 earthquake in the neo-classical style. It possesses many frescoes from churches destroyed in the earthquake, including one very important one of the 12th century. The entirely frescoed walls of a complete church are very impressive. There are many post-Byzantine icons and noteworthy works of the Heptanesian School which included artists such as M. Damaskinos N. Kallerghis, Victor, Tzanes, N. Doxaras, E. Koutouzis and N. Kandounis. Other exhibits include fine woodcarvings from the iconostases of the Pantokrator and Ayios Demetrios at Kolla, Hellenistic and Byzantine woodcarvings and escutcheons of the aristocratic Zacynthian families.

The *Solomos Museum and Mausoleum* possesses manuscripts of Dionysios Solomos, souvenirs of notable 19th century personalities, regional costumes and weapons.

KYTHERA

Although Kythera is one of the seven Ionian Islands, geographically and administratively it forms part of the Peloponnese. It is a beautiful island with wild rock-fringed beaches and deep gulfs. The villages were built in the time of the British occupation. The climate is that of the Southern Peloponnese. According to local mythological tradition, Aphrodite was born here. In some of the valleys there are remains of ancient walls. *Kastri* is the first Minoan settlement, so far discovered, which post-dates the destruction of Knossos (c. 1450 B.C.). In mediaeval times, before the Venetians occupied the island, Kythera was a lair for rapacious pirates.

Some Venetian towers, the cave of Mylopotamos and *countless churches* with exceptionally interesting frescoes are noteworthy.

Museum of Kythera

The museum, housed in a municipal building, possesses a rich collection of important finds from the recent excavations at Kastri, where a Minoan settlement was discovered, including a large number of clay and steatite vases of the Middle Minoan period, Mycenaean pottery and a 4th century B.C. head which belonged to a statue.

MACEDONIA AND THRACE

The history of Macedonia and Thrace is a more turbulent one than that of any other part of Greece. From ancient to modern times, the northern provinces, including Epiros, have undergone an endless series of invasions. The permanent state of alert in which the inhabitants were compelled to dwell delayed the process of evolution which is such a striking feature of the history of the rest of the country, including the Aegean islands. It should, however, be noted that archaeological research has provided evidence of the fact that Macedonia and Thrace were actually inhabited in the Neolithic period. In antiquity the fertile plains and wealth of raw materials were a never-ending source of attraction for Southern Greek colonizers, ever anxious to exploit the supplies of timber, pitch (an indispensable material in the construction of ancient vessels) and the gold and silver mines of Mt. Pangaion. Before Athens began to evince any interest in Macedonia, Chalcis, followed by Corinth and Thasos, had cast envious eyes on the Macedonian coasts along which they proceeded to establish important colonies. Thus large commercial centers, in which the arts also flourished, gradually grew up in Macedonia and later in Thrace. The development of the whole of this area was completed during the reign of Philip II of Macedon, ruler of a vast state, and that of his son and successor, Alexander the Great. Thus during the reigns of father and son, almost the whole country, with the exception of Sparta, formed a kind of *Greek Commonwealth*; as such it took part, at least symbolically, in Alexander's victorious campaigns in Asia.

Eventually, of course, Northern Greece became a Roman dominion and later formed part of the Byzantine Empire. After «God - Guarded» Constantinople, Thessaloniki was the most important city in the empire. Like the rest of Greece, which had already been conquered by the Crusaders in 1204, Macedonia and Thrace came under Turkish rule after the fall of Constantinople in 1453. Traces of the important role played by this part of the country in mediaeval times still survive at *Veroia, Kastoria, Didymoteichon* and *Thessaloniki*. In the 17th century learning flourished in Macedonia, and schools were founded. At the same time, many Greeks, with their acute sense of commerce, began to travel abroad, especially to Vienna, where they gained both knowledge and affluence. Their profits were subsequently expended in the superb interior decoration (frescoes and woodcarvings) of the large mansions at *Kozani, Veroia, Siatista, Kastoria* and other towns. Byzantine grandeur was preserved —as it is to this day— in the monastic communities of Mt. Athos.

The landscape of Macedonia is full of interest, and the beautiful *valley of the Nestos* is as yet hardly known to most travellers. Important sites, outstanding for their ancient and mediaeval ruins and monuments of later periods, include Thessaloniki, Pella, Philippi, Stageira, Vergina, Kavala, Kastoria,, Komotini, Nea Nikomedia, Amphipolis, Olynthos, Abdera, Potidaia, Leukadia, Siatista, Serres, Sidirokastro, Mt. Athos and the two offshore islands of Thasos and Samothrace which are geographically associated with Macedonia.

Archaeological research has not as yet made considerable progress, for the simple reason that both Macedonia and Thrace were not united with Greece until 1912.

THESSALONIKI

The Thessaloniki region was inhabited from at least the beginning of the 3rd millenium B.C., that is to say, during the Neolithic period. Archaeological excavations undertaken near the city have brought to light dwellings situated along the length of a stream that flows from the village of *Panorama* to the sea. The most important settlement is situated on a trapezoidal-shaped hill in the suburb of *Ano Toumba*; another extends across the right bank of the same stream, in the direction of Panorama, east of Anatolia College. The finds are less numerous than those of the former settlement, but they are of an earlier date.

At the beginning of the historical era, the settlements along the coast increased in number. During the Classical period *Therme* (from which the Thermaic Gulf derives its name) was the most important maritime city. Its position has not been precisely located. Sherds and other objects dated to a period earlier than the 5th century B.C. nevertheless indicate that a stettlement on the site of what was later to become Thessaloniki formed part of Therme. The city of Thessaloniki itself was founded in 314 B.C. by Kassandros, the Macedonian king, who named it after his wife, daughter of Philip II of Macedon and half-sister of Alexander the Great. Kassandros also founded Kassandreia, named after himself, on the site of ancient Potidaia in the Chalcidice.

In order to increase the population of Thessaloniki, Kassandros facilitated (or compelled) the inhabitants of the surrounding area to settle in the new city. After the defeat of Perseus by the Roman armies in the battle of Pydna in 168 B.C., Thessaloniki became the capital of one of the four administrative units into which the conquerors divided Macedonia. From 146 B.C. onwards the city developed rapidly, and when *Cicero* was banished to it in 58 B.C., Thessaloniki was already the pivot of the Roman *provinciae Macedoniae*. Its importance had acquired even greater proportions by the time it was visited by St. Paul in 49-52 B.C. Preaching the new faith, the Apostle founded a Christian community to whose members he subsequently addressed from Corinth the two great Letters to the Thessalonicians which contain the basic tenets of Christian doctrine. In about A.D. 300 Galerius, the Roman Emperor, made it his capital and commissioned the building of monumental edifices. In 303, in the course of the persecutions of Christians instigated by Galerius and Diocletian, the co-emperor Demetrios, subsequently patron saint of the city, suffered a martyr's death.

An artificial harbour was built by Constantine the Great, and Theodosios the Great, who often took up his residence in Thessaloniki, fortified the city with strong walls. But Theodosios also ordered the massacre of thousands of Thessalonicians as a retaliatory measure inspired by a revolt against officers of Gothic origin whom he had raised to the high civil and military rank.

A brilliant reflection of the thousand-year-old history of the Byzantine Empire of which it was the second capital, Thessaloniki can look back upon a past that was at once glorious and prosperous. Its monuments are the most representative examples of the art and architecture of the Byzantine and post-Byzantine periods, and the Byzantinist Charles Diehl once said that a study of the history of Thessaloniki was in itself a study of the history of Byzantium.

The oldest examples of Early Christian painting in Thessaloniki decorate the tombs which continue to be excavated regularly. Monumental art began in the 4th century A.D. with the raising of the circular *Church of St. George* (the Rotunda) which was probably intended as a mausoleum for Galerius (c. 306); at the beginning of the 5th century the exterior was decorated with superb mosaics, many of which are still preserved. Chronologically, the next church is the *Acheiropoietos*, a three-naved basilica of the 5th century, with fine mosaics in the soffits of the nave columns The five-naved *Basilica of St. Demetrios,* martyr, protector and patron saint of the city, occupies a very special place in the minds and hearts of the inhabitants. The church , dated to the 7th century, was burnt in the fire of 1917 which reduced the greater part of the city to ashes, and was subsequently rebuilt. The 7th century church, raised on the site of an earlier 5th century edifice, which was the scene of St. Demetrios' martyrdom, is an outstanding example of the magnificence of Early Christian architecture. Evidence of its original beauty still exists in fragments of the interior decoration which survived the 1917 conflagration. Of the mosaic decoration all that survives are a few fragments —all votive offerings— of the 5th, 6th and 7th, centuries. The few remaining wall paintings belong to different periods; the most interesting —the ones in the Chapel of St. Euthymios, dated by an inscription to 1303— are typical examples of the Macedonian School of painting in Thessaloniki during the Palaiologue period. Particular significance is attached to the Crypt, situated below the sanctuary, which is associated with the worship of the «myrrh-flowing» saint.

In the upper city nestles the small *Church of Hosios David*, once part of the Monastery of Latomos. In it is preserved part of the original 5th - 6th century edifice, the importance of which lies in the fact that the sanctuary apse is decorated

Thessaloniki.
Surviving part of the Arch of Galerius.

with a superb mosaic of a young and beardless Christ enthroned in a luminous circular 'Glory' between the symbols of the Evangelists and the prophets Ezechiel and Habbakuk.

First among the series of the city's Byzantine monuments is the *Church of St. Sophia*, raised in the Iconoclast period. The architectural form is a transitional one, foreshadowing the true Byzantine style. The dome and upper part of the sanctuary are decorated with brilliant mosaics. The original mosaics belong to the Iconoclast period; those which survive today are of the 9th century, that is to say, of the immediate post-Iconoclast period. The Church of the Panayia Chalkeon, dated by a surviving inscription on the lintel of the entrance door to the year 1044, is built wholly of bricks and presents an architectural innovation. It belongs to the type of composite four-columned church. The very damaged wall paintings of the interior are contemporary with the original structure.

An architectural development of the Panayia Chalkeon is found in the *Church of St. Panteleimon* which was consecrated in the year 1169. The 13th century *Church of St. Catherine*, architecturally related to that of St. Panteleimon, foreshadows the Holy Apostles (see below). It is a domed crossinscribed edifice surrounded on three sides by colonnades. The wall paintings are of the 14th century.

The *Church of the Holy Apostles*, once part of an important monastery of which little survives today, is of the same architectural type as St. Catherine's. The manner in which the materials have been used and applied is truly remarkable, and the visitor can let his eye roam with amazement over the brick revetments of the east wall, where the architect has succeeded in creating the impression of a woven carpet. The building in fact constitutes one of the finest architectural achievements of the Palaiologue period. Chronologically, it is of the early 14th century, having been commissioned by Nephon, Patriarch of Constantinople (1312-1315). The beautiful mosaics and wall paintings which decorate the interior belong to the same period.

There are five other 14th century religious monuments in Thessaloniki : the *Churches of Prophet Elia*, the *Archangels, St. Nicolas Orphanos*, the *Transfiguration of the Saviour* and the Katholikon of the *Monastery of Vlattadon*. The Church of St. Nicolas Orphanos holds a place apart from all others in the city —due to its extremely important wall paintings. This church is one of the few extant Byzantine monuments in which the entire —or almost entire— painted decoration survives in all its pristine brilliance and liveliness. The unique quality of this little church lies in the fact that unlike any other monument in Thessaloniki, it conveys an impression of the elements of sumptuousness inherent in Palaiologue painting.

After the fall of Constantinople the radiant light shed by Byzantium was of course dimmed. Life, however, continued; religious faith and worship provided inspiration for a new creativity into which new elements entered. During the period of the Turkish occupation a series of monuments, representative of the times, of which the most important are the Churches of Panagouda, Nea Panayia and St. Athanasios, were raised.

No description of Byzantine Thessaloniki would be complete without reference to its splendid fortifications. An immense enceinte of walls, the finest after that of Constantinople, encircles the city by land in the form of the Greek letter Π. In the course of a long history of successive barbarian invasions, the walls protected the city. The south walls are drowned by the acropolis, on the summit of which rises the Heptapyrgion. The walls, the first of which were raised in the time of the Emperor Theodosios, were built and restored in the course of many centuries, the most important being dated to the reign of the Emperor Justinian. Additional defence works were raised during the centuries that followed and some of these additions are even dated to the period of the Turkish occupation.

The White Tower, situated on the waterfront, marks the maritime extremity of the east walls which follow a steep line up the hillside to the crowning point of the Gingirli tower. The greater part of the east walls are, however, destroyed.

Thessaloniki possesses three fine museums: the Archaeological, the Ethnographical and Folklore, and the Museum of Popular Arts. The latter, now called the Museum of Northern Greece, situated at 51, Vasileos Konstantinou Street, possesses an important collection of textiles, embroideries, regional costumes, silver and bronze objects.

Archaeological Museum of Thessaloniki

The museum situated between the Public Gardens and the grounds of the International Fair is housed in a new building which is built in modern style. Some of the exhibits cover a range from the Neolithic period to the Iron Age (1000 - 600 B.C.). These include pottery, weapons and jewellery. There are also some interesting carvings and architectural fragments, figurines from Olynthos and vases from different areas, a series of Classical, Hellenistic and Roman bronze objects, gold jewellery and the large lavishly decorated bronze krater discovered at Derveni. A noteworthy papyrus, inscribed with part of an Orphic hymn, also found at Derveni, is exhibited in a special show-case. There are also mosaic pavements and glass objects of the Roman period and a fine collection of coins.

The Archaeological Collection of the Faculty of Philosophy of the University, housed in the *University of Thessaloniki*, consists of pottery, jewellery, coins and bronze objects. The university also possesses a *folklore collection* which includes embroideries, metal objects, woodcarvings and ceramics.

There are five private collections in the city: those of G. Philippou, G. Paralis, I. Papaïliakis, H. Vasiliou and V. Kyriazopoulos. Among their contents are ancient carvings, pottery, ancient Greek and Roman jewellery, coins, vases, icons and contemporary popular art ceramics (chiefly works by Minas Avramides).

PELLA

Pella, birthplace of Alexander the Great, became the capital of the Macedonian kings when they abandoned the ancient and beautifully situated fortified town of Aigai (modern Edessa) whence waterfalls cascade into the plain below. Before the advent of the Macedonian kings Pella was a small township known as *Vounomos*. Archelaos was the first king to transfer the capital to Pella in order that his headquarters might be in a more central situation near the sea. He commissioned the building of fine edifices and a magnificent palace, in which the most distinguished figures in the world of art and literature, including Euripides, were offered hospitality. The interior walls of the palace were decorated by the great painter Zeuxis.

During the reign of Philip II (359 - 336 B.C.), Pella was the centre of the political life of the whole of Greece, serving as a bulwark against foreign invasion, its monarch constantly intervening (in Macedonian interests) in the internecine strife of the Greek city states. Demosthenes and Aischines came to Pella as Athenian ambassadors with a view to establishing good relations between Athens and Macedonia.

Pella.
Mosaic floor of a house with a lion-hunt scene
(possibly depicting Alexander the Great and Krateros).

After Alexander's death, Pella maintained its supremacy throughout the regency of Antipater; and under the Diadochoi it continued to be an economic and cultural center of major importance. During the reigns of Antigonos Gonatas (276 - 239 B.C.) and Philip V the arts and literature flourished. The last Macedonian king was the unfortunate Perseus.

The excavation of Pella by the Archaeological Service began immediately after the liberation of Macedonia (the finds are now in the Archaeological Museum at Thessaloniki). Excavations were resumed in 1957, with impressive results. The acropolis was identified on twin hills : also the royal treasury, the central part of the town, paved streets 10 meters wide, reservoirs with immense jars which served as decant - wells for the water, large houses with beautiful mosaic decoration and inner colonnades and necropoles with impressive tombs constructed in the Macedonian style.

Pella is situated 38 kms west of Thessaloniki on the road to Edessa. The plain which extends to the left of the road is the reclaimed lake of Yannitsa, where Greek officers performed heroic exploits at the time of the liberation of all this part of the country, which is profoundly associated with the great patriot Pavlos Melas, from Bulgarian *commitadjis*.

A variety of subjects are depicted in the Pella mosaics. In the finest of all Dionysos is represented nude riding a panther. In his left hand the god holds a thyrsos; with his right hand he reins in the panther by holding on to its neck. In the other mosaics we see a griffin tearing a deer to pieces, two men hunting a lion, a pair of Centaurs. The houses which these mosaics decorated were lay buildings, dated to c. 300 B.C.

Museum of Pella

An enormous architectural fragment and a fine Doric capital were discovered among other remains in the part of the acropolis which has been excavated. A large number of smaller objects are displayed in the local museum. Chronologically, these begin with the Classical period; the greater number of exhibits are, of course, of the Hellenistic period. These include carvings, pottery, jewellery, a quantity of figurines and the mosaic pavements from the excavated houses. One of the finest exhibits is the sculpture of a dog, a masterpiece of the Severe Style.

CHALCIDICE

Ancient *Stageira*, Aristotle's native town, has been identified with the modern village of *Stratonion*. *Potidaia* (76 kms south - east of Thessaloniki) was a large city founded at the end of the 7th century B.C. by Corinthian colonizers. Athens and Corinth fought for its possession. Socrates saved the life of Alcibiades in the course of the Athenian campaign against Potidaia. Philip II of Macedon dismantled the city and depopulated it. Kassandros rebuilt the city and called it Kassandreia. At the site of ancient Olynthos (77 kms S.E. of Thessaloniki) there are also traces of Neolithic dwellings. Excavations carried out on the hill site have brought to light the town planning of the ancient city with its streets, houses, agora and acropolis. In many houses there are remains of mosaic pavements. Vestiges of the Neolithic settlement (c. 3000 B.C.) can be discerned on the west slope of the hill, as well as the ruins of a Byzantine castle.

MOUNT ATHOS

The place is unique. For over a thousand years a large monastic community has dwelt in a setting as often lush and verdant as it is barren and rocky, on the northernmost of the three prongs of the Chalcidic peninsula, the tip of which is crowned by the snow-capped peak of Mt. Athos. The Athos headland was known in antiquity, and parts of it were inhabited. Herodotos actually records the names of cities.

The fact that monks dwelt here during the first millenium A.D. is established, but there was no organised monastic community until the 10th century. St. Athanasios the Athonite played a decisive role in the development of Athonite monasticism. His friend, Nikephoros Phokas, general and later Emperor, provided lavish financial grants and in 963 the Monastery of the Great Lavra was founded. From that moment begins the extraordinary history of Athonite monasticism and its association with all the vicissitudes, disasters and renascences of the Byzantine Empire. This historical association with the fate of the Greek people continued throughout the Turkish occupation into the modern era. Monasteries were founded one after another; some survived; others were abandoned. Of many of the latter only the names survive. Others, however, have continued to prosper for a thousand years. Athonite monasticism is a unique phenomenon, a reflection of the strength of the Greek character, of the faith by which it is inspired, and of the powers of endurance of the Greek people.

There are now twenty monasteries on Mt. Athos. Twelve are of the coenobian class, eight of the idiorrhythmic, and are administered accordingly. The twenty monasteriers are the Great Lavra, Vatopedi, Iviron, Chilandari, Dionysiou, Koutloumoush, Pantokrator, Xeropotamou, Zographou, Docheiariou, Karakallou, Philotheou, Simopetra, St. Paul, Stavronikita, Xenophontos, Gregoriou, Esphigmenou, St. Panteleimon and Konstamonitou.

The monastic community is administered by the Holy Synod which is composed of representatives of the twenty monasteries, all of whom reside at Karyes, the capital of Mt. Athos. The executive organ of the Holy Synod is the *Iera Epistasia* (the Holy Superintendence), at the head of which is the Protos (the First). The Greek state is represented by a civil governor who supervises the application of the constitutional charter and is responsible for security and law and order.

From an artistic point-of-view, Mt. Athos is a very exceptional place. Its thousand-year-old history has bequeathed a rich legacy of *objets d'art* and architectural monuments. Architecture, painting and the minor arts (covering an enormous range of objects many of which are unique masterpieces) are so thoroughly represented that the Holy Mountain has acquired the character of an authentic Byzantine treasure-house.

Painting is represented by, among others, the outstanding Byzantine hagiographers Panselinos, who worked at the Protaton (Church of the Holy Synod) at Karyes in the 14th century, and Theophanes, who frescoed the walls of the Great Lavra in the 16th. A quantity of icons and a remarkable series of illuminated manuscripts ranging uninterruptedly over the centuries command sufficient attention in themselves to raise Mt. Athos to the front rank of art centers. Visitors and scholars alike are awe-struck by the architectural boldness and elegance of the monastic buildings. Mosaic icons, ecclesiastical and other objects, which cover a range so wide as to be unique, represent the various branches of the arts. Despite the materialistic technological age in which we live, the last chapter in the history of Mt.

Athos has not yet been written. In a spirit of profound faith and confidence in a future in which the Holy mountain shall one day relive the great days of the past, the torch continues to be carried alight - on high.

VEROIA

The site was inhabited in antiquity but only a few remains of those times survive. The main sights are the well-built ancient wall, the Byzantine churches, particularly the *Metropolis*, and the splendid mansions which slowly fall to ruins (the mansion of Sior Monalakis was a masterpiece of architecture and decoration; that of Sapountzoglou, at 12 Prophetou Elia Street, has stained-glass windows and finely carved wooden ceilings). The church of *Ayios Christos* is adorned with wall-paintings dating to 1314 and signed by Kallerges, one of the outstanding artists of those times. The church of *St. Nicholas* has a fine architecture and rich interior decoration, and the church of *St. Spyridon* shows remarkable specimens of Byzantine sculpture. Finally, the church of the *Sts. Kyrekos and Ioulites* is also worth visiting. In the central square of the town, the Bema from which St. Paul the Apostle is said to have preached, has been reconstructed.

Museum of Veroia

The Museum contains numerous and notable vases and figurines of the early Neolithic period and the Bronze Age uncovered in the course of excavations at Nea Nikomedeia. Also displayed are weapons and jewels of the Iron Age from excavations at the large cemetery of Vergina. Exhibits include pottery of the Geometric, Hellenistic and Roman periods, as well as sculptures, architectural members, important inscriptions and a great number of coins. There are also several fine Byzantine icons, and Mediaeval sculptures and manuscripts.

VERGINA

11 kms. S.E. of Veroia, after crossing the river Aliakmon, near the village Palatitsia (Vergina), a remarkable Macedonian tomb of the 3rd century B.C. has been discovered. The interior of this tomb is decorated with white, red and black paint. On the hill to the right, the visitor may see the ruins of a large palace with sides measuring 92 m., built during the reign of Antigonos Gonatas and destroyed by fire. In the south wing was uncovered a very fine mosaic floor of polychrome pebbles showing a floral design. The Macedonian tomb of Vergina is in the form of a temple with Ionic columns on the facade. In the interior stands a marble throne, 1.80 m. high, adorned with carved sphinxes. A vast necropolis with more than 200 graves, dating from 1000 to 600 B.C., was discovered near the palace.

After the bridge on the river Aliakmon the road bifurcates at 105 kms,. leading south towards the mountain range of Pieria, and right towards the fine *Moni Timiou Prodromou*, which has an exquisite iconostasis and affords a superb view. In the chapel of the Transfiguration —dated to 1325— have survived wall-paintings of the school of Panselinos. The visitor may also see the hermitage of St. Dionysios of Olympos.

At *Edessa*, the town of waterfalls, an archaeological collection is housed in the mosque and includes Hellenistic and Roman reliefs and inscriptions. In the church of the *Dormition of the Virgin* (Panaghitsa) at Nea Pella, are displayed post-Byzantine icons, and religious embroideries and sacred vessels brought over by the Greeks of Pontos (Black Sea).

The largest so far Macedonian tomb has been unearthed at *Lefkadia*, near Veroia. It has a two-storied facade with remarkable architectural and painting decoration. Paintings represent the large-sized figures of two judges of the Underworld, and of Hermes 'psychopompos' and the deceased. The painted decoration of the tomb is an example of monumental painting in the Hellenistic age.

KOZANI

The site was inhabited in the Stone Age, as testified by a truly unique find : a stone axe of the early Neolithic times. Bone tools and pottery sherds dating to the Neolithic period have also been found. The fossilized skeleton of an elephant has been discovered in the village Pentavryson Eordaias. The town, built in the 4th century and continuously inhabited since, was a principal cultural centre during the Turkish occupation. In the struggles before 1912, the inhabitants of Kozani supported at the cost of great sacrifices the fighters for Macedonia in their attempt to free this region. The national hero Pavlos Melas started his campaign from the Metropolis of Kozani. In the central square of the town stands a big Library founded in the 16th century. The building also houses the local *Museum,* which contains : pottery of Prehistoric times, of the Iron Age and of subsequent periods down to the end of the Roman rule; Hellenistic and Roman reliefs and Roman coins and inscriptions; fragments of wall-paintings of the basilica at Voskochorion and part of an Early Christian mosaic floor; post-Byzantine icons, silverware, and woodcarvings from local mansions; letters by Ali Pasha, old maps, and other documents.

At *Aiani* there is an *Archaeological and Folklore Collection* housed in the village hall. It comprises an interesting collection of Iron Age objects, Mycenaean finds, Geometric, Classical and Roman bronze jewellery, vases and statuettes, Hellenistic and Roman inscriptions and coins, post-Byzantine icons, wood-carvings, local costumes and jewellery.

At *Zavorda* the famous *Monastery of Hosios Nikanor* may be visited (women are not admitted). The sacristy contains icons, gold-embroidered vestments, woodcarvings, reliquaries, sacred vessels and manuscripts. At *Liknades*, Prehistoric tools and sherds, and pottery and coins dating from the Classical to the Roman periods, are kept in the Demotic School. Finally, at *Mavropighi*, a collection of vases and coins of Hellenistic and Roman times is housed in the Demotic School.

KASTORIA

Blessed by the natural beauty of its surroundings, the pride not only of Western but of the whole of Madeconia, the historic town of Kastoria spreads across the narrow neck of a headland jutting out into Lake Orestias. According to the historian Procopius, the town on the narrow isthmus was strongly fortified during the reign of the Emperor Justinian. Fragments of these fortifications still survive. All the vicissitudes experienced by the Greeks were shared by the inhabitants of Kastoria. Successive waves of conquerors came and went. But the fact that the town retained its identity is reflected in the large number —unique in Greece— of Byzantine churches which remain as intact as they are authentic. During the Turkish occupation Kastoria enjoyed, thanks to its thriving trade in furs, a prosperity that continues to this day. Merchants of Kastoria, settled abroad, controlled the fur trade, while maintaining close links with their native city. The numerous 17th, 18th and 19th century mansions constitute a testimony of their wealth. Something of the past glory and grandeur is still reflected in the Apozari and Doltso quarters which retain their former character, with narrow paved alleys between high walls surrounding fortified courts above which lofty mansions proudly tower.

Sixty churches and an even larger number of mansions compose into a uniform picture of outstanding interest which illustrates the history of regional art in this area. The churches of Kastoria, ranging over a period from the 11th to the 18th centuries, present a unique aspect of Byzantine painting without a single chronological break. The churches are all basilica-type, single- or three-naved, with only one exception: the Panayia Koubelidiki which is crowned by a dome (Turkish *koube*), to which it owes its name.

The exterior walls of the older churches, such as Ayioi Anargyroi, Ayios Stephanos, the Taxiarches (the Archangels), are decorated with intricate patterns of brick revetments which provide them with a special character. The interiors are decorated with frescoes which, owing to their unbroken chronological sequence, illustrate the range covered by the finest specimens of Byzantine art.

Within the narrow limits of this guide, it is only possible to refer to the principal churches to which dates have been either ascribed or proved by surviving inscriptions. In the older edifices there are often superimposed layers of wall paintings of different periods; alternatively, successive sections of fresco work range from the 11th to the 16th centuries. Among the former are Ayios Stephanos, the Panayia Koubelidiki, the Taxiarches and Ayios Nikolaos Kyritzis. Churches dated by inscriptions include, among others, Ayios Athanasios tou Mouzaki (1385), Ayios Nikolaos Kyritzis (14th century and 1654), Ayios Alypios (1422), Ayios Nikolaos of the Nun Eupraxia (1485), Ayioi Apostoloi (1547), Ayios Ioannis of the Monastery of the Mavriotissa (1552) and the Panayia Rasiotissa (1553).

The old mansions add much to the unique character of the town. Some of their most striking features include a distinctive architectural style, lavish painted decoration, ceilings of carved woodwork, wall revetments and polychrome skylights. Typical of these mansions, among others, are those of Natzis, of the brothers Emmanuel, of Tsatsapas, of Basaras and Nerantzis.

SIATISTA

The town consists of two districts (Ano Siatista and Kato Siatista) occupying two terraces. The small township was founded in the 14th century and has interesting Byzantine churches. In the 16th - 18th century it became a very prosperous center of trade with European cities, particularly Vienna. The old flowering of the town is still visible in the fine castle-like mansions of Poulko, Nerantzopoulos, Manousos, etc., remarkable not only for their architecture, but mainly for their decoration which consists of exquisite paintings and wood-carvings, stained-glass windows, etc. Siatista was one of the major centers of the movement for the liberation of Macedonia, and the seat of Pavlos Melas.

KAVALA

The city stretches amphitheatrically at the foot of Mt. Pangaion, crowned by a 14th century Byzantine citadel. It became very prosperous with the processing and trade of tobacco. Its history is associated with that of the island of Thasos. Initially the site was occupied by a colony of the Thasians (Neapolis), and was later included by the Athenians in their Alliance. The town was given the name of *Christoupolis* in the Byzantine era, and of *Kavala* during the Turkish occupation. St. Paul, the Apostle of the Nations, preached here. Near Kavala lies the ancient site of *Krenides*, which Philip of Macedon conquered and renamed *Philippi* after himself.

Museum of Kavala

This is an important local Museum housed in a new building and containing finds dating to Prehistoric and historic times : jewellery, tomb frescoes, pediments, a large chronological series of figurines from Amphipolis, notable vases and sculptures. The Museum antiquities have come from the city area, as well as from Drama, Xanthi, Serres, Amphipolis and Abdera. Architectural elements from the sanctuary of the Parthenos have been conventionally restored and exhibited. There is also a wonderful collection of gold jewels and wreaths, and gilded and painted ornaments from tombs at Amphipolis. Exhibits include Hellenistic and Roman bronze utensils and vases, coins and inscriptions.

The *Collection of the Kavala Metropolis* includes a number of Byzantine icons. Remains of the ancient city are to be seen in the area of the *Panaghia* quarter, where an ancient wall has been preserved, as well as ruins of the *sanctuary of the Parthenos*, which flourished from the 7th to the 1st century B.C. Other noteworthy sights are the Mediaeval castle (Byzantine), the aqueduct (16th century), the Imaret (19th century).

PHILIPPI

At the 15th kilometer NW of Kavalla on the road to Drama the ruins of the ancient city of Philippi extend across a plain surrounded by Mts. Orbylos, Symbolon and Pangaion.

Evidence of the fact that the site was inhabited in prehistoric times has been found in the Neolithic settlement of Dikili-tash. Later, in the historical era, various Thracian tribes dwelt around Mt. Pangaion. In 360 B.C. Greek colonists settled here and four years later Philip II of Macedon gave his name to the place, where he established the royal mint.

Time passed. In 43 B.C. the city's name was rendered famous throughout the ancient world by the great battle fought in the plain between Octavius and Antonius on the one hand and Brutus and Cassius, Caesar's assassins, on the other. The defeat of the republican leaders spelled the doom of the Roman Republic. The Romans then settled at Philippi, and for two to three centuries the character of the city remained a purely Roman one, as regards language, religion, administration and institutions.

In the earliest Christian years the city acquired further renown, for St. Paul preached here and was consequently imprisoned. His sojourn at Philippi is very vividly described in the Acts of the Apostles, and the site of his imprisonment became a place of worship. After the recognition of Christianity as the official faith, Philippi became the seat of a bishop.

The centuries that followed were very disturbed, with barbarian invaders, Goths, Slavs, Bulgars and Turks successively descending upon the place. In the 16th century Philippi was uninhabited. The cause of its abandonment is not known.

Kavala.
View of the town with the ancient aqueduct visible in the distance.

Immediately after passing the village of Krenides, the visitor beholds the ruins of the ancient city. To the left of the road extends a group of buildings which form a rectangle. This is the ancient forum, paved with stone slabs. Its dimensions are 100 x 50 m. In the middle of the north side is the rectangular structure of the *bema* from which public speeches were delivered. On the west side were the establishments of the Roman administrative authorities; on the east side a library and reading-room. The market place lay south of the forum. Two ramps connected the forum with the famous Via Egnatia which began at Dyracchium and ended at Byzantium.

The Roman forum communicated with the Early Christian Basilica B, whose majestic ruins rise in the middle of the now open area. The basilica was modelled on fine Constantinopolitan prototypes, such as St. Sophia and St. Irene. Structurally, it belonged to the architectural type of the domed basilica. The atrium was never built, although the space had been laid out for it. It is not, however, only the impressive ruins of the basilica which arouse admiration. The magnificently worked capitals, imposts and panels are admirable examples of the sculpture of the period.

The ruins of a palaistrà lie west of the basilica, beyond the narthex. It had the shape of a rectangular parallelogram, with chambers to the west, a small amphitheatre and latrines to the east. North-west of the palaistra are the ruins of the Roman baths with chambers which served as drying- and dressing-rooms.

North of the Kavalla-Drama road rises a terrace littered with the ruins of the Early Christian Basilica A. Tradition has it that the small building to the right of the entrance to the basilica is the site of the prison in which St. Paul was incarcerated. Fragments of wall paintings survive. A few steps lead up to another terrace on which the oldest building at Philippi, a small temple of the Ionic order, is situated.

Among other important buildings scattered about the site is Basilica A, whose dimensions are 130 x 50 m. The best preserved section is the Baptistery. Above the basilica, five chambers in a row have been identified by inscriptions as sanctuaries of the Egyptian gods. In the same area, to the north, are rock sanctuaries of the Roman period with apses in which objects of worship were placed.

Finally, there is the theatre, buttressed by a wall. Originally built in the 4th century B.C. it was one of the largest of ancient theatres. Alterations were made in the 2nd century A.D., including the enlargement of the orchestra. Further alterations were carried out in the 3rd century.

Philippi was enclosed within a circuit of walls 3500 m. long. Fragments of the Roman and Byzantine periods survive.

Archaeological Museum of Philippi

The Museum, situated in the area of the ancient town, houses exclusively local finds. Exhibits include the important Prehistoric finds — stone implements and pottery — from the excavations on the hill of Dikili - tash, interesting Roman and Early Christian sculptures, Hellenistic and Roman works of the minor arts from the site of Philippi, and a good series of inscriptions and coins of all periods.

THASOS

Thasos is one of the most beautiful Greek islands, covered with green woods and dense vegetation. In antiquity the island was a centre of marble and wine export, and was colonized by the Parians in the 7th century B.C. The islanders occupied important sites along the coast of Eastern Macedonia, which was hence named

Philippi.
Capital of a column.

Amphipolis.
Statue of a lion.

Thasion Epeiros. A dispute with Athens ended in defeat for the Thasians. Thasos was the birthplace of Polygnotos, the celebrated painter of the 5th century B.C.

Excavations at Thasos have been carried out for many years by the French School of Archaeology. The sites explored include the *acropolis* which is surrounded by an Archaic wall with monumental gates, the *Thesmophorion,* and the city *agora* with its outstanding monuments. The *temple of Athena,* the *sanctuary of Herakles* and the *sanctuaries of Poseidon* and *Dionysos* have been investigated in the area of the acropolis.

On the site of *Alykes,* a marble-yielding promontory, the sanctuary of Apollo is by the sea-shore; a cave near by containing ancient finds has been explored.

Museum of Thasos

The Museum includes notable finds dating to the Archaic period, funerary stelai, inscriptions, statues and sculptures. The colossal statue of the Kriophoros is outstanding among other Archaic, Archaising, Classical, Hellenistic and Roman sculptures. Also on display are several bronze and clay statuettes, and a large collection of vases and lamps of the Archaic and Classical periods, as well as many jewels and a few Early Christian sculptures.

SERRES

At *Serres,* an *archaeological collection* including Hellenistic and Roman sculpture is exhibited at the Bezistan (sheltered market - place), a Turkish building of the 15th - 16th century. A Byzantine castle stands on the pine-clad hill of the town. N.W. of the citadel is the Byzantine church of St. Nicholas.

AMPHIPOLIS

Amphipolis was in antiquity the principal city of Eastern Macedonia, the 'apple of discord' between Macedonians, Thasians and Athenians. It was originally named *Ennea Hodoi* (Nine Ways) and occupied a most important site, thanks to which it became very prosperous. The wealth and flourishing of the city are attested by rich funerary offerings from the ancient cemetery, which yielded among many other finds precious gold objects and exquisite figurines. A monumental marble lion marks the triumph of Philip II, who conquered Amphipolis.

DRAMA

The site was inhabited in the Neolithic period and life continued uninterrupted into the Bronze Age. Finds attest to the flourishing of the city from the end of the Classical era to the Byzantine age, when it prospered again. Sights include the Byzantine churches of *St. Sophia,* and the *Ayioi Taxiarchai,* and the *Byzantine walls* in the center of the town. There are also some fine old mansions (of Tzemos, Tsaprazis, etc.). Archeological finds consisting of Roman and Early Christian sculptures are displayed in the courtyard of the church of St. Sophia.

XANTHI

Xanthi is a very picturesque town and has some mansions with beautiful interiors. The town presents an unusual aspect combining Greek and Turkish features. In the Metropolis there are icons and manuscripts, and in the *Folklore Museum*, which belongs to the Municipality and is housed in a fine old mansion, there are local costumes and embroideries. At *Kosmeti* there is an *archaeological collection* of good Roman sculpture.

ABDERA

Situated at a distance of 26 kms. from Xanthi, Abdera is the birthplace of the philosopher Demokritos, the 'father of atomic science', of the sophist Protagoras, of Leukippos, etc. The city reached its zenith in the 5th century B.C., and had its own coinage.

Recent excavations brought to light part of the ancient *agora*, traces of the *theatre*, and countless clay figurines of all periods.

KOMOTINI

The history of the town was initially associated with the activity of the Thracians, their mythology and their singular cults. It occupied an important site crossed by the *Via Egnatia,* and is believed to have been a flourishing town in the Byzantine era, like *Myrsinoupolis,* whose ruins lie 5 kms. west of Komotini.

Museums of Komotini

The *Archaeological Museum* is in a new building and exhibits are finely set. It includes a great number of Prehistoric finds (tools and vases), some good sculpture dating from the Archaic age to Early Christian times (the local funerary stelai are remarkable). The most important exhibit is the *golden head of the Roman emperor Marcus Aurelius*. There are also many inscriptions and coins.

The *Folklore Museum of Thrace* was founded by the Komotini Cultural Society and contains local costumes, wood-carvings, silverware, ecclesiastical embroideries and bronze utensils. The silverwork displayed is very fine.

An *Ecclesiastical Museum* is housed in the Ioakeimideion Boys' Orphanage and includes icons, a gold-embroidered *epitaphios*, embroideries, earthenware and silverware of post-Byzantine date, as well as a few wood-carvings.

ALEXANDROUPOLIS

It is a new town, over 90 years old, built in 1876 and originally named Dede-Agatch, after the Turkish monk who was buried under a big tree near the Municipality. In 1920, it was renamed Alexandroupolis in honour of king Alexander who had visited the town. Today it is a notable cultural centre. In this town there is a large and rich collection of Sarakatsan aprons.

At *Maroneia* an *archaeological collection* is housed in the Demotic School. It contains Prehistoric finds from the cave of Maroneia (Neolithic and Early Helladic vases and tools), and Classical, Hellenistic and Roman sculptures and inscriptions. At *Traianoupolis* (Loutros) an *archaeological collection* is exhibited in a Roman building with later restorations (perhaps a staging post of the Via Egnatia), and includes Roman reliefs and inscriptions, and Byzantine architectural members and reliefs.

DIDYMOTEICHO

The town was one of the important centres of the region in Byzantine times, and the birthplace of John Batatzes, emperor of Nikaia. It suffered many adventures during the Frankish occupation. Didymoteicho is amphitheatrically built and surrounded by a twin Byzantine wall from which it derives its name. Part of the wall and the ruins of the Mediaeval town are visible on the summit of the hill. The Turks occupied the town in 1361 and made it their European capital before conquering Adrianople. The Sultan Bayezid was born here. Charles XII, king of Sweden, lay a prisoner at Didymoteicho until 1713, after his defeat by Peter the Great in the battle of Poltava. In addition to the walls and Mediaeval ruins, other sights of interest are the old mosque and the cold storage wells, where snow is kept during summer.

Gypsies live in caverns at Didymoteicho.

SAMOTHRACE

This strange island, which presents mainland features, is accessible by caique from Alexandroupolis, or steamer from Piraeus. Mt. Fengari rises to a height of 1500 m. in the centre of the island, which has abundant vegetation and a great number of hot springs known from antiquity and said to be superior than those of Karlovy Vary. A local legend relates that Zeus watched the fighting during the Trojan War seated on the summit of Mt. Fengari. Samothrace was the sacred island of the ancients and the sanctuary of the persecuted. The island was inhabited in the Neolithic period and colonized in the 8th - 7th century B.C. by the Greeks, who settled on the site of the modern town. Samothrace flourished in the 5th century B.C. and had a silver coinage. Its prosperity is also designated by the rich funerary offerings found in graves of the two necropoles. The cult of the Great Gods was initiated in very early times and had a mystical character unknown to us, for its secret has been well-kept. During festivities in honour of the Kabeiroi, who were the patrons of seafaring, the young Olympias and Philip II met and fell in love. Perseus, king of Macedon, sought refuge on the island after his defeat (in 168 B.C.). By reason of its being the meeting place of the parents of Alexander the Great, both the Macedonian kings, as well as the Diadochoi who ruled the dominions conquered by Alexander the Great, sought to make the island an important center and a sanctuary of Panhellenic prestige.

Arsinoe, sister and consort of Ptolemy, erected on the island the greatest circular building of antiquity — the *Arsinoeion*, probably used as hostel for persons of rank. Intellectual and cultural activity flourished on the site, which continued to prosper during the Roman occupation and was visited by Roman emperors. The sanctuary was raided by pirates in 84 B.C. and struck by earthquake in A.D. 200. Despite its decline, the ancient cult survived until its abolition by decrees of the Byzantine emperors.

In addition to Samothrace, Lemnos and Boiotia were also places of worship of the Kabeiroi. In the Kabeireia these deities were called Great Gods and their names corresponded to those of Demeter, Persephone and Hades. Diodorus Siculus records that following a deluge all the islands had been inundated by the sea, except for the summit of Mt. Fengari. Those who had managed to reach Samothrace were thus saved and as a sign of gratitude they dedicated the island to the Kabeiroi. According to local tradition, Herakles, Jason, the Dioskouroi, Orpheus, and even

Agamemnon and Odysseus had been initiated into the Kabeirian Mysteries. Samothrace was regarded as a place of fertility and fecundity.

It has been known that initiates wore an olive garland and a purple ribbon, which had the power to protect them from the greatest dangers. The faithful made some form of confession and were given absolution by the priest. Arsinoe, persecuted by Ptolemy Philadelphos, sought refuge in the sanctuary, and the same is related for other eminent persons. Festivals were celebrated annually, but lesser feasts were also held during the year.

The cult of Samothrace has several common elements with that of Eleusis. The Great Mother or *Axieros* was worshipped here (in pre-Hellenic times she was venerated as goddess of the rocks). After the Great Mother, *Kadmilos* was worshipped as a god of fertility (he was identified by the Greeks with Hermes). The *Kabeiroi* were next to those two divinities (they were identified by the Greeks with the Dioskouroi and symbolized by stars and snakes). These deities —the Great Mother, the god of fertility Kadmilos, and the Kabeiroi— dominated the pre-Greek local religion, which was maintained and accepted later by the Greeks. The Great Gods included another two divine figures, the god of the Underworld and his wife, whom the Greeks named Hades and Persephone, while in the local dialect they were called *Axiokersos* and *Axiokersa*. It seems that during the festival in the sanctuary of the Great Gods a reconstitution of the divine drama and a sacred marriage were performed in the *Temenos* founded in the 4th century B.C. on the site used earlier for cult purposes. The abduction of the goddess and her recovery and reunion with her mother were then added in the performance.

The *Mysteries of the Great Gods* were most celebrated and venerated over the whole Greek world.

Oracles were also pronounced in the sanctuary when sought by pilgrims during the annual festivals.

Unlike Eleusis, initiation to the Mysteries of Samothrace could be obtained by anyone, regardless of nationality or social status. Initiation ceremonies were not performed during festivals only, but at any time. The two degrees —*myesis* and *epopteia*— known from the Eleusinian Mysteries, existed here too, and could be obtained without interval.

The sanctuary received numerous and rich offerings from the faithful, just like any other Panhellenic sanctuary. The cult was modelled by the Greeks on the established pre-Hellenic religion. In the late 7th century B.C., a rock was enclosed by a double peribolos on the site where the Arsinoeion was later built. The buildings of the sanctuary were constructed on different periods. Several *altars* existed originally serving for the celebration of cult in the 6th century B.C. During the 6th century B.C. more sites of worship were founded. The *Stoa of Votive Offerings* was built in 550 B.C. to the north of the sacred temenos. In 500 B.C. was erected the *Anaktoron*, an oblong rectangular building with three doors on the long side and a square room adjoining one of the narrow sides by the south stoa and serving for the initiation into the Mysteries. This room did not communicate with the Anaktoron but had its own exit door. After the mid-4th century B.C. were founded the *Temenos* and an elegant *Propylon* facing N.E., near the altar of Hekate. A period of splendid building followed. The *Court of the Altar* was founded between 330 and 320 B.C., and a few decades later the *Hieron* was renovated, as a superb marble edifice with double colonnade on the façade and an arcade inscribed on the narrow west side. Its construction was completed much later, and it served for the initiation into the degree of Epopteia. Between 289 and 281 B.C., Arsinoe, Queen of Egypt, built the vast circular edifice used as hostel for official visitors and place of meetings. Between 280 and 265 B.C., Ptolemy II of Egypt built a new monumental marble entrance (*Propylon*) to the sanctuary of the Great Gods. Towards the late 3rd century B.C. the area of the sanctuary was enlarged and included a new section to the west. A monumental exedra was then erected between the great Stoa which bounded the sanctuary to the south and the Stoa of Votive Offerings. The exedra was surmounted by the celebrated *Nike of Samothrace*.

The *theatre* was constructed in the 2nd century B.C. in front of the Stoa of Votive Offerings.

Museum of Samothrace

Finds from the American excavations carried out at the sanctuary of the Great Gods are exhibited in the anteroom and three rooms of the local Museum. Antiquities are also displayed in the courtyard. Exhibits include fine Archaic, Classical and Hellenistic sculpture and architectural members. There is a restored drawing showing the main edifices of the sanctuary. Parts of bronze statues are also on display, as well as a rich collection of local pottery dating to the Bronze Age and the Archaic, Classical and Hellenistic periods. A great number of terracottas, jewels and other minor objects, displayed in several cases are of interest for they supply data regarding the cult of the Kabeiroi. There are also rich funerary offerings from graves of the Hellenistic period, coins, important inscriptions, bronze objects and Byzantine pottery.

Except for the exhibits of the local Museum, finds from Samothrace feature in the Louvre and the Museum of Constantinople.

THE AEGEAN ISLANDS

Lemnos, Mytilene, Samos and Chios are the northernmost of the Aegean islands. All Greek islands are of surprising beauty, each in its own particular way. With the exception of Lemnos, which has bare hills, small fertile plains and lovely resorts, the remaining three big islands are blessed with abundant and varied vegetation, where vines, olives, orange and lemon trees predominate.

LEMNOS

The island is associated with very old myths and legends. Hephaistos, the god personifying fire, who helped men escape the misery in which they had been living, was said to have his workshop on the island of Lemnos, whose volcanic origin made it appropriate for such a purpose. The Prehistoric period of the island is most interesting to scientists. At *Poliochni* on the east coast there are ruins of a whole city of the Bronze Age. The main finds, mostly precious gold jewels, date to 2300 B.C. and correspond to the jewellery found at Troy. The upper layer of Poliochni showed traces of an unfortified city dated to 1300-1100 B.C. The second layer revealed ruins of the Mycenaean period and there are remains of two more cities of the Neolithic period, the earliest one dating to 4000 B.C. The walls of the second city had towers and gates which have been preserved to a height of 5 m. *Hephaistia*, the principal city of the island in Classical times, was situated on the northern peninsula, where 8th century B.C. graves have also been uncovered. At *Kastro* (Myrina), the island capital, there are ruins of a Venetian fortress.

The *Kabeireion,* perhaps older than the corresponding sanctuary of Samothrace is on the coastal site, where a *Telesterion* or initiation hall, a *palace* and a *stoa* have been unearthed. Farther north, there was a larger edifice, a *Telesterion* with 12 Doric columns on the facade, dating to Hellenistic times.

Museum of Lemnos

The local Museum is situated at Myrina and contains important Prehistoric finds from the Italian excavations at Poliochni (tools, utensils, clay vases and figurrines). There are also tablets with representations, dark 'Tyrrhenian' vases, and a few sculptures, mostly of Roman date, some of which have come from Imbros. Also on display are bronze handles of Geometric and Archaic cauldrons, and inscriptions of various dates. The upper floor of the National Archaeological Museum of Athens houses finds from Lemnos (mostly clay objects) exhibited in a special case.

CHIOS

The fragrance of mastic and the smell of the sea blend in the air of Chios, which, despite its mountainous nature and sparse plains, has been transformed by human labour into a 'fragrant island'. Orchards, vines and lentisk trees grow everywhere. The meager soil of the hill slopes has been enriched with earth held on the small terraces by low stone embankments.

Chios has been inhabited since very ancient times, and, like all privileged Greek sites, is associated with many myths and traditions. British excavations have revealed traces of life on the island dating to the Neolithic period. An Early Helladic settlement was unearthed at *Emporio.* Chios is one of the alleged birthplaces of Homer, and visitors are shown the *Stone of Homer.* Local feasts have their origin in a very old tradition and offer a pleasing spectacle with folkloric dances and other performances. The Chians were of Ionian descent. Chios was occupied successively by the Romans, the Arabs in the Middle Ages, the Venetians and Genoese, and finally by the Turks. During the Turkish occupation the island enjoyed special privileges, having been ceded by reason of its mastic production to Valide Hanum, whose rule was milder.

In 1530 Chios was already a centre of letters. The island was the birthplace of scholars like Proios, Bambas, Rodokanakis, and, the most eminent of all, Adamantios Korais.

One of the outstanding figures in the War of Independence, the Samian Lykourgos Logothetis, instigated the uprising of the Chians in 1822. The vengeance of the Turks was dreadful. Under the admiral Kara Ali they massacred the population of the island, so that out of 100,000 only 15,000 survived. This tragic massacre ended in favour of the Greek cause, for it provoked the reaction of the European states. Great artists and men of letters (E. Delacroix, V. Hugo) were moved and inspired to create celebrated works on the massacre of Chios, and the political circles of the great powers became convinced that the Greeks should regain their liberty.

5 kms. south of the island capital is *Daskalopetra* (the Stone of Homer). Nearby is *Nea Moni,* an 11th century monastery, which was badly damaged in the earthquake of 1881. It is decorated with wonderful mosaics showing a Constantinopolitan influence. The south part of the island is occupied by the Mastichochoria —about

20 most attractive and picturesque villages which have maintained their old local features and grow lentisk trees, whence the mastic comes from.

In Chora, the capital of the island, the visitor may see the ruins of walls, the ancient theatre (to the north of the town), and the old quarter within the *Kastro*. This castle, built by the Byzantines and held later by the Genoese and the Turks, has nine towers and was outwardly protected by a moat 60 m. wide, filled with sea-water. Within the castle is the dungeon where the Turks emprisoned the 70 notables of the island before the great massacre of 1822. There is also a Roman fountain and many monuments marking the passing of the Genoese and the occupation of the Turks. A Turkish mosque stands outside the castle. In Plateia Syntri-vaniou is the tomb of Kapetan Pasha and his officers killed during the destruction of the Turkish flagship by K. Kanaris in June 1822. The excellent Library of Chios which contains over 100,000 valuable books is worth a visit.

The villages *Olympoi* and *Mesta* have a Mediaeval aspect. *Pyrgi* (25 kms from Chora) is noteworthy for the unusual architecture of its houses with their «scraped» decoration, the local costumes and strange customs. It has a fort and more than 50 churches with old wall-paintings.

Archaeological Museum of Chios

The local Museum is housed in the Turkish mosque and includes Neolithic and Early Helladic finds, mainly from Emporio. The sculpture and pottery exhibited date from the Archaic to the Roman age. There are also some Byzantine sculpture and pottery, Frankish sculpture, a collection of coins and a great many ancient and Turkish inscriptions.

Ethnological and Folklore Museum

Situated in the Korais Library, it includes local costumes, Chian and other woven fabrics, wood-carvings and embroideries. In the *Adamantios Korais Library* there are many mementos of the great scholar and other Chian men of letters. A collection of popular handicrafts is displayed in the *Boys' Gymnasium* where a History-room contains maps, scale models and other data relevant to the massacre of 1822.

In the Cultural Centre of Michael and Stamatia Xylas at *Ano Kardamyla*, are displayed icons, wood-carvings and woven fabrics. The Museum of the Society for Progress at *Vrontado*, is housed in the Xenieion Girls' School and includes wood-carvings, embroideries, pictures of ships painted by local artists, nautical objects and historic relics of the liberation of Chios.

In the church of *Nea Moni*, display cases contain post-Byzantine ecclesiastical embroideries and sacred receptacles.

SAMOS

The island lies very close to the coast of Asia Minor, being separated from it by a strait 2 kms. wide. It is a green island wooded down to the seashores. Orange-trees, vines, almond-trees, olives and chestnuts grow amidst myrtles and flowers.

Like Chios and Mytilene, Samos has a very ancient origin and gained great power in antiquity thanks to its prosperity. It was first inhabited by the Leleges or the Kares, while information regarding the first settlements of the Greeks is controversial. The island was initially ruled by a king, like the whole of Ionia, but royal authority was gradually restricted later. During the rule of the aristocracy the Samians came into possession of Mykale, on the opposite coast of Asia Minor. In the 7th century B.C. the islanders proved skilful ship-builders and audacious navigators. A spacious war vessel *(Samaina)* was named after the island. Kolaios, a native of Samos, sailed as far as the Spanish coast and became very rich. Their marine experience was of use to the Samians during the second colonization in the 7th and 6th centuries B.C., when they planted colonies in Amorgos, Thrace, Sicily, and Naucratis in Egypt.

In the Archaic period the Greek script spread on the island and the first coins were minted. The standard of living became higher and land-owners were supplanted by the traders who demanded access to authority, thus giving rise to tyranny. The first tyrant, Demoteles, who ruled in about 600 B.C., was easily overthrown by the aristocracy. The aristocrats were in turn ousted by the merchants and democracy prevailed. The passing of time was marked with further changes until 538 - 522 B.C., when Polykrates became for the second time tyrant of Samos. He made Samos an active cultural centre and founded great works and monuments, the *temple of Hera*, the *aqueduct of Eupalinos*, the *harbour mole* and the *city walls* (his statue is in the local Museum at Tegani). His court was frequented by the poet Anakreon. The island was liberated from a temporary occupation of the Persians, who killed Polykrates in 471 B.C. after the naval battle of Mykale. Owing to their naval power, Samos and perhaps the other two major islands were accorded special privileges by the Athenians. By the end of the Peloponnesian War, Samos was again ruled by the aristocracy established by Lysander of Sparta. Alexander the Great showed interest for the exiled Samian democrats and requested their return to the island. A new Samian state was founded again and experienced the adventures of that age, having fallen successively under the Ptolemies, the Macedonians and finally the Romans. The unequal distribution of wealth among the population was continued through the Roman and Byzantine periods. The Romans gave great importance to Samos. Antony and Cleopatra stationed their fleet here in 32 B.C., and Augustus spent two winters on the island. Many Roman emperors were honoured by the Samians. Towards the end of antiquity Samos belonged to the eparchy of the Cyclades, which had its seat in Rhodes. An organized Christian community was founded in the 4th century A.D., headed by an archbishop. The constant raids of the Arabs, Turks and, particularly, the pirates compelled the Byzantines in the 7th century to make Samos a 'theme' under the leadership of an admiral. The island was later occupied by the Franks, Venetians and Genoese. In 1475 it fell to the Turks, and the Genoese transferred the population to Chios and elsewhere. Thus, Samos remained deserted for a hundred years, and was re-inhabited in 1550. During the War of Independence Samos took an active part under Lykourgos Logothetis, and fought the Turks until 1834, when it was recognized by them as a subject hegemony. Samos was re-united with Greece in 1912.

An interesting sight is the *city wall,* a fortified circuit enclosing the ancient city of Samos both on the landward and seaward sides. Only the landward wall, equipped with 35 towers and 12 gates, has been preserved to a height of 6 m. The wall, erected in the 6th century B.C., probably by Polykrates, extends round the hill of *Kastelli.* Perikles encountered great difficulties in conquering the citadel and completely destroyed the wall in his attempt, but the Samians rebuilt it later. In the first half of the 2nd century B.C., the walls were again restored with fine masonry.

The *harbour* is today smaller than it was in antiquity, by reason of sand deposits. The bay was semicircular and protected on the east side by a mole 230 m. long, on a N.-S. axis. The solidly constructed mole is a work of Polykrates and constitutes an astonishing technical structure for those times (second half of the 6th century B.C.). The mole serves as a breakwater against the southwest winter winds. The summit of the hill of *Kastro* is dominated by the Castle of Logothetis and the church of the Transfiguration. The excavated area has revealed a Hellenistic villa.

On the way to Vathy, the visitor encounters the *Eupalineion*. Nearby is the ancient *theatre*, where very few stepped rows of seats have been preserved. The site affords a superb view of the town and the port. Eupalinos of Megara was commissioned by Polykrates to build the aqueduct, which was a true technical masterpiece. For this purpose he opened through the mountain a tunnel of 1045 m. length, which had been in use for one millennium.

At the west entrance to the city, by the sea, stand three large posts over 6 m. high, the so-called *Dontia*. These posts do not belong to the city wall, but supported, along with four similar ones, a large apsidal stoa dating to the end of antiquity. The remains of this stoa were later employed for the construction of a Christian church.

From Tegani, a 6 km. road leads to the *Heraion*, which was built on plans of the Samian architect Roikos. It was a vast temple, of which only one column has survived. The temple and altars of the sanctuary underwent successive phases. The Samians believed that Hera had been born on the island, by the banks of the river Imbrasos, under a willow, which like the oak of Dodona was a very old tree. The sanctuary enjoyed great prestige and was filled with rich votive offerings of every sort presented by Greek and foreign cities.

Museum of Samos

The Museum contains finds from the German excavations at the Heraion. Among them are important Archaic sculptures, and the base of Geneleukos surmounted by its statues, which constitutes the principal exhibit of the Museum. Exhibits include Classical, Hellenistic and Roman sculpture, as well as Geometric, Archaic and Classical pottery. Archaic works produced in workshops abroad are of special interest. There are also many figurines and bronze utensils, and remarkable ivory and wooden objects dating to the Geometric and Archaic times. Finds comprise objects imported from Egypt, Assyria and Cyprus.

The *Metropolitikon Megaron* of Samos contains post-Byzantine icons, vestments, sacred vessels and old prints.

16 kms. from the town of Samos is the *Monastery of Timios Stavros*. In the gallery of the narthex are kept fine ecclesiastical objects, manuscripts and rare prints. An *archaeological collection* is housed in the *Pythagoreion*; it includes Archaic and Roman sculptures, architectural members and inscriptions.

LESBOS

Traces of a settlement found near *Thermi* date to very ancient times and indicate that the island has been inhabited since a remote past. Lesbos is one of the most attractive and interesting Greek islands. Olive, pine and fruit-trees grow everywhere, and seashores are of exquisite beauty, particularly the bays of Kalloni on the S.W., and Gera on the S.E. coast. The climate is mild and pleasant.

The remains of settlements uncovered on the island are dated to 3000 B.C. Lesbos experienced the historical adventures of the other two large islands of the Aegean. The letters and arts flourished here to a remarkable extent, while political developments were particularly turbulent during the 6th and 5th centuries B.C. The tyrant Pittakos, one of the Seven Sages, and the lyric poets Alkaios and Sappho were famous natives. The island had a varied and active life to the end of antiquity. Lesbos shared the fate of the Byzantine empire and suffered successive occupations and plunders by the Venetians, Genoese, Franks, Catalans and Turks. Following fierce struggles, Lesbos was re-united with Greece in 1912.

Mytilene, the capital of the island stretches amphitheatrically on the slopes of a pine-wooded hill overlooking the harbour. An old castle crowns the summit of the hill and memories of the past survive in the monuments and ruins of the town. There is a famous 'Petrified Forest' at Sigri (53 kms. from Mytilene), the ruins of an ancient *theatre* at Mytilene, and a *temple of Artemis* at Thermi. Some towns like Molyvos and Eressos have developed into attractive tourist centres.

The *Kastro* of Mytilene was built by the Genoese Gateluzzi in 1373 on the site of a Byzantine castle, whose remains still show a carved Byzantine eagle. Opposite the Kastro are the ruins of the ancient theatre. Further down lie the remains of a Roman villa decorated with 3rd century A.D. mosaics depicting scenes from the comedies of Menander. To the north of the theatre are ruins of the 5th century B.C. city walls which extended along the ancient breakwater, now submerged.

Like all Greek islands, Lesbos has a multitude of interesting churches. In the sacristy of the *Monastery of St. John the Theologian* at *Antissa* are kept icons, sacred vessels, ecclesiastical embroideries, manuscripts and some wood-carvings. In the *church of Panaghia* at *Agiasos* some 100 icons are displayed in cases, and vestments, sacred vessels, manuscripts (some illuminated) and many old prints are kept in the sacristy.

The *Museum of Eressos* contains Hellenistic and Roman sculpture, pottery and statuettes dating to the 4th century B.C., and Early Christian sculptures and mosaic floors. The *Monastery of St. Ignatios Leimonos* at *Kalloni* has icons, sacred vessels, reliquaries, manuscripts, prints and Greek and Turkish documents. Finally the *archaeological collection* of *Molyvos* includes a few Hellenistic and Roman sculptures and a small collection of coins.

The *Museum of Mytilene* is housed in a Neoclassical building. Exhibits include Prehistoric, as well as Archaic, Classical and Hellenistic pottery. The Aeolian capitals and some of the Classical and Hellenistic sculptures are of great interest. Also on display are Roman sculptures and remarkable mosaics with scenes from the comedies of Menander. The inscriptions exhibited are very interesting. There are also some Byzantine icons and vases and a few carved chests, which are fine examples of popular art.

The *National Folk Museum of Lesbos* is housed in the Boys' 2nd Gymnasium and contains a collection of pottery, embroideries, lace, wood-carvings and metalwork. The library has interesting Byzantine and later manuscripts and old prints.

The *Picture Gallery of Mytilene* contains works of the popular painter Theophilos. At *Vareia*, the art-critic T. Eleutheriadis (Tériade) has organized a free exhibition with works by Theophilos and other modern painters. At *Petra*, the private collection of T. Eleutheriadis includes fine works by Theophilos, and some metalwork and pottery by popular artists. The private collections of M. Vlachos, Ch. Binos and M. Nikos, at Mytilene, include wood-carved chests, embroidered handkerchiefs (tsevredes), hand-woven materials and metalwork.

THE CYCLADES

The Cyclades are a cluster of islands and islets of 'dazzling whiteness', lying in the heart of the dark blue Aegean Sea. Beautiful sandy and rocky seashores are an invitation to swimmers. Narrow and winding paved lanes, whitewashed little houses and an infinite number of tiny churches, also whitewashed, compose a picture of unique charm. On some islands houses are practically outnumbered by churches. The Cyclades usually lack a luxuriant vegetation —except for the inland of Andros, Naxos and Paros. In spite of common features, each island has a different atmosphere and each can prove a source of delight to the traveller. Even the volcanic island of Thera has a characteristic beauty of its own. The Cyclades present an incomparable harmony of lines and colours with their white houses and churches set against a background of dark blue seas and azure skies. These enchanting islands and their unforgettable sunsets will satisfy even the most demanding sight-seer.

According to the local legend the islands were named Cyclades for they form a circle around Delos, the sacred island of Apollo and the most important one in antiquity.

DELOS

In remote antiquity the fame of Delos was such that even when the fierce Persians set out to conquer Greece, they showed respect for Delos and sent message to the islanders, who had fled in fright to Tenos, to have no fear and return to their homes. The island was inhabited in earliest times (3rd millennium B.C.), owing to the importance of its geographic position for ancient seafaring — a fact that explains the presence of Minoans on this tiny island (6 kms. long from north to south and just 1 km. wide). Low granite and schist hills cover most of the territory, while level areas are very few. The torrent *Inopos* connects Mt. Kynthos, the highest peak on Delos (112 m. height), to its most accessible shore.

The lower area to the north was flooded by the waters of the Inopos and formed the *Sacred Lake* (dry in our days). An ancient legend relates that by the lake grew a *palm tree,* against which Leto leaned when giving birth to Apollo. The best harbour of the island is situated in the middle of the west coast and was used as anchorage in antiquity.

A narrow channel separates Delos from the larger island of *Rheneia*, whilst Mykonos lies northwards, at a distance covered by motorship in 20 minutes. From Mt. Kynthos one has a wonderful view of the main Cycladic islands : Tenos and Mykonos to the north, Naxos and Paros to the south, Syros to the west. The remaining of the islands, which are not visible, lie farther away in circular formation, connecting Delos with the east and west ends of the Aegean.

The occupation of Delos was continuous from the Mycenaean period onwards. There exist traces of a Prehistoric cult associated with a female deity, who was succeeded by, or indentified with Artemis in historic times. According to local tradition, Artemis was also born on Delos and had even assisted her mother at the birth of her brother.

In what is perhaps the best *Homeric Hymn* (to Apollo), reference is made to the importance of the Sacred Island, and a wonderful description is given of the birth of the god. The fact that the palm tree is mentioned by Homer, suggests that Delos was a religious center of the Ionians since, at least, 1000 B.C. Whereas at Delphi Apollo was a demanding and severe Doric deity, on Delos he assumed completely different features. It is significant that here, at the «celebrated cult centre of the Ionians», the god was worshipped with songs and dances by youths and maidens, who accompanied as 'theoroi' the votive offerings of individuals and cities. This was the 'great gathering' of the Ionians, their great festival.

.   By the end of the 7th century B.C., under the undisputed supremacy of Naxos, the Delian sanctuary began to be enriched with votive offerings. In 530 B.C., Polykrates, tyrant of Samos, is said to have dedicated to Apollo the island of Rheneia, which he attached to Delos with a chain. Following the subjugation of the Ionians by the Persians, the festivals were continued though without their former magnificence. In the 5th century B.C. Athens had assumed the leadership of the Ionians and the Athenians exerted great influence over the sanctuary, which was made for a while the seat of the Attic-Delian Alliance. But the Athenian influence had started earlier, particularly in the age of Peisistratos, who carried out in 540 B.C. the first purification (by removing the tombs from the island). Athenian legends associate Theseus, Artemis, Apollo and Leto with Athens. The sanctuary was administered by the Athenian Amphiktyones from then on.

In 426/25 B.C., a second purification took place, which involved not only the sanctuary of Apollo, but the entire island of Delos. All graves were destroyed and remains of the dead were removed to Rheneia into a common tomb, unearthed during excavations —the finds are exhibited in the Museum of Mykonos. From 425 B.C., neither births nor deaths were allowed to occur on the island. In 422 B.C., the Athenians exiled the Delians to Adramyttion in Asia Minor, where they were practically exterminated by the Persians. Very few returned on the island following an oracle of the god. The Athenians then erected a separate temple to Apollo and restored the Delian festival under a new form. The annual festival was maintained, but a parallel quinquennial celebration was held, the majestic 'Theoria' of the Athenians, who sailed to Delos on the sacred trireme. The first such Delian festival was celebrated in 425 B.C., while the old games were resumed and equestrian contests were added. In the 4th century B.C., the Delians made an attempt to gain their independence, but it was only in the time of Demetrios Poliorketes that Delos became the religious centre of the *Island Confederacy* and was declared free and independent (314 B.C.).

Between 314 and 166 B.C., the monarchs of the Hellenistic states competed in expressions of piety towards Apollo by presenting precious offerings and the sanctuary experienced its most splendid era. New monuments were erected, and the island prospered as never before. Delos became a most important commercial port and many immigrants —mariners and merchants— settled on the island. New difficulties arose in 168 B.C. after the battle of Pydna, but in 166 B.C. the Romans ceded again the sacred island to the Athenians, who banished the Delians to Achaia, whence they never returned. Athenian 'klerouchoi' and other foreigners settled on Delos, which was made by the Romans into a *free port*, to counterbalance the economic growth of Rhodes. Romans, foreigners, and a few Athenian 'klerouchoi' benefited from the thriving activity of the port. During the Mithridatic War in 88 B.C., Mithridates attacked the island and destroyed it. 20,000 people were massacred in a single day and the treasure of the sanctuary was seized by Aristion, tyrant of Athens.

Henceforth the island began to decline. In the 2nd - 3rd century A.D., only a small settlement existed there with some humble houses amidst the ruins of the sanctuary. With the spreading of Christianity small Early Christian basilicas were built with reused ancient material. Delos became the seat of an episcopate which

Mykonos.
Courtyard of a house against a background
of the characteristic windmills.

included the neighbouring islands. At the end of the 5th century A.D., travellers reported Delos as 'adelos' (i.e. unseen). By the 6th century life on Delos was extinguished and the island was deserted. At a later date it was used as a refuge by pirates. For a short while in 1329 the Knights of St. John of Malta settled on the island. During the Turkish occupation Delos was undoubtedly a pirate's nest. The remaining few houses fell to ruins and Delos and Rheneia, whose name was already forgotten, became the *Deles*. Since then, the island was never re-inhabited. Official excavations of the site were begun in 1873 by the French School of Archaeology and are still carried out.

The visitor encounters numerous ruins. First of all, the *sanctuary of Apollo* with its three *temples,* and the *sanctuary of Artemis;* then the *Avenue of the Lions* (named Sacred Way in antiquity), traces of the *Sacred Lake* and the various residential quarters of Delos, where houses have survived to a considerable height with their interior arrangement clearly visible and their superb mosaics well-preserved — a unique instance in the historic period of ancient Greece. It is a truly moving experience to walk on the paved streets, cross the squares and pass by the shops of the deserted site, which seems to be still filled with the presence of its ancient inhabitants.

Museum of Delos

It is one of the most interesting local Museums containing a multitude of exhibits of all periods and works of outstanding rank. It has important Archaic, Classical and Hellenistic, as well as several Roman sculptures, and interesting architectural members. Similarly of interest are ceramic and ivory finds from the sanctuary of Artemis. The Museum includes a collection of pottery of all periods, gold and bronze jewellery, utensils of everyday use and minor objects.

MYKONOS

The island is a point of departure for a visit to Delos. Mykonos has developed into an international tourist centre and its beauty is greatly praised. Its white little houses, picturesque churches *(Paraportiani),* typical narrow lanes and characteristic windmills give it a singular charm. Mykonian houses are examples of the island architecture which is most interesting.

Museums of Mykonos

The local *Museum* houses mainly finds from Delos. The most remarkable exhibit is a huge clay pithos with appliqué reliefs depicting scenes from the sack of Troy. There are also a collection of pottery dating from Protogeometric to Roman times, statuettes of all periods, bronze vessels and lead funerary urns. Some very significant inscriptions are on display.

The *Folklore Collection of Mykonos* is housed in an early 18th century building with a modern extension and includes woven and knitted materials, embroideries, lace and ceramics of Aegean provenance, as well as remarkable stone-carvings. The Naval Archives are of interest. Models of stamped bread, specimens of basketry, weights and measures, are unusual items.

TENOS

In addition to its beautiful inland scenery, the great attraction of the island of Tenos is the *church of the Megalochari* (Panayia Evangelistria), a Panhellenic pilgrimage centre. Several collections belong to the Monastery : an exhibition of Tenian artists, which includes works by Gyzis, Lytras, Chalepas and Philippotis, post-Byzantine icons, vestments, sacred vessels, wood-carvings, and precious ex-votos. There is also an exhibition of works by the sculptor A. Sohos, and another picture gallery (donated by I. Papadopoulos) which includes works by Volonakis, Parthenis, etc., as well as copies of paintings of the Renaissance.

The *Archaeological Museum of Tenos* is situated in a fine building. The main room contains Archaic pithoi, with relief decorations, and other rooms include Archaic and Hellenistic sculpture, Geometric pottery and inscriptions.

An *archaeological collection* is exhibited in the Neoclassical building of the Town Hall, on the island of *Syros*. The collection includes Prehistoric marble and clay vases, and Hellenistic and Roman sculptures and inscriptions.

Paros is a very interesting island, and one of the most beautiful of the Cyclades. Paros was in antiquity a source of the finest marble, the raw material used for the production of a vast number of masterpieces. An important monument is the *church of Panaghia Katapoliani*, a huge building of the 5th century, recently restored to its original form by the removal of a picturesque 17th century external addition. The collection of Katapoliani, housed in cells, includes post-Byzantine icons, vestments, sacred vessels and Byzantine sculptures. The *Archaeological Museum of Paros* is one of the most interesting Cycladic Museums next to those of *Delos* and *Thera*. It contains Neolithic and Cycladic stone vases and statuettes, remarkable sculptures of all periods, pottery dating from Geometric to late Classical times, and important inscriptions. Mosaic floors from Katapoliani are also on display. For the friends of post-Byzantine art, there is a small ecclesiastical collection at *Naousa* on Paros, housed in the church of St. Nicholas and consisting of a few ancient finds and post-Byzantine icons, wood-carvings and minor objects.

On the island of *Siphnos*, excavations are being carried out at the site of the *Kastro of Ayios Andreas*. An archaeological collection is housed in the Frankish church of St. Antony at *Kastro*, and includes Hellenistic and Roman sculptures, as well as Archaic statuettes and vases. In the village hall of the attractive little island of *Seriphos* are exhibited sculptures of the Roman period.

NAXOS

Everything is appealing on this island and a visit to it affords a treasure of impressions. Naxos is of great interest for its Mediaeval and later buildings. A large number of Byzantine (about 48) and post-Byzantine churches are decorated with remarkable wall-paintings. Entering the harbour, the traveller sees on the left, on the islet of *Palatia,* the huge marble doorway of an ancient temple. The most picturesque *Chora* stretches as far as its Mediaeval castle. Within the castle are the decayed mansions of Barozzi and Sommaripa. Naxos has been explored for many years and investigations are continued by the Greek Archaeological Society. The majority of Cycladic stone statuettes and vases have come from Naxos, and the island has yielded excellent specimens of Mycenaean art. Naxos was an important island in antiquity, and a great artistic centre, particularly in the Archaic age. The famous *quarries* of the island were situated at *Apollonas,* the northernmost village of the east coast, where a gigantic (11 m. high) Archaic kouros still lies unnifished.

MELOS

Melos is a delightful island with a very old civilization. In antiquity it was the source of a then precious material, the obsidian, used for making blades and even vases (by the Minoans). The main archaeological site, *Phylakopi,* is worth a prolonged visit. The site has revealed three successive Prehistoric cities (dating from the 3rd milliennium. B.C. to the end of the Mycenaean period). A number of finds and beautiful frescoes are to be seen in the palace.

By the village *Trypeti* are the famous catacombs, where the earliest Christians secretly performed their religious ceremonies and buried their dead. The *Archaeological Museum* at *Plaka* contains Cycladic pottery and a vast number of obsidian blades, as well as some Greek and Roman sculptures, vases and inscriptions.

KIMOLOS

Kimolos is so closely associated with Melos that a reading of its history leaves one with the impression that they are one island. Separated by a strait less than one mile wide from Apollonia, the N.E. coast of Melos, the island is a source of chalk ('kimolia') from which it derives its name. It was inhabited in Prehistoric times (a settlement exists on the islet of Ayios Andreas). A necropolis has been unearthed on Kimolos. The island was later named *Echinousa.* Sights include the *Hellenikon* (now called Kophto), near the shore (its necropolis has been submerged since the Cycladic age), the *Palaiokastro* which has interesting antiquities (remains of a Mediaeval castle), the 17th century church of the Evangelistria at *Prasa.* In fact, the entire island is full of churches. There are also antiquities by the Lake Varvakaina, and in caves by the Lake Vromolimni and the river Kaos.

IOS

Ios is a pretty little island which has lately developed into a tourist centre. The island is said to have 400 churches. The remains of a Venetian castle can be seen at *Palaiokastro.* The island capital, *Ios,* lies on the site of the ancient city, which therefore cannot be explored. The church of St. Katherine has some incorporated ancient sculpture. *Epano Kampos* (the site is named Hellenika), has ruins of an ancient temple or fort. Ios is one of the islands claiming Homer as a native, and near *Plakoto,* the visitor is shown the *Tomb of Homer.*

Sikinos is an attractive island with sparse vegetation but lovely seashores. At *Chora,* lie the ruins of the *temple of Pythian Apollo,* which has been overlain by the church of the Dormition of the Virgin. At *Palaiokastro* there are ruins of an ancient temple which has not been excavated. Interesting local feasts take place on the islet of *Pholegandros,* whose capital, *Chora,* is built within the walls of the Mediaeval castle. At *Pounta* there is a cave with stalactites and stalagmites, the *Chrysospelia.* Outside the hamlet of Apano Meria stands the fine church of Panaghia.

Amorgos is an island with delightful scenery. At about the middle of the N.W. coast, near the present-day harbour of Katapola, are the remains of ancient *Minoa.* The celebrated *Monastery of Chozoviotissa* was founded in 1088 by the emperor Alexios Komnenos at the foot of a precipitous rock. The village *Arkesine* marks the site of the ancient homonymous city. Interesting inscriptions and other antiquities have been found at *Aïgiali*, where the fine *church of Exochoriani* was built over part of the *temple of Athena.*

KEA

An almost bare island, Kea, has beautiful shores and inviting deserted bays, as well as many antiquities. At the bay of *Ayia Eirene,* at the N.W. end of the island, excavations carried out for a number of years by the American School of Classical Studies have uncovered an important *settlement* and a small *temple* of the 15th century B.C., rebuilt in the 12th century B.C. Ruins of houses and walls are abundant and movable finds of various periods are exceptional — chief among them are the large female clay statuettes. Kea was inhabited in the Bronze Age. In the 15th century B.C., the Minoans planted a colony at Ayia Eirene. Above the town of *Chora* and the nearby site of ancient *Ioulis*, stands a ruined Frankish castle. Outside the town, an Archaic lion is carved out of the rock. The ruins of the *temple of Apollo* at ancient *Karthaia* are most impressive. The *archaeological collection* (at Chora) includes inscriptions and sculpture of all periods.

An island of many hot springs, *Kythnos* was important in antiquity and Aristotle mentions the 'constitution of the Kythnians' for its good organization. Very old customs have survived in the local wedding ceremonies and festivals. In the Middle Ages the town was transferred to the *Kastro tis Orias,* which was destroyed by the pirates in the 13th century. Near the west coast at about an hour's walk from *Chora,* is the village *Ovriokastro* on the site of ancient Kythnos. The *church of Panaghia tis Kanalas* is noteworthy. On the N.E. point of the island there are ruined Byzantine monasteries and a few churches with fine wall-paintings. Mediaeval churches at Chora are decorated with 17th and 18th century wall-paintings.

THERA

The island, known from the Middle Ages as Santorin, was named in antiquity *Kalliste* or *Strongyle*. It is an island of astonishing beauty with a very old life and outstanding culture which is being revealed by the current excavations of Professor Sp. Marinatos at *Akrotiri*. The site was selected because of its characteristic landscape and the fact that the layers of *tephra* are thinner at this point (elsewhere they reach a thickness of as much as 60m.). The aristocratic quarter of a large city stretching from one end of the coast to the other is being unearthed during these excavations which have so far yielded hundreds of superbly decorated vases of the 16th century B.C., and truly exquisite frescoes (Frescoes of the Spring, the Boxing Children, the Antelopes, the Blue Monkeys, the Priestess, the African, etc.). Each year (excavations on the site are continued) brings a new surprise. Strictly scientific methods are applied in exploring this site, and in a few years time Thera will prove comparable to Knossos, as far as finds are concerned, particularly frescoes. There has been already the unprecedented discovery of a whole room whose walls are covered with painting (Fresco of the Spring). The northern part of the city exploded during a terribly devastating volcanic eruption and sank to a depth of 500 - 800 m. in the 'Caldera' formed. This eruption which caused the destruction of the island occurred in circa 1500 B.C., and huge tidal waves and masses of volcanic ash covered everything on the island. As no human bones have been recovered so far, it appears that the inhabitants, forewarned by the earthquakes preceding the eruption, had abandoned

the island. This formidable volcanic eruption also destroyed the Minoan civilization. The ensuing tidal waves literally swept the north and east coasts of Crete, which
suffered a parallel damage and loss of human and animal lives, vegetation, etc.
According to Professor Marinatos' theory, which has been proved absolutely correct, the destruction of the palaces at Knossos, Phaistos, Mallia and Ayia Triada
occurred at that time. The best finds from the excavations at Thera are temporarily
exhibited in the upper floor of the National Archaeological Museum of Athens.

Although the soil of Thera consists now of rock formations of lava and volcanic ash ('aspa'), the island, like all volcanic areas, was most fertile in antiquity, a
true «oasis of peace, prosperity and good life», as Professor Marinatos suggests.
Olive and wild olive, palm and other luxuriant vegetation was growing on the island
as can be further deduced from the marvellous frescoes found at Akrotiri. (Until
1500 B.C. Thera was a round island, but the volcanic eruption of that date caused
the central section to sink, forming the separate little islands of *Thera* and *Thera-
sia* and the islet of *Aspronesi*). Before the catastrophe the island was well watered.
Some craters of the volcano had become lakes and there were streams and rivulets
flowing all year round. Above all, the art of Prehistoric Thera was developed to an
amazing extent. All this echanting setting, however, was destroyed all at once by
the volcanic eruption.

In historic times Thera, like Melos, sided with Doric Sparta. The island flourished in the Archaic period, as attested by excavations at *Sellada,* where the city
of that age was uncovered (excavations were carried out by German archaeologists
and, before them, by the French in the last century). Thera prospered most in the
7th century B.C., when the Therans founded the colony of *Cyrene* on the rich land
of Cyrenaica. Apollo Karneios was the patron god of the islanders, and the Gymno-
paidiai, an important festival of antiquity, were celebrated in his honour. A great
number of Archaic inscriptions recording names of gods and men are carved on the
rocks of the ancient city. The walls of a Byzantine fortress survive on the slope of
Mesa Vouno, and further down the church of the Annunciation overlies the ruins
of a 2nd century B.C. heroon. Nearby is the temenos of Artemidoros.

From ancient Thera the road leads down to *Perissa,* where there is an exquisitely charming little church built in the 19th century. At the west end of the
island, the church of Ayios Ioannis Marmarites overlies the ruins of a 3rd century B.C. marble temple. During the Peloponnesian War Thera sided with Sparta
but escaped disaster, having joined the Athenians at the last moment. In the Hellenistic period the Ptolemies made the island a religious center and their naval base
in the Aegean. Thera was deserted later and re-inhabited in the Byzantine era. It
was occupied by the Franks, included in the duchy of Naxos after 1204, raided by
Barbarossa, and later taken by the Turks. The modern name of the island derives
from the patroness saint, St. Eirene (Santa Irini).

In the ancient city there are ruins of a *Gymnasion,* the *temple of Pyrgian Apollo,*
the Hellenistic *shrines of Isis, Sarapis and Anubis* carved out of the rock, as well as
the *agora,* the *temple of Dionysos, etc.*

In the Archaic city at the foot of Mt. Prophetes Elias, where there is a *theatre*
of later date (3rd century B.C.) commanding a wonderful view, the Greek Archaeological Society has explored the Archaic *cemetery* of the city which yielded remarkable finds, now displayed in the *Museum of Phera.* The island has an endless
number of churches. Some fine mansions (particularly at Pyrgos) escaped destruction during the terrible earthquakes of 1956, which devastated the attractive town
of *Oia* and ruined the fine examples of local architecture at *Phera.*

Archaeological Museum of Thera

It is a remarkable Museum not only for its finds but also for the way these are presented. Exhibits are arrayed in the vestibule and the two large oblong rooms of the Museum, and include some very fine Prehistoric pottery (specimens from excavations at Akrotiri). There is also an outstanding collection of sculpture dating from the Archaic period to Roman times. Special cases contain excellent examples of Geometric, Archaic and Classical pottery, as well as Archaic statuettes. Also on display are Roman glassware and lamps, and a small number of inscriptions, some of which are of interest.

The *Ecclesiastical Museum,* housed in the Metropolitikon Megaron, contains a small collection of icons and wood-carved crosses. Finally in the *Monastery of Prophetes Elias* at Pyrgos, the visitor may see in the sacristy liturgical vessels, wood-

Thera.
Part of the Fresco of the Spring.

carved crosses, post-Byzantine icons, vestments, prints, and a few Turkish documents and firmans. The private *collection* of P. Nomikos includes fine woven materials, embroideries (some of which gold-embroidered) and metalwork, as well as a few paintings and porcelain ware. The mansions of *Pyrgos* are furnished with magnificent old glass, crystal and porcelain ware and old furniture which testify to the former prosperity of the island, when its inhabitants returning from their travels abroad brought with them these fine objects, which have been preserved to some extent.

ANDROS

Andros is the largest of the Cycladic islands with an age-long history. The unique round tower at St. Peter is a remnant of Prehistoric times. A settlement dating to the Geometric period is being excavated at Zagora. The statue known as the *«Hermes from Andros»*, now exhibited in the National Archaeological Museum of Athens, has come from Palaiopolis. The island prospered greatly in the Byzantine era, as evinced by the remains of that age : the splendid *church of the Taxiarches* at Messaria, and that of the *Taxiarches Melidas* (both are dated to the 11th century). The *Monasteries of Panachrantos* and *Zoodochos Pighi* are of Post-Byzantine date. A visit is recommended to Sariza, a well-known source of mineral waters.

THE DODECANESE

The Dodecanese is a group of islands of great beauty, each in its own particular way. Rhodes, the largest and most important of the Dodecanese, as well as the rest of these islands, shared the fate of Hellenism. At different periods each has known a great flowering, as local monuments denote. Situated between three continents, they occupy a strategic position in the Aegean Sea and various conquerors through the ages did not fail to set foot on them, either to plunder or take them into possession. The islands of the Dodecanese, particularly Rhodes and Kos, have beautiful sandy shores and an excellent climate. Some of them have been inhabited since Prehistoric times, occupied by Pre-Hellenic races from Asia Minor, before being settled by the Greeks. Later, they fell to the Persians, Romans, Venetians, Genoese, Turks and Italians (1911 - 1945), and were officially united with Greece on the 7th of March 1948.

RHODES

Rhodes is by far the largest of the Dodecanese. Its monuments have survived in good condition, so that today, after being restored, they show clearly the great flowering the island had enjoyed and the successive occupations it had suffered. Rhodes abounds in sights worth visiting. Occupation of the island in the Neolithic period has not been confirmed by excavation data. Only few Neolithic traces have been found accidentally. The Greeks made their appearance for the first time in about 1500 B.C. (in the Mycenaean period), when the Achaians dominated the Aegean with their navy and trade and established trading posts on the Greek islands and the west coast of Asia Minor. The Dorians under the leadership of Tlepolemos of Tiryns — who participated in the Trojan War — landed on the island in about 1100 B.C. With the passing of time three great centers were developed : Ialysos, Kameiros and Lindos. These cities formed part of the Dorian hexapolis founded in the early 7th century B.C.

According to the local legend, related by Pindar in his 7th *Olympian Ode*, when the gods divided the earth among them, Rhodes had not yet appeared «on the vast expanse of the sea», but lay hidden in its depths. As Helios however had been absent, no one remembered to include him in the distribution, and when he reminded them of it, Zeus offered to start the distribution anew. Helios refused, saying that he saw emerging from the sea a land that would feed many people and have abundant cattle. Thus, Rhodes — for this was the island — became the possession of Helios «who gives birth to the sharp rays». Out of his union with the nymph Rhodos, he begot seven sons and these in turn begot Kameiros, Ialysos and Lindos, who divided among them the land of their fathers and gave each his name to his share.

The island has a long and rich history. In Archaic times the Rhodian cities planted colonies in Sicily and Pamphylia in Asia Minor. When the Persians launched their campaign against Greece, the cities of Rhodes were under the rule of the barbarians and were hence obliged to fight on their side. When the invaders were defeated thanks to the incomparable valour of the Greeks, the Rhodians were among the first who sought to join the First Athenian Alliance in order to secure their independence. The year 408 B.C. is a memorable date for Rhodes; it was then that the Rhodians decided to leave their three cities and form a synoecism, a larger and stronger centre on the N.E. end of the island, which they named after the island itself *Rhodes*. Dorieus of Ialysos, a descendent of a noble family (the Diagoridai), played a leading role in the formation of the synoecism and its political organization. His family was celebrated because of the successive victories won by several of its members in the Panhellenic games (the first victor was Diagoras). The language, customs, political system and religious cult of the island were Dorian. Rhodes owed her commercial expansion to her most favourable situation. The fact that Kameiros in the 6th and Ialysos and Lindos in the 5th century B.C., minted their own coins is a sign of the prosperity of the three Rhodian cities. By reason of the very old local cult of Athena Lindia, Lindos had remained a great religious centre. Kleoboulos of Lindos, son of Euagoras, a contemporary of Solon, was an outstanding personage of Rhodian antiquity. He was the 'tyrant' of Lindos for 40 years and acquired Panhellenic fame as a just ruler and one of the Seven Sages of Greece. The 'demes' of the three early Rhodian cities had been preserved, but administrative and political matters were debated and settled in Rhodes by the ecclesia (assembly), the boule (parliament) and five prytaneis. The Priest of Helios was annually appointed as eponymous.

In the 4th century B.C., the island was disturbed by great political conflicts. Rhodes became a member of the Second Athenian Alliance. By the middle of the century it escaped the possessive intentions of Mausolos of Halikarnassos. Later, the independence of the Rhodians was storm-tossed between the Persians and the Greeks. Memnon the Rhodian was one of Darius' mercenary generals who fought against Alexander the Great. Henceforth, the island's commercial interests dictated its political alignment.

Rhodes attained great prosperity in the Hellenistic period, after the foundation of Alexandria. Demetrios Poliorketes, having vainly tried for a whole year to conquer the strongly fortified island, was compelled to raise his siege and sign a treaty which guaranteed the Rhodians their independence and honour. A great number of votive offerings were then dedicated to the gods. In the 3rd century B.C., the policy of the Rhodians, always subject to their commercial interests, saved them from the fierce rivalries of that age. In fact, the prestige of their city was so great that it often played the role of mediator. A disastrous earthquake in 227 or 226 B.C., caused the fall of the Colossus and the destruction of part of the city, her walls and her shipyards. Rhodes maintained a friendly attitude towards Rome, and sometimes even fought on the side of the Romans against the Hellenistic monarchs, in order to benefit her trade and avoid an open clash with Rome. The island reached its zenith in the first decades of the 2nd century B.C. and gained supremacy over the *Island Confederacy*. Henceforward, in order to protect her interests, Rhodes sided with the Romans. From the 2nd century B.C., and particularly in the 1st century B.C., the island became celebrated as a great intellectual and artistic center. Prominent orators (Apollonios Molon and Apollonios Malakos), as well as great philosophers (Poseidonios) taught at Rhodes. They were even entrusted with diplomatic missions, which they carried out successfully, for many prominent Romans had attended the Rhodian school as their pupils, or travelled there for political purposes (Tiberius Gracchus in 165 and 161, B.C., Scipio Aemilianus Africanus in 129 B.C., Cicero on several occasions from 78 B.C. onwards, the poet Lucretius Carus, Julius Caesar, etc.). Following the naval battle of Actium (31 B.C.), the Rhodians found it increasingly difficult to retain their independence. The island became a refuge for many exiled Romans (Tiberius), for this was permitted by decree of the emperor Augustus, and the home of those in quest of an intellectual and cultural centre. Whereas Nero plundered Olympia, Delphi and Pergamon, he spared Rhodes. Finally in A.D. 297, Diocletian united Rhodes with the Roman Provincia Insularum.

In the 1st century A.D., the city of Rhodes still preserved its old magnificence, while life began to decline. After the terrible earthquake of A.D. 155, and in spite of the help of Antoninus Pius, Rhodes never recovered her old glory.

At the ancient harbour (on the site of the present-day harbour) stood the famous *Colossus of Rhodes* (30 m. high), which was considered as one of the seven wonders of the world. The statue was made in 290 B.C. and the cost defrayed by the sale of the siege material of Demetrios Poliorketes; it was destroyed in 225 B.C.

The ancient *acropolis* of Rhodes lies by the S.W. edge of the city, on the east slope of a hill named *Monte Smith* (after the admiral stationed there at the time of Napoleon to keep watch on the movements of the French fleet). The visitor encounters on the site a small *theatre* of quadrilateral shape, the restored ancient *Stadion,* and the ruins of two *temples* consecrated to *Apollo* and *Athena.* The view from the hill is indeed unforgettable. At *Phileremos* (15 kms. from the city) there are remains of a 3rd century B.C. *temple of Athena* and a small Byzantine church. The ancient *fountain* of Phileremos is celebrated and marks the site of ancient *Ialysos.* Its necropolis has been explored by the Italians who investigated about 500 graves dating from the Mycenaean age to the Classical period. 26 kms. from the city of Rhodes is the valley of Butterflies (*Petaloudes*), where there are thousands of beautiful butterflies. *Kameiros* (36 kms. from the city of Rhodes) is regarded as the Rhodian Pompeii. It was founded by Tlepolemos on the slope of a pretty hill. Kameiros was the birthplace of the poet Peisander. Among the ruins have survived a 3rd century B.C. *temenos* a Doric *temple,* the *agora,* a few remains of the *temple of Athena,* a Doric *stoa* and a cistern.

Lindos, with her acropolis crowning a gigantic rock rising abruptly from the sea, makes an indellible impression on the sight-seer. It is bathed in a dazzling sunlight and commands a magnificent view. On the *acropolis* are the ruins of the *sanctuary* of Athena Lindia. Passing under the lower Gate of the Mediaeval wall, the visitor reaches a terrace with the relief of a ship carved into the rock; the deck served as the base of a statue of Hagesandros (180 B.C.) made by the Rhodian artist Pythokritos. The purpose for which this work was founded is unknown. The sanctuary

Rhodes.
Decorative Arts Collection.

of Athena Lindia. was modelled in the Hellenistic period. A large Π-shaped Doric *stoa* has been restored. The stoa included in its central part a monumental staircase (of earlier date, for it provided access to the temple of Athena since the age of Kleoboulos). The stairway leads to the *Great Propylaia,* which were constructed after 408 B.C. and served as monumental entrance. Beyond stands the *temple of Athena Lindia,* built after 342 B.C., when the older temple, founded by Kleoboulos, was destroyed by fire, along with the old wooden cult statue of the goddess. According to a local legend, the sanctuary of Athena and her cult statue were founded by Danaos, in 1510 B.C., when he went with his daughters by Lindos on his way to Argolis. In any event, the cult was earlier than the settlement of the Dorians on the island, and was associated with a female deity, perhaps named *Lindia,* later identified by the Greeks with Athena Lindia. The cult was originally performed in the sacred grove of the acropolis, which was preserved throughout antiquity.

By the end of Geometric times, a small temple and a small wooden statue representing a seated figure were consecrated to the goddess. Kleoboulos renovated the sanctuary and erected on the highest point of the rock a similar Doric temple with four columns on the facade and another four at the back. This building has been probably overlain by the temple we see at present. When the later temple was constructed in 342 B.C., it housed the new acrolithic statue of the goddess (the body was of gilt wood and the head and extremities of marble or ivory). The goddess was represented standing, holding a phiale in the right hand, her shield in the left. A colonnade stood on the west side of an enclosed court in front of the temple. Excavations at Lindos were carried out by the Danes and many finds are now exhibited in the Museum of Copenhagen, while some are displayed in the Museum of Constantinople. The monuments on the acropolis were restored during the Italian occupation.

The town of Lindos has some excellent 16th and 17th century houses decorated with woven fabrics and Rhodian plates. The ancient *theatre* of Lindos (the koilon and orchestra have been preserved) is situated west of the acropolis. Traces of a *Gymnasion* exist near the church of St. Stephanos. By the site *Vigli,* north of the acropolis, there is a small ancient shrine in a natural niche of the rock, named *Boukopion,* where oxen were sacrificed to the gods during the festival of the Boukopia, for it was not permitted to sacrifice on the acropolis. Finally, a large circular monument of the Classical period is said to be the *Tomb of Kleoboulos.* It is situated on the edge of the promontory stretching north of the great harbour. The monument, originally surrounded by a peribolos, was later converted by the Christians into the church of St. Aimilianos.

Archaeological Museum of Rhodes

The Museum is situated in the Mediaeval building of the Hospital of the Knights and includes fine collections of pottery and sculpture. It contains Prehistoric pottery and other finds of the Neolithic period discovered within caves on the islands of Kalymnos and Kos (tools, blades, vases). Exhibits include finds of the Mycenaean period from excavations at the necropolis of Ialysos (vases, gold jewels, ivory or glass finger-rings, scarabs). Funerary offerings from graves of historic times (from the Geometric to the Classical age) are finely displayed and include superb Rhodian, Corinthian, a few Laconian, and a greater number of Attic black-figure and red-figure vases, terracotta statuettes, etc. Some Klazomenean clay sarcophagi are decorated with painted floral designs or human portraits (the latest are dated to the

Museum of Rhodes.
Statue of Aphrodite.

early 5th century B.C.). There are numerous finds from the sanctuary of Athena on the acropolis of Ialysos and finds from the rich graves of Kameiros, similar to those from Ialysos. Finally, there are finds from the *sanctuary of Zeus Atabyrios*, situated on the summit of the homonymous mountain (mostly bronze votive offerings, statuettes of oxen, etc.).

On the upper gallery of the Museum are exhibited Archaic large clay pithoi decorated with embossed geometric ornaments. These were often used as sarcophagi for the burial of children or youths. There are also many Rhodian amphoras with stamped handles and inscriptions, used for transporting or storing wine.

Exhibits include architectural members and funerary monuments (the stele of Krito and Timaresta from the necropolis of Kameiros is an Ionic work of outstanding sensibility, dating to the last decades of the 5th century B.C.), Christian mosaics, coats-of-arms and tombstones of the Knights. There is also an interesting collection of ancient and Mediaeval coins and medals. Of exceptional interest are two Archaic kouroi found in the acropolis of Kameiros, on the site of an altar of Helios of later date. Both statues show an influence of Ionic art and are dated to the third quarter of the 6th century B.C. One of the kouroi was made by a Naxian and the other by a Parian sculptor. Other exhibits of interest are : a male statue (2.30 m. high) from Kos dated to circa 150 B.C.; a Hellenistic female portrait statue of the end of the 4th century B.C.; a head of Helios (0.55 m. high including the neck) bearing holes on the hair for the insertion of metal rays, found at the top of the Kastello, which is believed to have been the site of the sanctuary of Helios (the head is dated to the mid-2nd century B.C.); a fine headless statuette of a Nymph (0.63m. high) seated on a rock (dated to the early 1st century B.C.). There is also a remarkable statuette of a nude Aphrodite (0.49 m. high) represented kneeling and about to take a bath (a 1st century B.C. copy of the famous work of the sculptor Doidalsas). Another fine female statue represents a Nymph covering the lower part of her body with a sliding himation and resting her right foot on a rock (dated to the 1st century B.C.). A most interesting exhibit is a marble tropaion (1.90 m. high) from the necropolis of Rhodes, the tombstone of a Rhodian soldier of the Mithridatic War (1st century B.C.).

Decorative Arts Collection of the Museum of Rhodes

The Collection is also housed in the Hospital of the Knights (entrance from Argyrokastrou Square). It includes very fine embroideries, woven materials, carved chests and wood-carvings, and some Symian pottery.

In the *Palace of the Grand Masters*, at the end of the Street of the Knights, there is an interesting collection of 16th and 17th century West European furniture and tapestries. Roman and Early Christian mosaics have been transferred from Kos and Karpathos to decorate the floors of the Palace, which also houses some Early Christian sculptures. At *Lindos*, the fine typical house of Papaconstantinou, adorned with relief decorations on the facade and painted ceilings, contains an *archaeological collection* which includes some Classical and Hellenistic sculptures and inscriptions. The private collections of Ch. Georgiou and Em. Koskines include popular ceramics and the collection of P. Ioannides ornamental plates.

The Byzantine and Postbyzantine monuments of Rhodes

The Mediaeval period

By the end of the 3rd century A.D. the island of Rhodes had become the metropolis of the *Provincia Insularum* of the Aegean and, with the partition of the Roman world into an Eastern and Western empire, the capital of the theme of Kibyratis. Rhodes' destiny was thus bound up with that of the Eastern Roman Empire. From the 7th century onwards it suffered Persian attacks, followed by Arab incursions which continued unremittingly for three centuries: that is to say, until the beginning of the 9th century. Byzantine domination of Rhodes was complete during the 11th century, and, when Constantinople fell to the Crusaders, Leon Gavalas, the Greek governor of Rhodes, proclaimed the island his personal heritage in order to prevent it from being captured by the Venetians. The island thus remained independent. From 1258 onwards it came under Genoese rule. In 1306 the latter offered hospitality to the Knights of St. John who were obliged to leave Jerusalem under Moslem pressure. In three years the Knights had become masters of the island and their rule lasted for two centuries. They successfully withstood both Turkish and pirate raids, and during the period of their domination Rhodes attained a high state of prosperity. But, in spite of the Knights' spirited resistance, the island was conquered by the Turks in 1522, after which it became the capital of the Aegean and an important commercial center. In 1912 it was annexed by the Italians and in 1947 ceded, together with the other islands of the Dodecanese, to Greece.

The Monuments

During the Early Christian period Rhodes was a very important center and, from the end of the century, the metropolis of all the neighbouring islands. Tradition has it that St. Paul landed here and stayed for a while. Numerous basilicas have been excavated in different parts of the island which include, among others, Philerimos, Arnitha, Lardos, Aphandou and Messanagros.

Many Byzantine and post-Byzantine edifices, both lay and ecclesiastical, survive. Among the most outstanding lay buildings of the Byzantine period are the castles of the capital, of Lindos, of Pharaklos and Philerimos, on all of which the Knights of St. John built additional fortifications. Among the most impressive monuments of the period of the Knights are those that lie outside the perimeter of the acropolis of Rhodes: namely, the strong walls with bastions, towers and ramparts, the palace of the Chief Magistrate, the Senate house and the magnificent Street of the Knights. So numerous are the Byzantine and post-Byzantine churches scattered about the town and countryside that it is only possible to mention a few of the most typical ones with the most interesting features, whether interior or exterior. Of the basilica type, the majority are single-naved. These include Ayios Demetrios at Lindos, Ayios Ioannis Baptistis within the castle of Rhodes and the 12th century Ayia Paraskevi on Mt. Paradeisi on the west coast of the island. The 14th century Ilk - Mihrab, which was converted into a mosque during the Turkish occupation 'and is situated within the castle of Rhodes, is a double-naved basilica. Cross-inscribed edifices include the remains of a 10th century church on the acropolis of Philerimos, the 13th century Panayia within the precincts of the castle of Rhodes which combines Byzantine and Gothic architectural features and the 13th century Ayios Ioannis within the castle of Lindos. Among the churches with a free Greek Cross plan are those of Ayia Irene at the village of Koskinou and of Ayios Phanourios within the castle of Rhodes. The former Katholikon of a Byzantine monastery, also within the precincts of the castle, converted during the Turkish occupation into a medresse which went under the name of Hourmali-Medresse, is tri-apsidal in form.

A number of monuments whose architectural style was influenced by the sojourn of the Knights are also worth noting. This type of edifice continues to be raised to the present day. It generally consists of a rectangular basilica, single- or three-naved, with a cross vault roof. Among these is the church at Apolakkia.

All the Byzantine and post-Byzantine churches in these categories were for the most part built of local limestone, the walls of the more modest ones consisting entirely of ordinary stonework without any bricks. Windows were few and narrow. And only the domes of some 14th century churches give an impression of architectural modelling which serves as a contrast to the —on the whole— bare austerity of the exteriors. The painted decoration of the interiors of the Rhodian churches is by no means without interest. We consequently have examples of a provincial adaptation of the formal art of Constantinople, such as in the 13th century Church of Ayios Georgios Vardas near the village of Apolakkia; other examples betray the infiuence of the Cretan school, of which the Church of the Panayia on the castle of Lindos is one. Distinctly Eastern-Cappadocian trends are also observed in the 14th century Ilk-Mihrab within the castle of Rhodes.

KOS

A most attractive island with a serene landscape, Kos was renowned in ancient times for its Asklepieion. It is the birthplace of Hippokrates, the greatest physician of antiquity. The island lies very close to the coast of Asia Minor and has beautiful seashores and picturesque bays. It is dominated by Mt. Oromedon, which is surrounded by pretty green valleys sloping towards the sea. In the 4th century B.C., thanks to the sanctuary of Asklepios, the island became a Panhellenic cult center. The celebrated painter Apelles was also born here (4th century B.C.). Kos followed the historic course of the rest of the Dodecanese. In the 4th century B.C., the island is said to have had 160,000 inhabitants. Devastated in 142 B.C. by a severe earthquake, Kos was rebuilt in more magnificent style, with baths, gymnasia, a stadion and an odeion. In A.D. 469, another earthquake caused great damage. Early Christian basilicas were erected over the ruins of old buildings. Finally, the earthquake of 554 destroyed everything and the island was deserted by its inhabitants.

The Crusaders conquered Kos in 1391, and marks of their passage are the Palace of the Regent to the east of the harbour, and the fine Castle of the Knights in the town itself. There are also some Turkish buildings, reminiscent of the Turkish occupation of Kos (it fell to the Turks in 1523). Among the most interesting monuments of the island are the *Odeion* and a Roman villa with exquisite mosaics. The so-called *plane-tree of Hippokrates* is a sight to be seen; the perimeter of the trunk measures 12 m., and the tree is supposed to have been planted by Hippokrates himself, who cured his patients under its shade. Nearby is a *stoa* dated to the 4th or 3rd century B.C., and an Early Christian basilica of the 5th - 6th century. In the town there are many ruins dating to the ancient and Early Christian times : a Doric temple, the basilica of St. John, a very well preserved Roman street, and the remains of the ancient gymnasion overlain by a basilica. Among the ruins there is an interesting mosaic representing gladiators.

The *Asklepieion* is situated 4 kms. from the town. The site had been selected with the usual sensible criterion of the ancients, so as to provide a most suitably peaceful environment. The *temple* of the god is Doric, built on an elevated platform accessible by a large staircase. The buildings have been restored by the Italians (therapeutic springs, stoas). Halikarnassos is visible in the distance on the ccast of Asia Minor. The sanctuary occupies three terraces.

Kos.
Ruins of the Asklepieion.

Museum of Kos

The local Museum contains Prehistoric pottery and excellent sculpture dated from the Classical era to the Roman age. Similarly of interest are the vases and numerous inscriptions.

The Metropolitikon Megaron houses a *Museum of Popular Art* with many fine post-Byzantine icons and gold-embroidered and hand-woven textiles.

There is an *Archaeological collection* at the *Kastro*, which contains a few sculptures of Classical and Early Christian date, as well as some inscriptions dating from Hellenistic to Byzantine times.

Kalymnos is the island of sponge-divers, renowned for the bravery and kindness of its inhabitants and for its interesting local customs, whose origins are traced to antiquity. The colourful houses of the town are perched on the mountain slope. The *Archaeological Museum,* housed in an old carpet-weaving workshop, includes Neolithic and Classical pottery, as well as sculptures and inscriptions of different periods. *Nisyros* is an extinct volcano, all wooded now. The island, which is mentioned by Homer, has good therapeutic springs. Among the sights are the castle with the monastery of Panayia Speliani, and Mandraki, the island capital, with its pretty white houses. The *Archaeological collection* of Nisyros is housed in the Town Hall and the Demotic School, and includes sculpture, pottery, and inscriptions of the Hellenistic and Roman times, as well as post-Byzantine icons of the 18th and 19th century.

Chalke is the smallest of the Dodecanese. It is a picturesque island with many antiquities. Initially colonized by the Dorians and later occupied by the Romans, it was liberated by the Byzantines and taken by the Crusaders, the Turks and the Italians.

Kasos played an important role in the War of Independence of 1821. Kastro, the island capital, was destroyed in 1824 by the Turks. *Syme* is an attractive island with its fine castle and the monastery and church of Panayia, which is decorated with remarkable wall-paintings (at Nemporeio, near the chapel of the Transfiguration, there is a mosaic representing a camel-driver and twelve caves). The famous *monastery of Panormites,* consecrated to St. Michael the Taxiarch, is built at the S.W. extremity of the island on a wooded bay. The monastery, which has a fine bell-tower and a wood-carved iconostasis, contains historic relics and rich ex-votos. Panormites is the patron saint of Syme. The picturesque island of *Kastellorizo* as well as the islands of *Leros* and *Astypalaia* are worth a visit. They all have post-Byzantine churches and are interesting for their local customs.

PATMOS

History: It was in Patmos, the holy island of the Dodecanese, that St. John was commanded to write his apocalyptic vision. One of the smallest islands of the Aegean archipelago, it is bare and rocky, with a deeply broken coastline, a crystalline atmosphere and a wonderful climate.

Of prehistoric Patmos it is only possible to form a very general picture, for there is little evidence to go upon: only a few references by ancient writers; some scanty archaeological remains (Mycenaean and Geometric sherds, fortifications of the Classical period, Hellenistic inscriptions). The island, of which Artemis was the tutelary goddess, was obviously of little significance. All we know of it in Roman times is that it served as a place of exile. The island's historical fame began in A.D. 95, when St. John the Divine was banished to it and spent the two years of his exile composing the Apocalypse. According to an ancient tradition. the site where the Book of the Revelation was written is the cave now incorporated within the precincts of the 17th century Monastery of the Apocalypse.

On the evidence of some architectural sculptures embedded in the walls of the churches of Chora, the island capital, Patmos must have enjoyed a measure of prosperity during the period of the 4th - 6th centuries. From the 7th to the 11th it was, like many Aegean islands, depopulated. It reappears in the historical limelight in the 11th century when the Monastery of St. John the Divine was founded by Hosios Christodoulos (1088). This blessed man was one of the outstanding representatives of the monastic way of life and a personality typical of the turbulent Comnene age. In the 12th century the diligence of the monks, the donations of pious persons and, above all, the patronage of the Emperor and the Patriarch, contributed to the consolidation of the status of the monastery and ensured its prosperity. It was then inhabited by 150 monks; it owned dependencies in other islands and disposed of a fleet of commercial vessels. The inhabitants' nautical tradition served them well and they soon began to export goods in the form of local handicrafts. From the 16th century onwards mansions and churches were built and the island entered upon a new way of life. This first period of prosperity came to an end when the Venetians devastated the island in 1659.

The foundation of the Patmian School in 1713 and the commercial enterprise shown by the Patmian merchants, who had settled in the Balkan countries, in Austria, Russia and Egypt brought about a renascence in the 18th century. The Patmians, one of whom was Emmanuel Xanthos, participated energetically in the activities of the Philiki Hetaireia and in the War of Independence which broke out in 1821. But the creation of the modern Greek state contributed to the decline of the island merchant fleet. In 1912 the Turks ceded the island to Italy and in 1947 Patmos, together with the other Dodecanesian islands, was reunited with Greece.

The Monuments

The most important Byzantine monument on the island is the Monastery of St. John the Divine. One of the oldest and wealthiest monasteries in the Orthodox world, it constitutes a particularly fine example of a mediaeval fortified monastic complex. The 11th century Katholikon is of the four-columned cross-inscribed architectural type, decorated with 12th century wall paintings, as is also the 12th century Chapel of the Panayia. Other monastic buildings, dated to different periods, complement an architectural ensemble which is, however, deprived of uniformity. The various buildings crown the interior part of the peribolos and the monks' cells. The chapels, courts and halls are connected by means of galleries and winding alleys. The Library of the monastery possesses 895 codices and about 2000 printed books; the Treasury contains numerous precious icons, silverware objects and other relics.

Other Byzantine monuments on the island include the Churches of Ayios Demetrios tis Choras, Ayia Marina ston Kambo, Ayios Nikolaos at Evdylos and the Church of the Asomatoi which forms part of the Monastery of the Evangelismos. There also countless post-Byzantine shrines of the domed single-aisled architectural type. These include Ayioi Apostoloi, the twin chapels of Ayios Ioannis and Ayios Spyridon which have vaulted roofs and the Koimesis, a rather more late architectural type of a double chapel with a single dome and vaulted roof.

Although it was during the period of the 16th - 19th centuries that Patmos developed and prospered, it is in the mediaeval layout of its little streets and squares, in its ancient customs, in the nature of the sites and quality of the works of art that the modern visitor is most likely to be able to conjure up a vivid image of the past.

CRETE

Crete is the largest of the Greek islands and a tour of it affords a most thrilling experience to sight-seers, particularly those who visit it for the first time. Crete enjoyed an active life originating in the remotest Prehistoric times and continuing all through the historic period, marked by magnificence and splendour and characterized by wonderful achievements in the domain of the arts and letters. The remains of its glorious past are still visible on the island. For several long decades after the liberation of the other Greek territories, Crete suffered, fought and paid the price of costly sacrifices, in order to be re-united with Greece and enjoy «sweet freedom», in the words of the poet.

Three towering massifs, the White Mountains in Western, Ida in Central, and Dikte in Eastern Crete, dominate the island from west to east. Densely wooded, they slope softly or abruptly into lower ranges, deep ravines and upland plains; in some places large caves have been formed. The entire island is very fertile and the endless variety of its landscape is ever attractive and fascinating. Many sandy shores and safe little bays along the coast offered every possibility for the growth of navigation in antiquity. On the other hand, the facility of communication with the three continents created the prerequisites for *the development of the first important civilization on European territory*. Central and Eastern Crete have been extensively explored, while Western Crete has not been sufficiently investigated yet, though whatever has come to light so far is of great interest.

Life existed on the island from the Neolithic period. The most characteristic site showing clearly signs of that period is the *cave of Eileithyia* at Amnisos, a few kilometres from Herakleion. (Finds from the cave, together with other objects dating to that age, are exhibited in the Archaeological Museum of Herakleion).

Neolithic Crete presents no outstanding features; by contrast, the life which was developed on the island from 2600 to 1450 B.C. is truly admirable. It is not known how many peoples had inhabited Crete at that time : apparently races from Asia Minor had moved towards Crete, the Cyclades and mainland Greece. The people who settled on Crete, the Minoans, were a lively, active and intelligent stock, superb artists and ingenious architects; they attained a remarkable standard of culture and lived in an atmosphere of prosperity, joy and lasting peace. They were fond of colour, movement, and nature —the faunal, floral and marine world— and their accomplishments in every domain of life are indeed astounding. Thanks to their joyous and expansive nature, and the prevailing so-called 'Pax Minoica', they reached an incredible for those times degree of progress. Unlike the peoples who had created the Oriental civilizations, the Minoans were not dominated by a mighty priesthood or local sovereigns, and their activities seem to have been unhindered. They experienced neither fear towards gods, nor problems with men. They lived happily and peacefully in their unfortified cities, free even from the fear of death, which had preoccupied so much the Egyptians. Until 1450 B.C., two kinds of script had been developed on the island : the hieroglyphic and the Linear A, both of which have not been deciphered yet. Nevertheless, owing to its expressive character, the Minoan civilization is quite well-known from works of art. In the Pre-Palatial period, from 2600 to 2000 B.C., the Minoans established relations with Asia Minor and Cyprus to ensure their supply of copper, imported gold from Sinai and Nubia, and produced works of the minor arts, which are true masterpieces : hair ornaments, fine chains, diadems, necklaces, and miniature figurines of animals. With the silver obtained from Siphnos and Cilicia they manufactured jewellery and daggers. They also used precious or semi-precious stones, rock-crystal, amethyst, sard and glass to make necklace beads. At that time they began to employ sealstones, initially made of bone, steatite, ivory, and later of semi-precious stones exquisitely carved. Pottery was similarly developed and the knowledge acquired during voyages to Egypt served for the manufacture of vases from steatite, serpentine, limestone, alabaster, etc. Thus the island presented an unprecedented degree of prosperity and progress, its population living in kinship groups and forming densely inhabited inland or coastal settlements.

An important change occurred from 2000 to 1700 B.C. (Early Palatial period). Authority became centralized and for the first time large palaces were built in the three fertile plains of Central Crete : *Phaistos, Knossos* and *Mallia*. The advanced knowledge of technical methods made possible the undertaking of technical works (such as the levelling out of the hills of Knossos and Phaistos). All sorts of precious metals continued to be imported and used by artists for the production of master-pieces. The development of commercial contacts and transactions with both Greek and foreign countries resulted in the growth of the Cretan marine. The economy of that period was based on barter conducted by the kings themselves, who had control of the trade activities. This led to a form of bureaucracy in the palaces, and the ensuing development of the hieroglyphic script (the most remarkable example of which is the Phaistos disk displayed in the Museum of Herakleion) and the Linear A script, both of which have remained so far undeciphered. The royal work-shops were intensively active with the production of outstanding works of art. Seal-engraving, the minor arts, goldwork, small sculpture, architecture, as well as sea-faring and trade flourished to a great extent. In 1700 B.C., the three Minoan palaces were simultaneously destroyed either by earthquakes or a barbaric invasion.

New and more majestic palaces with numerous storerooms were erected at Knossos, Phaistos, Mallia and Zakro between 1700 and 1450 B.C. In addition, vil-las were built and a paved road network was constructed. The Minoan ships roamed the seas. This was the most splendid era of Crete. Painting, especially, became an expressive branch of art, and exquisite frescoes and superb vases were produced. In about 1450 B.C., all this magnificent setting was suddenly destroyed as a result of the eruption of the volcano of Thera (according to the verified theory advanced by Professor Sp. Marinatos). After 1450 B.C., the palaces were not rebuilt. The pal-ace of Knossos was only partly repaired and inhabited by the Achaians who had landed on the island. The Achaians employed the Linear B script, of which more than 3,000 tablets have been recovered. Art continued to flourish, but its splendour was dimmed. The Palatial style emerged at Knossos, while the clay sarcophagus of Ayia Triada, decorated with remarkable representations, is a work of that time; a series of sarcophagi, discovered quite recently in the Nome of Chania, are also dated to the same period. A further catastrophe occurred in 1400 B.C., following an earthquake or a new invasion of the Achaians. The palace of Knossos was never rebuilt.

The last phase of the Minoan civilization is very poor in accomplishments. The radiance of the Cretan world was extinguished and henceforth other centers —Mycenae, etc.— emerged and gained maritime supremacy. On mainland Greece were produced numerous works of art inspired by Minoan prototypes. Artistic activity declined on Crete, and in 1150 B.C. the island was conquered by a Greek race from the northwest — the Dorians.

The Minoan civilization and its outstanding development survived in ancient Greek myths associated with Minos, the Labyrinth, the Minotaur, Ariadne, etc. A local legend cites the island of Crete, whose name is mentioned for the first time by Homer, as the birthplace of Zeus. According to a Panhellenic tradition, the infant Zeus was raised there. His mother Rhea had hidden the infant in a cave of the island, to save him from his father Kronos who devoured his children. The child was looked after by the Nymphs of Mt. Dikte and fed with the milk of the goat Amaltheia, while the Kouretes beat their shields to cover the infant's cries so that Kronos would not hear him. Another legend relates that Zeus in the form of a bull led Europe, whom he had abducted from Phoenicia, to Crete. Out of their union were born Minos, Rhadamanthys and Sarpedon. According to the Greek tradition, Minos, whose seat was at Knossos, ruled over the whole of Crete and his reign was renowned for the prosperity and peace which prevailed in his age. The consort of Minos was Pasiphae, and their children were Ariadne, Glaukos, Androgeo and Phaidra. The Minotaur, whom Minos confined in the Labyrinth, was born of the union of Pasiphae with the sacred bull. During the reign of Minos the Cretans were masters of the seas; they planted many colonies throughout the Aegean, and forced even Attica to pay a tribute, until Theseus freed his country from this dreadful burden by slaying the Minotaur with the help of Ariadne.

This and other associated legends reflect memories of an age when Crete was all-powerful — a fact further attested by excavations at various sites which had an intensively active life in Prehistoric times.

Historic times. The transition from Prehistoric to historic times was quite smooth, without essential changes, except of course for the generalized use of iron. People continued to live in the earlier settlements, while houses, graves and even art present no basic differences from those of the previous period (between 1000 and 900 B.C.).

The first changes occurred from 900 B.C. : remote settlements were abandoned and, as in the rest of Greece, city-states were formed, the most important being *Axos, Dreros, Knossos, Aptera,* etc. Excavations have not yielded sufficient data : known sites are the cemetery of Fortetsa near Herakleion, the Geometric temple of Apollo and the Prytaneion at Dreros, while the cemetery of *Arkades* is dated to the late Geometric times (circa 700 B.C.) and the subsequent period. Crete became Dorian.

In the Archaic age (after 700 B.C.) the city-states of Crete followed the example of Sparta in organizing their form of government and way of life. They were ruled, of course, by an aristocracy, and the archons, who were called Kosmoi, were of the new settlers, not the autochthonous old inhabitants. It was only towards the end of the 3rd century B.C. that democracy prevailed in Crete, when the institution of the Kosmoi assumed a merely formal character. To judge from the writings of Plato and Aristotle about Crete, the legislation of that time was excellent (e.g. the laws of Gortyn). In the Classical era the city-states declined and so did local art. Confederacies of cities were formed and endless wars were fought among them, which led to the exhaustion of all parties. The most important cities were *Knossos, Gortyn* and *Kydonia. Lyktos,* which Plato considered as a model city-state, was destroyed by the Knossians in 220 B.C. Many Cretans left the island to serve abroad as mercenaries. The early 2nd century B.C. was marked by total anarchy, and pirates from

Cilicia settled along the coasts using the island as a base for their raids. Their attacks against the Romans provided Rome with an excuse to interfere in the internal affairs of the island. A first attempt by the Romans to conquer Crete in 74 B.C. failed. In 69 B.C., however, the Roman consul Caecilius Metellus occupied Kydonia. Knossos and all the other cities which had resisted the Romans were occupied in turn. Gortyn, which had submitted to the Romans, became the capital of the island and the seat of the Roman governor. And so, Crete became a Roman province. In the age of Augustus Crete was administratively united with Cyrenaica. The Cretan cities retained some form of local autonomy, and the *Cretan Koinon* minted its own coins. Gortyn was embellished with splendid edifices : temples, the Prytaneion, theatres, the Odeion, Nymphaia, baths and other public buildings.

Very scant information is available from the earliest Byzantine period. Constantine the Great annexed the island to the Illyrian theme. When the Roman state was divided into East and West, Crete remained as part of the East Roman empire (A.D. 395). In the age of Justinian, Crete was made into a separate theme governed by generals. Leo III Isaurus imposed heavy taxes on Crete and placed the island outside the ecclesiastical jurisdiction of the Pope of Rome. The island was a center of strong resistance to the iconoclastic policy of the Isaurians. The interest of the Arabs for Crete began in the mid-7th century and culminated in the conquest of the island by the Saracens of Spain in 824. Crete was turned into an independent piratic state with Chandax (Herakleion) as its capital. The Byzantines attempted to liberate Crete on six different occasions, until this was achieved in 961 by Nikephoros Phokas, who had laid a siege to Chandax for many months. Information on the Arab occupation of Crete is scarce. The Byzantines demolished the wall built by the Arabs and removed all traces of the Arab occupation. Mosques were converted into churches and Hosios Nikon Metanoeite re-converted to Christianity the part of the population who had become Moslems. After a subjugation of 138 years, Crete was re-united with Byzantium and recovered her Christian and Greek character. It was colonized by Nikephoros Phokas with new settlers and remained till 1204 part of the Byzantine empire, governed by a duke appointed by Constantinople. *Chandax* (Kandak means 'ditch' in Arabic) became the political and religious center of the island, while Gortyn fell into oblivion. Peace prevailed and a political development was noted. Eminent scholars appeared (the Metropolite Elias, Hosios Ioannis Xenos, etc.), and monasteries and churches were founded. Alexios Komnenos sent twelve noblemen, descendents of prominent Byzantine families, to colonize the island anew. They were the founders of the great Cretan families who played a leading role in the history of the island in the period of the Venetian occupation and in subsequent times. In 1206 Boniface of Montferrat, to whom Crete was given in 1204 after the conquest of Constantinople by the Franks, sold the island to the Venetians. It was later occupied by the Genoese, who built 14 fortresses in strategic points of the island. Finally, Crete was reoccupied by the Venetians, who proclaimed it a kingdom and made *Chandax* the seat of the Duke appointed as governor. The Venetians attended to the political and military organization of Crete, for the island was indispensable for the growth of their trade and the mobility of their fleet, by reason of its most important situation in the Mediterranean. Although the Venetians tried to latinize the island, they did not interfere with the monasteries and the lower clergy.

27 uprisings were made against the Venetian rulers of Crete, some at the instigation of monarchs ruling the then independent Greek states. Revolts, famine, poor crops and earthquakes annihilated the Greek population of the island. In 1645

Chania fell to the Turks after a siege, and so did Rethymno in 1646. In 1647 began the siege of Chandax which lasted until 1669, when the whole island was occupied by the Turks. The Turkish domination lasted 250 years, during which revolutions and the abduction of children ('paidomazoma') reduced the population further. Trade was neglected and works of public utility were no longer undertaken. A guerrilla warfare was waged by the 'Chaïnides', as they were called by the Turks. The uprising of 1692 against the Turks failed and so did the revolution of Daskaloyiannis in 1770. When the War of Independence was declared in 1821, the Turks applied harsh measures. From that date onwards a series of insurrections by the Greek population of the island were literally drowned in blood. In 1830 Crete was ceded to Mehmet Ali of Egypt, whose occupation lasted till 1840, when the island was reoccupied by the Turks. In 1841, 1858 and 1860 new revolts occurred, the last one culminating in the holocaust of Arkadi. The revolution ended in 1869 but unrest continued until 1878, when with the help of the great powers the 'Charter of Chalepa' was signed, which provided for the appointment of a Christian governor. The breach of the agreement led to the revolution of 1897, which was in turn followed by the Greko-Turkish War. In November 1898 the Cretan problem was given a temporary solution. The great powers appointed as High Commissioner Prince George, who landed at Souda in December 1898. The Cretan parliament, founded at that time, voted on repeated occasions resolutions demanding union with Greece. The great powers refused, and in March 1905 the revolution of Therisos broke out, with Eleutherios Venizelos as protagonist. The great powers blockaded the island, but unrest continued. In 1908, following the revolution of the Young Turks, the Cretans abolished the provisional regime of the High Commissioner and proclaimed the union of Crete with Greece.

A five-member committee, in which participated the new hero of Crete Eleutherios Venizelos, undertook the formation of a provisional government. The Greek flag was hoisted on the castle of Phirka at Chania. The foreign powers exerted pressure on Greece to refrain from supporting Crete, and a new Greko-Turkish war was threatened. After 1909 Eleutherios Venizelos was invited to join the Military League as political adviser (September 1910), and on 1st October 1912 the Cretan delegates were received in the Greek Parliament. On 14th October 1913 the Cretans lowered the flags of the great powers and Turkey at Souda. At last, after the end of the Balkan Wars, a separate treaty between Greece and Turkey ratified the union of Crete with Greece. King Constantine and the Prime Minister Eleutherios Venizelos arrived in Crete on the 1st December 1913 and union with Greece was officially celebrated with the flying of the Greek flag on the castle of Phirka.

Crete never surrendered to any conqueror. During the Second World War, the heroic 'battle of Crete' lasted from 20 to 31 May 1941. A great number of Cretans lost their lives as the inhabitants joined the soldiers in their fight against the German paratroopers, who finally occupied the island. The airport of Maleme was taken by the Germans, whilst the surviving Cretan defenders retreated to Sphakia, whence they made their way to the Middle East. The 'battle of Crete' caused heavy losses to the Germans—it was the first attempt at occupation by airborne invasion, which was not repeated elsewhere by reason of the heavy losses it had caused.

Excavations. Knossos was first explored by the Greeks, when they were still under Turkish rule (by Minos Kalokairinos, in 1878). In 1886 the Turkish authorities refused Schliemann permission to undertake excavations. In 1894 the island was visited by Evans, who carried out extensive excavations at Knossos from 1900 to 1931, and restored the great Minoan Palace he had discovered. The Italians explored

Phaistos and Ayia Triada and investigated Axos and Arkades. The French unearthed the palace and cemetery of Mallia; excavations are still continued there, and the site of Lato has been investigated recently. The Americans explored some Minoan settlements (Vasiliki, Pseira, Mochlos, Gournia). The British continue their excavations at Knossos and have been lately carrying out excavations at other Cretan sites in collaboration with the Greek Archaeological Service. Greek archae- ologists investigated and uncovered the palace of Zakro (N. Platon), the megara of Vathypetro (Sp. Marinatos), Tylissos, Sklavokampos, Archanes, the settlement of Kydonia, the peak sanctuaries of Piskokephalo, Kophina, etc., the tholos tombs of Mesara, the cemeteries at Katsamba, Lebena, Armenoi, Kyparissi, the tholos tombs at Maleme, Stylos etc., the graves at Archanes, and the caves of Platyvola, Geranion etc.

HERAKLEION

The city occupies a central position for the visit of most of the archaeological sites of the island. Herakleion itself has many sights, for there are preserved the Mediaeval wall with its gates, Venetian and Turkish monuments (mosques and fountains), the Cathedral of St. Menas, the church of St. Catherine where there is on display a collection of Byzantine and post-Byzantine works of art, including six icons by the celebrated 16th century painter Michael Damaskenos, the basi- lica of St. Mark (where there is a collection of copies of wall-paintings of se- veral Cretan churches). Similarly of interest is the local architecture of houses with the famous 'Herakleiot courtyards'.

Fine castles are also to be seen at *Rethymno* and *Chania* — where the Venetian harbour and the old quarter of the city have been preserved.

KNOSSOS

Knossos lies at a distance of 5 kms. from Herakleion. The Minoan city extended around the hill of Gypsades. There were sumptuous villas near the palace, and be- yond the city, in all directions. The cemeteries were farther away.

Knossos (like Phaistos) enjoyed an important position, which explains its re- markable development. Communication was easy with the rest of the island, and the city lay at a short distance from the north coast where there were sandy bays suitable for pulling ships ashore. Within a distance of only 10 kms., Knossos had three ports: Katsamba, Amnisos and Ayioi Theodoroi, which served her large fleet and flourish- ing trade. Knossos was not surrounded by walls. Gardens, vineyards and olive groves grew around the city, which Pindar describes as 'polydendre' (i.e. of many trees). The vast palace dominated the hill (the one we see at present is of the Early Palatial period and occupied an area of 20,000 sq. m. including its two courts). Like all Minoan palaces it has a west court and a large central court flanked by the two main wings of the palatial complex. The wing which included the Room of the Throne and the storerooms had three storeys; the other wing with the king's and queen's quarters and the workshops had five storeys. The walls were covered with superb frescoes. Life in this, as well as the other palaces, was pleasant, rich and comfortable. Grand staircases, multiple doors, terraces, small shrines, etc., were the main features of the palace, which (like that of Phaistos) also had an open-air space for gatherings, a sort of quadrilateral theatre with flights of steps.

Crete. Knossos.

Crete. Palace of Knossos.
Room of the Throne.

GORTYN

Situated at a distance of 47 kms. from Herakleion, Gortyn has many ruins showing the glory of the city in Roman times. Among the sights are the basilica of St. Titus (consecrated to the memory of the episcope sent by St. Paul the Apostle to preach the Christian religion on the island), and the Roman Odeum. Into the walls of this are incorporated slabs with the laws of Gortyn inscribed in boustrophedon Doric script (17,000 words). The legislation refers to matters of civil and penal code, land property, inheritance, divorce, etc. There is a small *Museum* at Gortyn containing sculpture and inscriptions found on the site.

At *Lenda*, 35 kms. from Gortyn, near the homonymous promontory, there are ruins of an Asklepieion with hot springs. The visitor is well advised to pay a visit to the beautiful *Kamares* cave (Idaion antron), the gorge of *Samaria* (in the Nome of Chania), and the town of *Sphakia*, celebrated for the traditional bravery and pride of its people. In fact, the whole island of Crete has interesting customs and morals that have been preserved intact through the centuries. Finally, a visit to *Anogeia*, near Herakleion, would be worth while.

PHAISTOS

The Minoan palace of Phaistos is smaller than that of Knossos, but it presents the same principal features and a luxurious construction. Its theatre is larger and its monumental staircase grander; the palatial workshops are excellent. Recent excavations at the site of this palace have revealed that life continued uninterrupted into the historic times. The ruins seen at present belong to the second palace built after the destruction of 1700 B.C.

AYIA TRIADA

After a walk of half a kilometre from Phaistos, the visitor reaches the site of Ayia Triada, where there is a small palace, probably the residence of a local ruler, subject to the sovereign of Phaistos. Very fine frescoes have been found there.

At *Tylissos* (13 kms. from Herakleion) there are ruins of three Minoan villas with the characteristic features of Minoan palaces, that had probably served as residence of local rulers appointed by the Minoan kings. The villas overlay the ruins of earlier buildings. The finds —magnificent bronzes— are displayed in the Archaeological Museum of Herakleion. Recent excavations at *Archanes* (12 kms. from Knossos) have brought to light important funerary monuments and a large building. Excavations conducted by Professor Sp. Marinatos at *Amnisos* have unearthed a large villa decorated with fine frescoes (exhibited in the Archaeological Museum of Herakleion).

The third large Minoan palace was uncovered at *Mallia* (35 kms. east of Herakleion), near the sea. The palace, which was surrounded by large houses, has features similar to those of the other two. The remarkable yield of finds from the palace and the necropolis of the site is now exhibited in the Archaeological Museum of Herakleion.

Similar characteristic and valuable finds have come to light during excavations at the palace of *Zakro* (Eastern Crete). *Gournia* is a rather well-preserved Minoan township with its houses, narrow paved lanes, and official center.

Crete.
A typical lane of the old town of Chania.

The whole island of Crete abounds in archaeological sites, Museums and collections. The most important of the latter are the following :

Archaeological Museum of Herakleion

This is one of the richest Museums in the world. A number of rooms on the ground floor house finds which offer a comprehensive picture of the Minoan civilization (pottery, small sculpture, sealstones, weapons, implements, bronzes, goldwork, and many cult objects). The last rooms of the ground floor contain Gretan pottery of historic times, and a room at the back has most important Archaic sculpture (Crete was believed by the Greeks of historic times to have been the point of departure of the mythical artist Dàidalos and the wandering sculptors Dipoinos and Skyllis, who travelled to Greece and Sicily and imparted the secrets of their craft to the Greeks).

The last room includes sculpture of the remaining periods of antiquity. Outside the Museum, to the east, are displayed important inscriptions. The Museum houses all finds from Central and Eastern Crete uncovered during the Greek, British, French, Italian, etc. excavations. On the upper floor are exhibited a wooden model of the palace of Knossos, as well as sarcophagi and the frescoes which have been preserved.

Historical Museum of Crete

The Museum belongs to the Society of Cretan Historical Studies and contains Cretan works dating from the Early Christian period to present times. Among the exhibits are sculptures, inscriptions, Byzantine, Venetian and Turkish works, a good collection of wall-paintings, post-Byzantine icons, vestments, wood-carvings, liturgical vessels, and 17th century pottery.

The Folklore collection includes models of Cretan houses and many handicrafts. The Historic collection, housed together with the Folklore collection on the upper floor, comprises weapons, relics, flags and documents from the many Cretan revolts. Two rooms are dedicated to N. Kazantzakis and Em. Tsouderos. After the Archaeological Museum, a visit to the Historical Museum completes the picture of the Cretan civilization and gives a comprehensive idea of the island's life and history which cover a period of 8,000 years.

Archaeological Museum of Ayios Nikolaos

The Museum contains a representative collection of various finds from excavations carried out in Eastern Crete. Exhibits include remarkable Minoan vases, figurines and sarcophags, as well as bronze weapons and stone vessels and tools. There are also on display finds of the historic times, dating from the Geometric period to the late Hellenistic age. The visitor may see some weapons of the last century, and some ancient inscriptions and coins.

Museum of Ierapetra

The Museum is situated in the old Town Hall and contains vases and fine painted clay sarcophagi of the Late Minoan period. There are also some red-figure vases, Hellenistic statuettes, sculpture and inscriptions.

Archaeolological Museum of Rethymnon

In the *Archaeological Museum of Rethymnon* (in the Venetian building of the Officers' Club) are displayed Prehistoric pottery, Minoan figurines, sarcophagi, sealstones, scarabs, and Minoan double axes. There are also some Hellenistic and Roman sculpture, bronze statuettes, mirrors, Byzantine and Venetian reliefs, and a large collection of coins of all periods.

The *Collection of the Girls' Lyceum at Rethymnon* includes fine local embroideries and ceramics by popular artists.

Archaeological Museum of Chania

The Museum is housed in the Venetian Monastery of St. Francis, and contains Neolithic pottery, weapons and statuettes of all periods, Greek and Roman sculpture, pottery dating from Geometric to Roman times, lamps, glassware, a mosaic floor, Roman inscriptions and coins.

In the *Historical Museum and Cretan Corner*, a section of the Historical Archives of Crete, there are relics of the political and military activity from the 19th century to the Second World War. A room is dedicated to Eleutherios Venizelos and contains personal possessions and documents. The Folklore collection of the Cretan Corner includes woven materials, embroideries and other local handicrafts.

THE BYZANTINE MONUMENTS OF CRETE

In terms of archaeology, Crete derives its major fame from the fact that it was the cradle of Minoan civilization. But archaeological interest is not confined to those remote prehistoric centuries. History did not bypass Crete during the Christian era, nor throughout long centuries punctuated by endless vicissitudes, mostly of a tragic nature. The soul of the heroic Cretan people, strengthened by their faith, rose above adversity. Irrefutable evidence of their creative impulse exists to this day. Over eight hundred frescoed churches are scattered across the length and breadth of the island. But let us take first things first.

The earliest examples of Christian art in Crete belong to the 5th and 6th centuries. Christianity, now the officially recognised religion of both Church and State, had acquired its definitive form. The earliest large Christian churches, in town and country alike, were episcopal seats. Basilica-type, they constitute the most representative examples of Early Christian art on the island. The basilica was a large rectangular edifice with an apsidal sanctuary at the east end. The interior was divided into three or more naves by colonnades, and the roof, as commonly throughout the Eastern Mediterranean, was of timber. To the rectangular edifice were added a narthex (west side), a large colonnaded court or atrium, a baptistery, treasury and other complementary chambers. The main decoration of the naves, apart from the sculptured capitals crowning the columns and a low marble iconostasis, consisted of mosaic floors with various polychrome geometrical and foliate patterns and animal designs. Archaeological research has brought to light more than forty basilicas throughout the island. Noteworthy examples of this type of edifice, with fine mosaic floors, have been excavated at, among other places, Chersonesos, Elounta, Knossos, Onythe and Panormos.

The tri-apsidal type of church, generally raised above the tomb of a Christian martyr, evolved contemporaneously with the basilica. One of these edifices, probably raised over the tomb of Ayioi Deka, martyred under the Emperor Decius, has recently been excavated in the diocese of the Messara. Three large apses project from the basic rectangular edifice which is entered through the narthex (west). A fine mosaic pavement with beautiful geometrical designs and a slab in which birds are depicted, is preserved in the south apse.

Another interesting architectural type is the circular structure in the diocese of Kissamos to which the Venetians added side chapels and a narthex. It is one of the rare extant examples of a circular building of the Early Christian period in Greece.

The large church of St. Titus at Gortyna, in which the architectural types of the basilica and the domed cruciform church are combined, was built at about the same time, namely the 6th century. This church is a rare example of a transitional type which derived from the Hellenistic basilica and evolved into the Byzantine domed cruciform edifice. The structure of the walls of St. Titus, composed of large carved slabs of limestone of equal size, betrays evidence of Syrian models and is a characteristic feature of the period. The provenance of the single-aisled edifice, with a dome above the centre of the arch, such as the Church of St. Nicolas Merambello (8th - 9th centuries) is also found in the Eastern provinces of the Byzantine Empire. In this church are preserved the oldest wall paintings of the island, dated to the Iconoclast period, with which the first phase of Byzantine art in Crete comes to an end. The wall paintings consist of extremely stylized geometric and foliate designs from which the human image is banished, as it indeed was from all Byzantine art, in accordance with the proscriptions of the Iconoclast emperors. The significance of this decoration in a Cretan church clearly indicates the Cretan population's reaction to the Iconoclast policy of Byzantinum.

Following the tribulations undergone by the population at the hands of Saracen pirates and the recapture of Crete from the Arabs by Nikephoros Phokas (961), the great art of Byzantium, distinguished by the highly evolved style associated with the Macedonian dynasty, spread throughout the island. Impetus was added to its diffusions by the activities of the missionaries, Nikon Metanoite and Ioannis Xenos. Of the art of this period all we know is that which has survived in creations of later times. The 11th century Church of Ayios Ioannis at Roukani, a typical example of a Byzantine church with a cross vaulted roof, a dome and a plastic disposition of interior surfaces, indicates that architectural trends fashionable in the capital were, from the beginning of this period, adapted to Cretan provincial traditions. On the other hand, the 11th century wall paintings of Ayios Eutychios and Kera at Chromonastiri, like those of the preceding period, suggest the influence of Eastern traditions. For even in the old Cappadocian wall paintings the main purpose of art was the expression of religious emotion. Disregard of the principles of accurate symmetry consequently deprived the figures of physical beauty. They remained elongated, flat, with clear-cut outlines and large expressive eyes.

Evidence of the fact that the Hellenizing art of the Comnene era, with its characteristic feeling for sobriety and symmetry and its expressionist style, underwent a wide dispersal during this period is found in surviving works of the 13th century. But Crete, when conquered by the Venetians, remained isolated, clinging tenaciously to regional traditions, impervious to the bold artistic innovations that were being tried out in centers where Hellenism had found a refuge after the capture of Constantinople by the Crusaders in 1204. Traditional art prevailed in Crete, as illustrated in a series of 13th century churches in whose wall paintings the feeling for the monumental still predominates. Among these are Ayios Georgios Sklavopoulas (1290), Ayios Panteleimon Vizarianos (1300) and Panayia Kera at Kritsa (1250-1300).

The 14th century witnessed a new flowering of Byzantine art in Crete. Church fresco painting was diligently and enthusiastically developed throughout the centuries of Venetian occupation (the painted decoration of more than eight hundred churches survives), and Orthodox hagiography in Crete survived the fall of Constantinople to the Turks.

Apart from a few examples of monumental architecture, namely, the domed cross-inscribed churches, the main architectural structure, whose interior walls were decorated with frescoes. that underwent development, was the small simple church with tiled roof and apsidal sanctuary. Whereas its origins are to be found in the East, which influenced Crete in many ways, its propagation and predominance throughout the island was due to contemporary social and economic factors. This simple popular form of church architecture remained unchanged for a long time, subject to foreign influences only in respect of pointed arches and carved limestone lintels in the Gothic and Late Gothic styles. The skill with which the larger iconographical cycles, intended for the decoration of churches in the monumental architectural style, were adapted to the confined surfaces of these small churches is remarkable. A variety of subjects from the Evangelical liturgy and the cycle of the Saints' calendar were systematically disposed in specially allocated areas in the interior of the church.

The whole evolution of Cretan art, firmly orientated in the ways of the great Palaeologue «Revival», and inspired mainly by the imperial artistic centres of Constantinople and Macedonia, may be followed in these admirable iconographical cycles. The Macedonian School of painting, distinguished by the sturdiness of its forms, its realism and a characteristically dramatic manner of expression, both in respect of figures and compositions, enters the scene during the first half of the 14th century with a whole series of wall paintings. Admirable examples of these are found in the Monastery of Gouverniotissa, as well as, among others, in the side aisles of the churches of Kera at Kritsa, Ayios Georgios at Apostoloi and Ayios Andreas at Hodeghetria. The tone set by the official school of the capital had thus prevailed throughout the island by the middle of the century. The wall paintings of the Monastery of Valsamonero, admirable examples of the conservative school of Constantinople with its characteristic idealism, ushered in a brilliant period of Byzantine art in Crete. Similar trends ae to be found in, among others, the Churches of Ayios Georgios at Melissourghaki, of Ayios Ioannis at Margharites and Ayios Ioannis at Hodeghetria. Examples of the conservative trend, whose decisive supremacy was due to the triumps of the Hesychast movement, multiplied to such an extent during the 15th century that after the fall of Constantinople in 1453 the island's great artistic heritage survived in the humblest Cretan chapels. The genesis and development of a new style, in which the influence of the portative icon plays an important role, is evident in the paintings of these chapels. For examples, see the Churches of the Panayia in the plain of Sklaverochori, of Ayios Georgios at Symi Viannou and the Monastery of Kardiotissa Voron. This style had developed by the beginning of the 16th century (the Church of the Panayia at Ayia Paraskevi is an example) into a fully-fledged Cretan school of painting, with its own individual features which were destined to be disseminated by Cretan painters on the Greek mainland (at Meteora and on Mt. Athos, for example), in the Balkan countries and throughout the Orthodox world. It was the last beautiful swan song of Byzantine art.

TABLE OF CONTENTS

PRINTED: BY J. MAKRIS S.A. ATHENS